The Homework Myth

"Kohn takes many of the things we assume about homework and shreds them, showing over and over how little research there is to back up all the accepted theories. . . . [He] chip[s] away at the conventional thinking that homework improves achievement, that homework improves grades, that homework builds character and all the other things we've heard about it since we were doing it . . . Worse, [it] may have the adverse effect of dulling a child's interest in learning altogether. . . . The crucial thing parents and teachers take away from the book: Challenge the status quo."

—*San Diego Union Tribune*

"A convincing case against homework. . . . Engaging, informative, and. . . well-researched. Kohn has never been better at challenging the status quo and declaring that the emperor has no clothes."

—*Kappa Delta Pi Record*

"Like all Kohn's books, *The Homework Myth* provokes thought and encourages activism. But best of all, it brings back the now almost forgotten question: 'What is good for the child?'"

—*Our Schools/Our Selves*

"*The Homework Myth* passionately and systematically challengc[s] the idea that more homework yields more learning."

—*The New York Sun*

"Thought-provoking. . . . Kohn calls into question the long-held belief that homework is good for kids."

—*Scholastic Parent and Child*

"Kohn . . . exposes the lack of evidence for many of the standard arguments in favor of homework: that it boosts achievement, that it inculcates good study habits, that it teaches kids to take the initiative, that it's better than . . . whatever else kids do in their free time. . . . In *The Homework Myth* [he asks], why make homework the rule rather than the rare and thought-through exception?"

—Slate.com

ALSO BY ALFIE KOHN

No Contest: The Case Against Competition

The Brighter Side of Human Nature:
Altruism and Empathy in Everyday Life

You Know What They Say . . . : The Truth About Popular Beliefs

Punished by Rewards: The Trouble with Gold Stars,
Incentive Plans, A's, Praise, and Other Bribes

Beyond Discipline: From Compliance to Community

Education, Inc.: Turning Learning into a Business [editor]

What To Look For in a Classroom . . . And Other Essays

The Schools Our Children Deserve:
Moving Beyond Traditional Classrooms and "Tougher Standards"

The Case Against Standardized Testing:
Raising the Scores, Ruining the Schools

What Does It Mean to Be Well Educated?:
And More Essays on Standards, Grading, and Other Follies

Unconditional Parenting:
Moving from Rewards and Punishments to Love and Reason

THE HOMEWORK
MYTH

Why Our Kids Get
Too Much of a Bad Thing

ALFIE KOHN

Da Capo
LIFE
LONG

A Member of the Perseus Books Group

Set in Granjon by the Perseus Books Group

Cataloging-in-Publication data for this book is available from the Library of Congress.

First Da Capo Press paperback edition 2007
First Da Capo Press edition 2006
HC: ISBN-13 978-0-7382-1085-8; ISBN-10 0-7382-1085-4
PBK: ISBN-13 978-0-7382-1111-4; ISBN-10 0-7382-1111-7

Published by Da Capo Press
A Member of the Perseus Books Group
www.dacapopress.com

Da Capo Press books are available at special discounts for bulk purchases in the U.S. by corporations, institutions, and other organizations. For more information, please contact the Special Markets Department at the Perseus Books Group, 2300 Chestnut Street, Suite 200, Philadelphia, PA 19103, or call (800) 255-1514, or e-mail special.markets@perseusbooks.com.

CONTENTS

PART I

The Truth About Homework

CHAPTER 1

"Missing Out on Their Childhoods"

AFTER SPENDING MOST of the day in school, children are typically given additional assignments to be completed at home. This is a rather curious fact when you stop to think about it, but not as curious as the fact that few people ever stop to think about it. It's worth asking not only whether there are good reasons to support the nearly universal practice of assigning homework, but why that practice is so often taken for granted—even by vast numbers of parents and teachers who are troubled by its impact on children.

The mystery deepens in light of the fact that widespread assumptions about the benefits of homework—higher achievement and the promotion of such virtues as self-discipline and responsibility—aren't substantiated by the available evidence. As we'll see later, supporting data are either weak or nonexistent, depending on the specific outcome being investigated and the age of the students. But, again, this has rarely prompted serious discussion about the need for homework, nor has it quieted demands that even more be assigned.

Parents frequently talk about homework when they get together, and it's one of the first subjects to come up when they meet with teachers, either individually or in group sessions. There's no more reliable way to pack the house at a PTA meeting than to promise advice for dealing with homework woes. Likewise, there's a seemingly limitless demand for books that offer help, books with titles like: *The Homework Solution: Getting Kids to Do Their Homework; Seven Steps to Homework Success; Homework Rules and Homework Tools; Ending the Homework Hassle; How to Help Your Child with Homework; Hassle Free Homework*, and so on.

Clearly this is an issue of acute relevance to just about everyone who's involved with children—and it's one that leaves many of us feeling frustrated, confused, or even angry. But the assumption that homework should, even *must*, continue to be assigned despite our misgivings is rarely called into question.

This posture of basic acceptance would be understandable if most teachers decided from time to time that a certain lesson ought to continue after school was over, and therefore assigned students to read, write, figure out, or do something at home on those afternoons. We might have concerns about the specifics of certain assignments, but at least we'd know that the teachers were exercising their judgment, deciding on a case-by-case basis whether circumstances really justified intruding on family time—and considering whether meaningful learning was likely to result.

That scenario, however, bears no relation to what happens in most American schools. Homework isn't limited to those times when it seems appropriate and important. Most teachers and administrators aren't saying, "It may be useful to do this particular project at home." Rather, the point of departure seems to be, "We've decided ahead of time that children will have to do *something* every night (or several times a week). Later on we'll figure out what to make them do." This commitment to the idea of homework in the abstract is accepted by the overwhelming majority of schools—public and private, elementary and secondary. Even many schools that see themselves as progressive have adopted homework policies specifying that children at a given grade level will be required to do a set number of minutes of some kind of schoolwork at home.

Has anyone spoken up to challenge this state of affairs? Consider the following passage from an article in *Parents* magazine:

> *If* children are not required to learn useless and meaningless things, homework is entirely unnecessary for the learning of common school subjects. But when a school requires the amassing of many facts which have little or no significance to the child, learning is so slow and painful that the school is obliged to turn to the home for help out of the mess the school has created.

If you're a regular reader of *Parents* but don't recall coming across that provocative statement, it may be because the article appeared in the November 1937 issue.[1] The author was a school superintendent named Carleton Washburne, for whom a school in his hometown of Winnetka, Illinois, was named after his death. As if to impress upon us how drastically attitudes have changed since then, the first thing a visitor to the Washburne School's website notices today is a "student homework link." But of course readers of mainstream magazines and newspapers already know how the subject is apt to be treated nowadays. The February 2004 issue of *Parents*, for example, includes an article that uncritically accepts the proposition that all children should be given homework, beginning in first grade, and then proceeds to offer practical suggestions for how to help kids "focus and finish" whatever they've been assigned.[2]

Anyone who is dissatisfied with that sort of advice may feel a twinge of nostalgia for the pointed questioning and progressive thinking that were more common in the 1920s through the 1940s.

Sadly, it seems necessary today to make the same arguments and fight the same battles against the same practices and premises that Washburne and his colleagues faced. But that doesn't mean the supposed "pendulum swings" of educational philosophy are matched by changes in practice. With respect to schooling in general, progressive theory has periodically generated a surge of excitement among researchers and theorists but has never made serious inroads into most American classrooms. The phrase "back to basics" is a misnomer: We never really left.[3]

With respect to homework in particular, it's equally important to recognize that shifts in attitudes on the part of scholars—or even the public at large—don't necessarily translate into significant variations in the amount of homework that students actually have to do. It's easy to confuse what's being discussed with what's being done. For example, a 1999 article in the *New York Times* included this observation: "Once the pendulum swings one way, it takes a long time to reverse direction, but there are signs that heaping on homework for young children is taking its toll."[4] The second half of that sentence is surely true and, as has happened during other periods, some writers have taken notice.[5] But that doesn't mean the pendulum is swinging or, mechanistic metaphors aside, that anything is being done to relieve children of this toll.

The Amount

The most striking trend regarding homework in the past two decades is the tendency to pile more and more of it on younger and younger children. Even school districts that had an unofficial custom not so many years ago of waiting until the third grade before assigning it have abandoned that restraint.[6] Today it is the rare educator who is brave enough to question whether first graders really need to fill out worksheets at home. A long-term national survey of several thousand families discovered that the proportion of six- to-eight-year-old children who reported having homework on a given day had climbed from 34 percent in 1981 to 58 percent in 1997, and the weekly time spent studying at home more than doubled for youngsters of these ages.[7]

In 2002, that survey was updated. Now the proportion of young children who had homework on a specific day had jumped to 64 percent, and the amount of time they spent on it had climbed by another third. Not only do these new numbers confirm the trend of more homework (as well as a greater likelihood of getting it) for children in the primary grades, but the *rate* of increase is remarkable given that only five years elapsed between the last two surveys. The proportion of six- to eight-year-olds who are assigned homework is now almost the same as that for nine- to twelve-year-olds.[8] In fact, homework is even "becoming a routine part of the kindergarten experience," according to a 2004 report in *Teacher* magazine: "Some parents say nightly assignments are too much of a strain on children who, not long ago, were still taking afternoon naps to make it through dinner."[9]

By age nine, according to the 2004 National Assessment of Educational Progress, only 21 percent of children said they'd been assigned no homework on the previous day, a significant decline from the 36 percent who gave that response two decades earlier.[10] (As with the previous survey, this doesn't mean that such children get no homework at all. Even those who said they had none to do "yesterday" may well have had assignments over the course of the week.)

When schooling becomes departmentalized, sometimes years before high school, there is often no coordination among a student's teachers, which means that each may assign homework without regard to how much other teachers have already given. Anecdotally, many parents of teenagers report being astounded by how much more homework their kids get as compared with what they themselves were required to do a generation ago, and many are also struck by how much more difficult these assignments seem. This is particularly true for high school students who are taking the kinds of courses required for admission to selective colleges.

The hard numbers for older students are mixed; everything depends, as is so often the case, on how the question is framed. As with younger children, the proportion of thirteen-year-olds who reported having no homework yesterday dropped dramatically— from 30 percent in 1980 to 20 percent in 2004. For seventeen-year-olds, there was also a decline, from 32 percent to 26 percent.[11] U.S. Department of Education analysts continue:

> The amount of time students spend doing homework each day, however, has not changed significantly. A greater percentage of 17-year-olds said they do homework for mathematics classes often in 1999 than in 1978. A greater percentage of 9- and 13-year-olds read more than 20 pages each day for school or for homework in 1999 than in 1984. There was no significant change, however, in the pages read per day by 17-year-olds.[12]

As for international comparisons, a 1995 study found that U.S. twelfth graders reported spending less time on homework than did their counterparts in most of the other nineteen countries that participated in the survey—1.7 hours a night as compared to an average of 2.7 for students elsewhere. This may have been related to another finding in the same survey: American seniors worked at a paid job for an average of three hours a day, about triple the time for those in other nations.[13]

On the other hand, U.S. twelfth graders who took *advanced* math and science classes "reported being assigned homework. . . more frequently than the international average."[14] Even more striking is a cross-national comparison published in 2005. The United States, it turns out, is now "among the most homework-intensive countries in the world for 7th and 8th grade math classes."[15]

Recently, a few writers who strongly support homework (and sometimes other traditional education policies as well) have attracted considerable press attention by claiming that American children actually get too little homework.[16] They contend that any concerns we may have about excessive assignments, or even about the growing burden on younger children, are misplaced. Interestingly, back-to-basics advocates in Japan have lately been making the same claim about *their* children—sometimes even warning that they're falling behind harder-working American students.[17] Presumably these polemicists theorize that if we accept their account of the way things are (kids have it too easy!), we'll be more receptive to their advice for the way things should be (kids ought to be made to work harder!). Data always can be cited selectively to support the conclusion that the homework burden really isn't so onerous and that students could be doing more. But it may not be so easy to sell this argument to parents who have a front-row seat every evening from which to watch their kids toiling away.

More troubling is the number of scholars and journalists whose reports assume that if U.S. students really did have less homework than kids elsewhere (or than their grandparents did), that would of course be a bad thing. But why? On what basis do so many people regard the prospect of less homework, or even none, as reason for concern? Clearly, we need to look carefully at the data and evaluate the arguments on both sides. The two questions to be investigated in this book, then, are as follows:

1. On balance, does homework turn out to be beneficial?
2. Why not?

The Impact

To sort out the complaints one frequently hears about homework is to identify five basic themes.

1. A burden on parents. Gary Natriello, a professor of education at Columbia University's Teachers College, once wrote a paper supporting the value of homework. That recommendation, tossed off without a second thought, continued to make sense to him until a few years later when his "own children started bringing home assignments in elementary school." Only then did he begin to understand just how much is required of moms and dads.

> Not only did we need to establish a time and place for the homework to be done, but we found ourselves working through the directions and checking progress each step of the way. For you see, not only was homework being assigned as suggested by all the "experts," but the teacher was obviously taking the homework seriously, making it challenging instead of routine and checking it each day and giving feedback. We were enveloped by the nightmare of near total implementation of the reform recommendations pertaining to homework.

Even "the routine tasks sometimes carry directions that are difficult for two parents with only advanced graduate degrees to understand," Natriello discovered, while the more creative assignments can be even more burdensome for parents. At a minimum, "they require one to be well rested, a special condition of mind not often available to working parents."[18] Many mothers and fathers return each evening from their paid jobs only to serve as homework monitors, a position for which they never applied.

2. Stress for children. One frustrated father declared that homework is "a curse put on parents." Unfortunately, he made that declaration in front of his child, who shot back, "If you think it is difficult for parents, you should be a kid. It's horrible."[19] Most attentive parents can testify that their children are chronically frustrated by homework—weepy, stressed out, and fed up. Some are better able than others to handle the pressure of keeping up with a continuous flow of assignments, getting it all done on time and turning out products that will meet with the teacher's approval. Likewise, some of those assignments are more unpleasant than others. But only an individual squirreled away in the proverbial ivory tower could deny—and only someone bereft of human feeling could minimize the importance of—the fact that an awful lot of homework is emotionally trying for an awful lot of children. In the words of one parent, it simultaneously "overwhelms struggling kids and removes joy for high achievers."[20]

Often homework feels like an endurance contest. "School for [my son] is work," one mother writes, "and by the end of a seven-hour workday, he's exhausted. But like a worker on a double shift, he has to keep going" once he gets home.[21] Exhaustion is just part of the problem, though. The psychological costs can be substantial for a first grader who not only is confused by a worksheet on long vowels but also finds it hard to accept the idea of sitting still after school to do more schoolwork.

The situation plays out differently for a high school student, buried under endless assignments in chemistry and literature, French and history and trigonometry. ("It is not at all rare for our 11th-grader to be up after the rest of us go to bed and also before we get up," laments one father.)[22] A study published in 2002 found a direct relationship between how much time high school students spent on homework and the levels of anxiety, depression, anger, and other mood disturbances they experienced.[23] A young child may burst into tears; an adolescent may try to cope with the stress in more troubling ways. Both may be unhappy on a regular basis.

No discussion about homework should be taken seriously if it fails to address the impact on real children. When I hear self-satisfied pronouncements from adults about the importance of demanding "higher expectations" and insisting on the need to teach children "good work habits," or when I read academic monographs that talk about "extending a value-added education production function to treat homework as an additional measure of school inputs" (that's a real quote, incidentally), I want to ask, Do these people have a clue? Do they have a *child*? Can they really be oblivious, or indifferent, to the impact on flesh-and-blood kids: the loss of cheer, the loss of self-confidence, the loss of sleep—in extreme cases, over time, the loss of childhood? Forget the abstractions. This is the reality experienced by millions of families.

Homework is tough on parents, then, and it's also tough on children. Moreover, these two effects are related. If parents feel pressure from school authorities to make sure their kids are buckling down and keeping up, then that pressure is passed along to the kids. When Mom senses that her parenting skills are being evaluated, you may be sure her offspring will share the burden. In an interesting study conducted by Wendy Grolnick and her colleagues, third graders and their parents were asked to work together on a homework-like task involving the rhyme scheme of poems. The parents who had heard from the experimenter that their children would soon be tested on the skills became more controlling in their interactions. Later, each child was left alone to tackle a similar assignment, and those whose parents had been warned of an evaluation ended up not doing as well.[24]

3. Family conflict. Beyond its effects on parents and children, homework's negative impact—and specifically the nagging, whining, and yelling that are employed to make sure assignments are completed on time—affects families as a whole. As one writer remarked, "The parent-child relationship. . . is fraught with enough difficulty without giving the parent a new role as teacher" or enforcer.[25] Ironically, the sorts of relaxed, constructive family activities that could repair this damage are among the casualties of homework's voracious consumption of time.

More than a third of fifth graders in one study said they "get tense working with their parents on homework." And in a survey of more than 1,200 parents whose children ranged from kindergarteners to high school seniors, exactly half reported that they had had a serious argument with their child about homework in the past year that involved yelling or crying.[26] (Since so many people admitted this to a stranger, one can speculate how much higher the actual numbers may be.) The more that parents helped with homework, moreover, the more tension children experienced—and without any apparent long-term academic benefit from the assistance.[27]

When an assignment is particularly challenging—or simply unclear—the probability of unpleasant interactions is even higher. "Despite my years of professional experience," the eminent educator Nel Noddings remarked, "I'm often hard put to figure out what the teacher wants. . . [on] some assignments given to second graders. . . . I can well imagine these exercises adding to the tensions of home life instead of bringing parents and children together." She added parenthetically, "Picture what happens when, in addition to the original struggle, the assignment gets a poor grade!"[28]

Family conflict is also more common when the children are struggling. In fact, every unpleasant adjective that could be attached to homework—time-consuming, disruptive, stressful, demoralizing—applies with greater force in the case of kids for whom academic learning doesn't come easily. Curt Dudley-Marling, a former elementary school teacher who is now a professor at Boston College, conducted interviews with some two dozen families that included at least one such child. In describing his findings, he talked about how "the demands of homework disrupted. . . family relationships and den[ied] parents and children many of the pleasures of family life." The "nearly intolerable burden" imposed by homework was partly a result of how defeated such children felt; how they invested hours without much to show for it; how parents felt frustrated when they pushed the child but also when they didn't push, when they helped with the homework but also when they refrained from helping. "You end up ruining the relationship that you have with your kid," one father told him.[29] Such parents have often accepted what they've been told—that homework is useful and kids ought to be made to do it. But what they experience directly are "the tensions and frustrations, the angry words, the frequent yelling, the storming away, and the slamming of doors."[30]

Even when children *are* able to keep up, and even when they get along well with their parents, homework reshapes and directs family interactions in ways that we have learned to expect but are troubling to consider. Leah Wingard, a linguist at the University of California–Los Angeles, videotaped thirty-two families in their homes and then pored over the results to analyze who said what to whom, when, and how. For starters, she discovered that when the subject of homework was brought up, it was almost always by the parent—and usually within five minutes of greeting the child. (How can a relationship *not* be affected when one of the first things out of our mouths is, "So, do you have any homework?" It may be useful to consider what else we might say to our children after not having seen them all day—what other comments or questions they might experience as more welcoming, more supportive, or even more intellectually engaging.)

On those rare occasions when it was the child who raised the topic first, the study found that he or she invariably did so either to announce with relief that there was no homework (or it had already been done at school), which generally elicited a positive response from the parent, or to ask the parent for permission to do something or go somewhere. "Children orient to homework as an organizer of their time, and a gatekeeper from other activities if there is homework to complete."

Mostly, though, Wingard was struck by how "homework talk and the doing of homework are one of the organizers of children's afternoon weekday activities and have a significant impact on the time and activity planning of family life."[31] In most of these interactions, homework is viewed by parent and child alike as something to be gotten over. Conversations typically deal with what kinds of assignments the child has, how long it will take to do them, and the ways in which activities will be scheduled around them. Wingard's data indicate that even when homework is not an occasion for outright misery or hostility, it is, at best, something mildly unpleasant that families have learned to live with. (This is certainly consistent with other anecdotal reports: Even parents who defend homework against its critics often do so by insisting that it doesn't do *too* much harm, or it's *no longer* a significant source of conflict for their families.)

One of the fathers in this study is shown on tape raising his hand at the dinner table to high-five his daughter upon learning that she has finished her homework. But there are virtually no exchanges—in this or any other family—that deal with the *content* of the homework. No parent asks, "So, did the assignment help you to understand this topic?" or "What's *your* opinion of [the issue you were working on]?" As a rule, the point of homework generally isn't to learn, much less to derive real pleasure from learning. It's something to be finished. And until it is, it looms large in conversations, an unwelcome guest at the table every night.[32]

4. Less time for other activities. Quite apart from the often disagreeable effects that homework has on parents, kids, and family interactions is the simple fact that an hour spent doing schoolwork at home is an hour not spent doing other things. There is less opportunity for children just to hang out with their parents. There is less opportunity for the kind of learning that doesn't involve traditional academic skills. There is less opportunity to read for pleasure, make friends and socialize with them, get some exercise, get some rest, or just be a child.

In the mid–1960s, the American Educational Research Association released an official policy statement that said, in part: "Whenever homework crowds out social experience, outdoor recreation, and creative activities, and whenever it usurps time that should be devoted to sleep, it is not meeting the basic needs of children and adolescents."[33] Those basic needs apparently *aren't* met in many cases. One clinical psychologist, for example, recalled "what my children and I used to do before homework took over our lives. We ate dinner together, telling stories about our days. We read together. Sometimes we played cards or Monopoly. Once we made an entire gingerbread town. The children had time to themselves, too. Time to play, time to go outside, time to do nothing."[34]

It is the rare school that respects the value of those activities—to the point of making sure that its policies are informed by that respect. One independent school in Colorado has taken the position that, in the words of its director,

> 6½ hours a day in school is enough. . . . Kids and families need the rest of the days/evenings/weekends/holidays for living—playing, having friends and pets, shopping, solving problems, cooking, eating, [doing] chores, traveling, playing on sports teams, communicating, finding out about world news, playing musical instruments, reading for pleasure, watching movies, collecting things, etc., etc., etc.[35]

To fill in those "et ceteras" with activities of one's own choosing is to tally what homework displaces. This is not to imply that the presence of homework entails the complete absence of other activities. Most children do homework and they also do other things. But often there just isn't enough time left for some of those nonacademic pursuits once all the homework is done. This objection, in other words, is predicated on how much of a child's day is absorbed by academics. Other critics, meanwhile, offer a stronger objection, arguing that there is a principle involved: Schools shouldn't be dictating to families how *any* of their children's time in the late afternoon or evening must be spent.

Either way, the loss of time is not like other adverse effects, which at least in theory could be tested empirically. Here, research isn't relevant. This is a matter of value judgments: To what extent do we believe children (and families) should be able to decide how to spend their time together? For that matter, what do we think childhood ought to be about? To require students to do homework on a regular basis is to give one kind of answer to these questions. If we don't like those answers, then homework should come in for sharp scrutiny. After all, it is not a fact of life that must be accepted but a policy that can be questioned.

5. Less interest in learning.   Homework's emotional effects are obvious, but its adverse impact on intellectual curiosity is no less real. Kids' negative reactions may generalize to school itself and even to the very idea of learning. This is a consideration of overriding importance for all of us who want our children not only to know things but to continue *wanting* to know things. "The most important attitude that can be formed is that of desire to go on learning," said John Dewey.[36] (Then again, perhaps "formed" isn't the most appropriate verb. As the educator Deborah Meier reminds us, a passion for learning "isn't something you have to inspire [kids to have]; it's something you have to keep from extinguishing.")[37]

Anyone who cares about this passion will want to be sure that all decisions about what and how kids are taught, every school-related activity and policy, is informed by the question, "How will this affect children's interest in learning, their desire to keep reading and thinking and exploring?" In the case of homework, the answer is disturbingly clear. Most kids hate homework. They dread it, groan about it, put off doing it as long as possible. It may be the single most reliable extinguisher of the flame of curiosity.

A father in Massachusetts wrote to me not long ago about having asked his thirteen-year-old son whether he (the son) liked something he had just read. "Well, it was a good book," his son replied, "but I really never enjoy reading when I have an assignment hanging over my head." Mused the father, "Yup, that'll teach a lifelong love of learning."

Phil Lyons, a high school social studies teacher in California, came to much the same conclusion. Homework, he told me, basically contributes to a situation where students see learning as just an unpleasant means to an end, "a way to accrue points":

> It simply reinforces what is already a terrible problem in America's archaic educational system; it emphasizes reading because there will be a quiz on the reading, it mandates dozens of identical math problems because the test will contain dozens more just like the ones on the homework, and it asks students to respond to end of chapter questions like, "Which country did Napoleon invade in 1812?" All of these tasks are time-consuming, dreary, uninspiring and serve only to kill whatever motivation remains in students.

This teacher concluded that trying to improve the quality of homework assignments wouldn't solve the problem. He finally decided to stop giving homework altogether. Later I'll say more about his reasons and results—as well as those of other teachers and schools that have also pulled the plug. For now, I want to report one thing Lyons noticed immediately: In the absence of homework, "students come in all the time and hand me articles about something we talked about in class or tell me about a news report they saw. When intrigued by a good lesson and given freedom [from homework], they naturally seek out more knowledge."[38]

Precisely because most kids find most homework so unappealing, parents often feel compelled to offer them praise and other incentives for doing it—or threaten punitive consequences for failing to do it. So, too, do many teachers. Elsewhere, I've written at length about how the main effect of such carrots and sticks is to reduce people's interest in whatever they were rewarded for doing (or punished for not doing).[39] People who rely on these tactics to make kids complete an assignment end up making the learning itself seem even less appealing, which then makes bribes and threats seem even more necessary, creating a vicious circle. But the problem isn't due merely to these crude techniques employed by desperate adults. It's a function of the homework that drove them to do this to children.

The Attitudes

The effects I've listed here, if not universal, are surely pervasive. Every child won't experience all of them, but most of them will be familiar to the majority of families. The next logical question, then, would be: What conclusions about homework do people form in light of these consequences?

It would appear that the positions taken by parents are more varied than the reality to which they're responding. Some endorse homework enthusiastically and without reservation. Quite a number of educators will tell you that "excessive homework has been brought about to a very large extent by parental pressure."[40] Occasionally the parent's motive may just be to keep children busy: One New York teacher reports that she has "actually had parents come up and tell me to give their child lots of homework because if the kid does not have anything to do, [he or she] will drive them (the parents) crazy."[41]

What seems to be more common, though, is a simple desire on the part of parents for their children to succeed academically, accompanied by the belief that homework is a critical means to that end. Thus, a Washington elementary school teacher, who concluded after ten years in the classroom that homework is a waste of time, has been thwarted in her attempts to stop assigning it by the fact that "parents want it. I have actually been told that by not requiring homework I am setting their children up for failure later in life."[42] And from an Ohio middle school teacher: "Most of what the other core subject teachers in my building assign is what I consider 'busywork.' Many students don't bother to do it and most who do complete it don't learn anything from it. In my opinion the other teachers assign homework because parents and administrators expect it."[43] *Yes!*

In fact, some parents seem to figure that as long as their kids have lots of stuff to do every night, never mind what it is, then learning must be taking place. Educational quality is assumed to be synonymous with "rigor," and rigor, in turn, is thought to be reflected by the quantity and difficulty of assignments. "I have been contacted by parents on a number of occasions who demand that their children do 'something,'" reports a high school English teacher in California. "They don't seem to care what their children think *about*, so long as there is plenty of homework to be done."[44] This perspective isn't limited to any single demographic, by the way. It can be found among parents of overachieving students and underachieving students, among rich and poor, liberal and conservative.

Other parents, by contrast, wind up endorsing the institution of homework despite misgivings based on how it affects their children. Some send mixed messages to teachers and principals: They complain about lost family time but also assume that too little homework reflects a worrisome lack of seriousness about academics on the part of the school. They object to the burden placed on their children but at the same time are suspicious of teachers who don't give as many assignments.

Still other parents can't be described as active supporters of homework, but neither do they oppose it. They've never taken a position on the subject one way or the other; they just go with the flow of assignments their kids get. One politically progressive, well-educated New Hampshire mother spoke to me with remarkable candor about how it can be appealing to avoid looking too hard at what's going on. After reading an early description of this book, she wrote, "As a total type A good girl, it never occurred to me to actually check the value of [my high school son's] homework. I just make him do it. So this weekend. . . I took a look. Holy cow—how stupid it all is. Of course, now I'm just ticked off at you because I either have to admit to my son that it's all stupid or go talk to the high school principal about its being stupid. Neither conversation is very appealing."[45] Needless to say, many parents in this camp never end up having such conversations—or even ruminations. They just continue to treat homework as a fact of life and make their children do it.

But some parents *do* think about it and find themselves moved to take a stand. They conclude that homework is "more a hindrance than a help" as far as learning is concerned; they describe it as "busywork, with zero redeeming qualities"; they are anguished that their children "have grown up in their rooms doing homework," "missing out on their childhoods."[46] And they resent the fact that they, along with all other parents, are pressured to swallow their doubts and push their children to do whatever has been assigned, even if they can see little benefit. National policy documents, as well as memos from school, frequently give the impression that the objective is to ensure compliance from parents as much as from students.

That compliance, even for willing parents, often entails walking a tightrope. On the one hand, teachers and policy makers blame parents for doing too little. Nearly four of every five teachers in one survey said they "believe parents are barely involved in their children's homework."[47] A front-page article in the *Washington Post* sounded an extended note of indignation about students who fail to do what they've been assigned, and it quoted teachers who said "the fault ultimately lies with parents who don't pressure children" to do so.[48] On the other hand, parents are often faulted for getting *too* involved. It's not unusual to find teachers (and journalists) for whom this is the primary grievance when the topic of homework is raised. And indeed, some parents do take over their kids' assignments.[49] It may be because of competitiveness (they want their child to outshine his peers), or enmeshment (their own self-esteem is bound up with their child's success), or misplaced priorities (they become so concerned about the quality of the product that they forget the point is supposed to be about the process—that is, learning). You know something is amiss when parents talk about the homework "we" had last night.

What's lost in criticizing such behavior, though, is the real dilemma that almost all parents face. It's one thing to agree in theory that children should be responsible for doing their own homework; it's something else to put the abstract principle of self-sufficiency ahead of pleas from your child who is overburdened, frustrated to the point of tears, and begging for your help. Some caring parents provide that help because they've concluded it's the least bad way of dealing with a difficult situation; other parents step back and chew their knuckles for the same reason. The tendency to blame parents for doing too much—or too little—is, above all, a way of deflecting attention from problems with the homework itself.

If parents sometimes feel squeezed—"Get more involved. . . but not *too* involved!"—so, too, do many educators. One teacher who worked at three different elementary schools over the course of a decade told me, "No matter how much or how little homework I assigned, I always had some parents asking for more homework, and others asking for less."[50] You can find teachers—just like parents—at all points on the continuum. Some are strong believers in the value of homework. (When Chicago teachers were asked by researchers what the negative effects of homework might be, one out of three replied that there weren't any.)[51] But others detest homework or at least find it unhelpful, and assign it only because they feel pressured to do so. Based on their years of classroom experience, many have concluded that homework has little pedagogical value. Some, however, had to see things from the other side before the light dawned. I've spoken to several teachers who rarely, if ever, give homework, and when I ask what led them to this practice, their first words were, "Well, I'm a parent myself, and when I watched *my* kids . . ." Disturbingly, some teachers seem to lack this perspective unless, or until, they have their own children. "Now that I'm a parent myself," one fourth grade teacher in North Carolina said, "I realize they have lives at home."[52]

It's understandable that parents critical of homework would fault teachers, teachers critical of homework would fault parents, and students critical of homework would fault both. But it's important to recognize that all three constituencies often have a substantial burden in common, along with a feeling of powerlessness. To blame any of the victims here is to miss the structural issues, the forces that discourage us from asking whether homework is really desirable or inevitable.

Moms often sit on playground benches and commiserate about what homework is doing to their families, but then limit the questions they ask of their children's teachers to those dealing with the details: When is this assignment due? What sorts of binders will our kids need? It's acceptable to ask, "How much time should they be spending on this each evening?" but not to ask, "Is it really necessary to assign homework on this topic?" Teachers, too, may catch themselves wondering just how useful it really is to send children home with those packets, but then assume their only option is to revise the packets' contents.

Why do so many of us recognize the detrimental effects of homework and yet continue to put up with it, even defend it? Several possible answers will be reviewed in the course of this book. But the most obvious response is that we assume homework's benefits outweigh its costs. It's hard for us to watch as our children mechanically, joylessly grind out their assignments, perhaps frustrated by those that are too difficult, perhaps exhausted from having to do too much. At least it's doing them some good, we tell ourselves. At least it's improving their achievement, teaching them independence and good work habits, helping them become more successful learners.

But what if none of this is true?

CHAPTER 2

Does Homework Improve Learning? A Fresh Look at the Evidence

BECAUSE THE QUESTION in the title of this chapter doesn't seem all that complicated, you might think it has a straightforward answer. You might think that open-minded people who review the evidence should be able to agree on whether homework really does help.

If so, you'd be wrong. "Researchers have been far from unanimous in their assessments of the strengths and weaknesses of homework as an instructional technique," according to an article published in the *Journal of Educational Psychology*. "The conclusions of more than a dozen reviews of the homework literature conducted between 1960 and 1989 varied greatly. Their assessments ranged from homework having positive effects, no effects, or complex effects to the suggestion that the research was too sparse or poorly conducted to allow trustworthy conclusions."[1]

When you think about it, any number of issues could complicate the picture and make it more or less likely that homework would appear to be beneficial in a given study: What *kind* of homework are we talking about? Fill-in-the-blank worksheets or extended projects? In what school subject(s)? How old are the students? How able and interested are they? Are we looking at how much the teacher assigned or at how much the kids actually did? How careful was the study and how many students were investigated?

Even when you take account of all these variables, the bottom line remains that no definite conclusion can be reached, and that is itself a significant conclusion. The fact that there isn't anything close to unanimity among experts belies the widespread assumption that homework helps. It demonstrates just how superficial and misleading is the declaration we so often hear to the effect that "studies show" homework is an important contributor to academic achievement.

Research casting doubt on that assumption goes back at least to 1897, when a study found that assigning spelling homework had no effect on how proficient children were at spelling later on.[2] By 1960, a reviewer tracked down seventeen experimental studies, most of which produced mixed results and some of which suggested that homework made no difference at all.[3] In 1979, another reviewer located five more studies. One found that homework helped, two found that it didn't, and two found mixed results.[4] Yet another review was published a few years later that described eight articles and seven dissertations from the mid-1960s to the early 1980s. The authors, who included a longtime advocate of traditional educational policies, claimed the results demonstrated that homework had "powerful effects on learning."[5] But another researcher looked more carefully and discovered that only four of those fifteen studies actually compared getting homework with getting no homework, and their results actually didn't provide much reason to think it helped.[6]

"The literature reviews done over the past 60 years . . . report conflicting results," one expert concluded in 1985. "There is no good evidence that homework produces better academic achievement."[7] Four years later, Harris Cooper, an educational psychologist, attempted to sort things out by conducting the most exhaustive review of the research to date. He performed a metaanalysis, which is a statistical technique for combining numerous studies into the equivalent of one giant study.[8] Cooper included seventeen research reports that contained a total of forty-eight comparisons between students who did and did not receive homework. About 70 percent of these found that homework was associated with higher achievement. He also reviewed surveys that attempted to correlate students' test scores with how much homework they did. Forty-three of fifty correlations were positive, although the overall effect was not particularly large: Homework accounted for less than 4 percent of the differences in students' scores.[9] Worse, most of the studies included in the review had such serious "methodological shortcomings" as to raise doubts about the validity of any conclusion based on them, according to two experts.[10]

Cooper and his colleagues published a review of newer studies in 2006. Those that compared students with and without homework found a stronger association with achievement than the earlier studies had, but these new experiments measured achievement by students' scores on tests that had been designed to match the homework they had just done. As for more recent studies looking for a relationship between achievement and time spent on homework, the overall correlation was about the same as the one found in 1989.[11]

But several new studies weren't included in Cooper's recent review, and they "do not support the notion that students who spend more time on homework have higher achievement gains than do their classmates."[12] Still another study—the same one that found younger students are spending a lot more time doing homework these days (see pp. 6–7)—confirmed that the time commitment was "not associated with higher or lower scores on any [achievement] tests." (By contrast, the amount of time children spent reading for pleasure was strongly correlated with higher scores.)[13]

Taken as a whole, the available research might be summarized as inconclusive. But if we look more closely, even that description turns out to be too generous. The bottom line, I'll argue in this chapter, is that careful examination of the data raises serious doubts about whether homework enhances meaningful learning for most students. Of the eight reasons that follow, the first three identify important limitations of the existing research, the next three identify findings from these same studies that lead to questions about homework's effectiveness, and the last two introduce additional data that weaken the case even further.

Limitations of the Research

1. At best, most homework studies show only an association, not a causal relationship.   Statistical principles don't get much more basic than "correlation doesn't prove causation." The number of umbrellas brought to a workplace on a given morning will be highly correlated with the probability of precipitation in the afternoon, but the presence of umbrellas didn't *make* it rain. Also, I'd be willing to bet that kids who ski are more likely to attend selective colleges than those who don't ski, but that doesn't mean they were accepted *because* they ski, or that arranging for a child to take skiing lessons will improve her chances of being admitted. Nevertheless, most research purporting to show a positive effect of homework seems to be based on the assumption that when students who get (or do) more homework also score better on standardized tests, it follows that the higher scores were due to their having had more homework.

There are almost always other explanations for why successful students might be in classrooms where more homework is assigned—let alone why these students might take more time with their homework than their peers do. Even Cooper, a proponent of homework, concedes that "it is equally plausible," based on the correlational data that comprise most of the available research on the topic, "that teachers assign more homework to students who are achieving better. . . or that better students simply spend more time *yes!* on home study."[14] In still other cases, a third variable—for example, being born into a more affluent and highly educated family—might be associated with getting higher test scores *and* with doing more homework (or attending the kind of school where more homework is assigned). Again, it would be erroneous to conclude that homework is responsible for higher achievement. Or that a complete absence of homework would have any detrimental effect at all.

Sometimes it's not easy to spot those other variables that can separately affect achievement and time spent on homework, giving the impression that these two are causally related. One of the most frequently cited studies in the field was published in the early 1980s by a researcher named Timothy Keith, who looked at survey results from tens of thousands of high school students and concluded that homework had a positive relationship to achievement, at least at that age. But a funny thing happened ten years later when he and a colleague looked at homework alongside other possible influences on learning such as quality of instruction, motivation, and which classes the students took. When all these variables were entered into the equation simultaneously, the result was "puzzling and surprising": Homework no longer had any meaningful effect on achievement at all.[15] In other words, a set of findings that served—and, given how often his original study continues to be cited, still serves—as a prominent basis for the claim that homework raises achievement turns out to be spurious.

Several studies have actually found a *negative* relationship between students' achievement (or their academic performance as judged by teachers) and how much time they spend on homework (or how much help they receive from their parents).[16] But researchers who report this counterintuitive finding generally take pains to explain that it "must not be interpreted as a causal pattern."[17] What's really going on here, we're assured, is just that kids with academic difficulties are taking more time with their homework in order to catch up.

That sounds plausible, but of course it's just a theory. One study found that children who were having academic difficulties actually *didn't* get more homework from their teachers, although it's possible they spent longer hours working on the homework that they did get.[18] But even if we agreed that doing more homework probably isn't responsible for lowering students' achievement, the fact that there's an inverse relationship seems to suggest that, at the very least, homework isn't doing much to *help* kids who are struggling. In any event, anyone who reads the research on this topic can't help but notice how rare it is to find these same cautions about the misleading nature of correlational results when those results suggest a *positive* relationship between homework and achievement. It's only when the outcome doesn't fit the expected pattern (and support the case for homework) that it's carefully explained away.

In short, most of the research cited to show that homework is academically beneficial really doesn't prove any such thing.

2. Do we really know how much homework kids do?   The studies claiming that homework helps are based on the assumption that we can accurately measure the number and length of assignments. But many of these studies depend on students to tell us how much homework they get (or complete). When Harris Cooper and his associates looked at recent studies in which the time spent on homework was reported by students, and then compared them with studies in which that estimate was provided by their parents, the results were quite different. In fact, the correlation between homework and achievement disappeared when parents' estimates were used.[19] This was also true in one of Cooper's own studies: "Parent reports of homework completion were. . . uncorrelated with the student report."[20] The same sort of discrepancy shows up again in cross-cultural research (parents and children provide very different accounts of how much help kids receive)[21] and also when students and *teachers* are asked to estimate how much homework was assigned.[22] It's not clear which source is most accurate, by the way—or indeed whether any of them is entirely reliable.

These first two flaws combine to cast doubt on much of the existing data, according to a damning summary that appears in the *Encyclopedia of Educational Research*: "Research on homework continues to show the same fundamental weaknesses that have characterized it throughout the century: an overdependence on self-report as the predominant method of data collection and on correlation as the principal method of data analysis."[23]

3. Homework studies confuse grades and test scores with learning. Most researchers, like most reporters who write about education, talk about how this or that policy affects student "achievement" without questioning whether the way that word is defined in the studies makes any sense. What exactly is this entity called achievement that's said to go up or down? It turns out that what's actually being measured—at least in all the homework research I've seen—is one of three things: scores on tests designed by teachers, grades given by teachers, or scores on standardized MCAS exams. About the best thing you can say for these numbers is that they're easy for researchers to collect and report. Each is seriously flawed in its own way.

In studies that involve in-class tests, some students are given homework—which usually consists of reviewing a batch of facts about some topic—and then they, along with their peers who didn't get the homework, take a quiz on that very material. The outcome measure, in other words, is precisely aligned to the homework that some students did and others didn't do—or that they did in varying amounts. It's as if you were told to spend time in the evening learning the names of all the vice presidents of the United States and were then tested only on those names. If you remembered more of them after cramming, the researcher would then conclude that "learning in the evening" is effective.

In the second kind of study, course grades are used to determine whether homework made a difference. The problem here is that a grade, as one writer put it long ago, is "an inadequate report of an inaccurate judgment by a biased and variable judge of the extent to which a student has attained an undefined level of mastery of an unknown proportion of an indefinite amount of material."[24] Quite apart from the destructive effects grades have on students' interest in learning, their depth of understanding, and their preference for challenging tasks, the basis for a grade is typically as subjective as the result is uninformative. Any given assignment may well be given two different grades by two equally qualified teachers—and may even be given two different grades by a single teacher who reads it at two different times. The final course grade, moreover, is based on a combination of these individual marks, along with other, even less well-defined considerations.[25]

As bad as grades are in general, they are particularly inappropriate for judging the effectiveness of homework for one simple reason: The same teacher who handed out the assignments then turns around and evaluates the students who completed them. The final grade a teacher chooses for a student will often be based at least partly on whether, and to what extent, that student did the homework. Thus, to say that more homework is associated with better school performance (as measured by grades) is to provide no useful information about whether homework is intrinsically valuable. Yet grades *are* the basis for a good number of the studies that are cited to defend that very conclusion. The studies that use grades as the outcome measure, not surprisingly, tend to show a much stronger effect for homework than studies that use standardized test scores.[26]

Here's one example. Cooper and his colleagues conducted a study in 1998 with both younger and older students (from grades 2 through 12), using both grades and standardized test scores to measure achievement. They also looked at how much homework was assigned by the teacher as well as at how much time students spent on it. Thus, there were eight separate results to be reported. Here's how they came out:

YOUNGER STUDENTS

Effect on grades of amount of homework assigned	No sig. relationship
Effect on test scores of amount of homework assigned	No sig. relationship
Effect on grades of amount of homework done	Negative relationship
Effect on test scores of amount of homework done	No sig. relationship

OLDER STUDENTS

Effect on grades of amount of homework assigned	No sig. relationship
Effect on test scores of amount of homework assigned	No sig. relationship
Effect on grades of amount of homework done	Positive relationship
Effect on test scores of amount of homework done	No sig. relationship

Of these eight comparisons, then, the only positive correlation— and it wasn't a large one—was between how much homework older students did and their achievement as measured by grades.[27] If that measure is viewed as dubious, if not downright silly, then one of the more recent studies conducted by the country's best-known homework researcher fails to support the idea of assigning home-work at any age.

The last, and most common, way of measuring achievement is to use standardized test scores. Purely because they're standardized, these tests are widely regarded as objective instruments for assessing children's academic performance. But as I've argued elsewhere at some length, there is considerable reason to believe that standardized tests are a poor measure of intellectual proficiency.[28] They are, how-ever, excellent indicators of two things. The first is affluence: Up to 90 percent of the difference in scores among schools, communities, or even states can be accounted for, statistically speaking, without knowing anything about what happened inside the classrooms. All you need are some facts about the average income and education lev-els of the students' parents. The second phenomenon that standard-ized tests measure is how skillful a particular group of students is at taking standardized tests—and, increasingly, how much class time has been given over to preparing them to do just that.

not all people test well

In my experience, teachers can almost always identify several students who do poorly on standardized tests even though, by more authentic and meaningful indicators, they are talented thinkers. Other students, meanwhile, ace these tests even though their thinking *isn't* particularly impressive; they're just good test takers. These anecdotal reports have been corroborated by research that finds a statistically significant positive relationship between a shallow or superficial approach to learning, on the one hand, and high scores on various standardized tests, on the other. What's more, this association has been documented at the elementary, middle, and high school levels.

Standardized tests are even less useful when they include any of these features:

- If most of the questions are multiple choice, then students are unable to generate, or even justify, their responses. To that extent, students cannot really demonstrate what they know or what they can do with what they know. Multiple-choice tests are basically designed so that many kids who understand a given idea will be tricked into picking the wrong answer.

- If the test is timed, then it places a premium not on thoughtfulness but on speed.
- If the test is focused on "basic skills," then doing well is more a function of cramming forgettable facts into short-term memory than of really understanding ideas, making connections and distinctions, knowing how to read or write or analyze problems in a sophisticated way, thinking like a scientist or historian, being able to use knowledge in unfamiliar situations, and so on. *Companies are seeking this kind of thinking!*
- If the test is given to younger children, then, according to an overwhelming consensus on the part of early-education specialists, it is a poor indicator of academic skills. Many children under the age of eight or nine are unable to demonstrate their proficiency on a standardized test just because they're tripped up by the format.
- If the test is "norm-referenced" (like the Iowa Test of Basic Skills, Terra Nova, Stanford Achievement Test, and others used widely in classrooms and also by researchers), then it was never designed to evaluate whether students know what they should. Instead, its primary purpose is to artificially spread out the scores in order to facilitate ranking students against each other. The question these tests are intended to answer is not "How well are our kids—or our schools—doing?" but "Who's beating whom?" We know nothing about academic competence in absolute terms just from knowing what percentage of other test takers a given child has bested. Moreover, the selection of questions for these tests is informed by this imperative to rank. Thus, items that a lot of students answer correctly (or incorrectly) are typically eliminated—

regardless of whether the content is important—and replaced with questions that about half the kids will get right. This is done in order to make it easier to compare students to one another.

My purpose in these few paragraphs has been to offer only a brief summary of the reasons that informed educators and parents would never regard a standardized test score as meaningful information about the quality of a student's thinking—or about the quality of a school. (In the latter case, a high or rising average test score may actually be a reason to worry. Every hour that teachers spend preparing kids to succeed on standardized tests, even if that investment pays off, is an hour not spent helping kids to become critical, curious, creative thinkers.) The limitations of these tests are so numerous and so serious that studies showing an association between homework and higher scores are highly misleading. Because that's also true of studies that use grades as a stand-in for achievement, it should be obvious that combining two flawed measures does nothing to improve the situation.[29]

I'm unaware of any studies that have addressed the question of whether homework enhances the depth of students' understanding of ideas or their passion for learning. The fact that more meaningful outcomes are hard to quantify does not make test scores or grades any more valid, reliable, or useful as measures. To use them anyway calls to mind the story of the man who looked for his lost keys near a streetlight one night, not because that was where he dropped them but just because the light was better there.

If our children's ability to understand ideas from the inside out is what matters to us, and if we don't have any evidence that giving them homework helps them to acquire this proficiency, then all the research in the world showing that test scores rise when you make kids do more schoolwork at home doesn't mean very much. That's particularly true if the homework was designed specifically to improve the limited band of skills that appear on these tests. It's probably not a coincidence that, even within the existing test-based research, homework appears to work better when the assignments involve rote learning and repetition rather than real thinking.[30] After all, "works better" just means "produces higher scores on exams that measure low-level capabilities."

Overall, the available homework research defines "beneficial" in terms of achievement, and it defines achievement as better grades or standardized test scores. It allows us to conclude nothing about whether children's *learning* improves.

Cautionary Findings

Assume for the moment that we weren't concerned about basing our conclusions on studies that merely show homework is associated with (as opposed to responsible for) achievement, or studies that depend on questionable estimates of how much is actually completed, or studies that use deeply problematic outcome measures. Even taken on its own terms, the research turns up some findings that must give pause to anyone who thinks homework is valuable.

4. Homework matters less the longer you look. The longer the duration of a homework study, the less of an effect the homework is shown to have.[31] Cooper, who pointed this out almost in passing, speculated that less homework may have been assigned during any given week in the longer-lasting studies, but he offered no evidence that this actually happened. So here's another theory: The studies finding the greatest effect were those that captured less of what goes on in the real world by virtue of being so brief. View a small, unrepresentative slice of a child's life and it may appear that homework makes a contribution to achievement; keep watching and that contribution is eventually revealed to be illusory.

5. Even where they do exist, positive effects are often quite small.   In Cooper's review, as I've already pointed out, homework could explain only a tiny proportion of the differences in achievement scores. The same was true of a large-scale high school study from the 1960s.[32] And in a more recent investigation of British secondary schools, "the payoff for working several more hours per week per subject would appear to be slight, and those classes where there was more homework were not always those classes which obtained better results."[33] As one scholar remarked, "If research tells us anything" about homework, it's that "even when achievement gains *have* been found, they have been minimal, especially in comparison to the amount of work expended by teachers and students."[34]

6. There is no evidence of any academic benefit from homework in elementary school.   Even if you are untroubled by the methodological concerns I've been describing, the fact is that after decades of research on the topic, there is no overall positive correlation between homework and achievement (by any measure) for students before middle school or, in many cases, before high school. More precisely, there's virtually no good research on the impact of homework in the primary grades—and therefore no data to support its use with young children—whereas research *has* been done with students in the upper elementary grades, and it generally fails to find any benefit.

The absence of evidence supporting the value of homework before high school is generally acknowledged by experts in the field, even those who are less critical of the research literature (and less troubled by the negative effects of homework) than I am. But this remarkable fact is rarely communicated to the general public. In fact, it's with younger children, where the benefits are most questionable (if not absent), that there has been the greatest increase in the quantity of homework!

In 1989, Cooper summarized the available research with a sentence that ought to be e-mailed to every parent, teacher, and administrator in the country: "There is no evidence that any amount of homework improves the academic performance of elementary students."[35] In revisiting his review a decade later, he mentioned another large study he had come across. It, too, found minuscule correlations between the amount of homework done by sixth graders, on the one hand, and their grades and test scores, on the other. For third graders, the correlations were *negative*: more homework was associated with lower achievement.[36]

In 2005, I asked Cooper if he knew of any newer studies with elementary school students, and he said he had come across exactly four, all small and all unpublished. He was kind enough to offer the citations, and I managed to track them down.

The first was a college student's term paper describing an experiment with thirty-nine second graders in one school. The point was to see whether children who did math homework would perform better on a quiz taken immediately afterward that covered exactly the same content as the homework. The second study, a master's thesis, involved forty third graders, again in a single school and again with performance measured on a follow-up quiz dealing with the homework material, this time featuring vocabulary skills. The third study tested sixty-four fifth graders on social studies facts.

All three of these experiments found exactly what you would expect: The kids who had drilled on the material—a process that happened to take place at home—did better on their respective class tests. The final study, a dissertation project, involved teaching a lesson contained in a language arts textbook. The fourth graders who had been assigned homework on this material performed better on the textbook's unit test, but did not do any better on a standardized test. And the third graders who *hadn't* done any homework wound up with higher scores on the standardized test.[37] Like the other three studies, the measure of success basically involved memorizing and regurgitating facts.

It seems safe to say that these latest four studies offer no reason to revise the earlier summary statement that no meaningful evidence exists of an academic advantage for children in elementary school who do homework.[38] And the news isn't much better for children in middle school or junior high school. If the raw correlation between achievement (test scores or grades) and time spent on homework in Cooper's initial research review is "nearly nonexistent" for grades 3 through 5, it remains extremely low for grades 6 through 9. The correlation only spikes at or above grade 10.[39]

Such a correlation would be a prerequisite for assuming that homework provides academic benefits, but I want to repeat that it isn't enough to justify that conclusion. A large correlation is necessary, in other words, but not sufficient. Indeed, I believe it would be a mistake to conclude that homework is a meaningful contributor to learning even in high school. Remember that Cooper and his colleagues found a positive effect only when they looked at how much homework high school students actually did (as opposed to how much the teacher assigned) and only when achievement was measured by the grades given to them by those same teachers. Also recall that Keith's earlier positive finding with respect to homework in high school evaporated once he used a more sophisticated statistical technique to analyze the data.

All of the cautions, qualifications, and criticisms in this chapter, for that matter, are relevant to students of all ages. But it's worth pointing out separately that no evidence exists to support the practice of assigning homework to elementary students. No wonder "many Japanese elementary schools in the late 1990s issued 'no homework' policies."[40] That development may strike us as surprising, particularly in light of how Japan's educational system has long been held out as a model, notably by writers trying to justify their support for homework.[41] But it's a development that seems entirely rational in light of what the evidence shows right here in the United States.

Additional Research

7. The results of national and international exams raise further doubts about homework's role. The National Assessment of Educational Progress (NAEP) is often called the nation's report card. Students who take this test also answer a series of questions about themselves, sometimes including how much time they spend on homework. For any number of reasons, one might expect to find a reasonably strong association between time spent on homework and test scores. Yet the most striking result, particularly for elementary students, is the absence of such an association. Even students who reported being assigned no homework at all didn't fare badly on the test.

Consider the results of the 2000 math exam. Fourth graders who did no homework got roughly the same score as those who did thirty minutes a night. Remarkably, the scores then *declined* for those who did forty-five minutes, then declined again for those who did an hour or more! In eighth grade, the scores were higher for those who did between fifteen and forty-five minutes a night than for those who did no homework, but the results were worse for those who did an hour's worth, and worse still for those did more than an hour. In twelfth grade, the scores were about the same regardless of whether students did only fifteen minutes or more than an hour.[42] Results on the reading test, too, provided no compelling evidence that homework helped.[43]

International comparisons allow us to look for correlations between homework and test scores *within* each country and also for correlations *across* countries. Let's begin with the former. In the 1980s, thirteen-year-olds in a dozen nations were tested and also queried about how much they studied. "In some countries more time spent on homework was associated with higher scores; in others, it was not."[44] In the 1990s, the Trends in International Mathematics and Science Study (TIMSS) became the most popular way of assessing what was going on around the world, although its conclusions can't necessarily be generalized to other subjects. Again, the results were not the same in all countries, even when the focus was limited to the final years of high school (where the contribution of homework is thought to be strongest). Usually it turned out that doing some homework had a stronger relationship with achievement than doing none at all, but doing a little homework was also better than doing a lot.[45] This is known as a "curvilinear" relationship; on a graph it looks like an upside-down U.

But even that relationship didn't show up in a separate series of studies involving elementary school students in China, Japan, and two U.S. cities: "There was no consistent linear or curvilinear relation between the amount of time spent on homework and the child's level of academic achievement." These researchers even checked to see if homework in first grade was related to achievement in fifth grade, the theory being that homework might provide gradual, long-term benefits to younger children. Again they came up empty-handed.[46]

What about correlations across cultures? Here we find people playing what I'll later argue is a pointless game in which countries' education systems are ranked against one another on the basis of their students' test scores. Pointless or not, "a common explanation of the poor performance of American children in cross-cultural comparisons of academic achievement is that American children spend little time in study."[47] The reasoning, in other words, goes something like this:

·Premise 1: Our students get significantly less homework than their counterparts across the globe.

Premise 2: Other countries whup the pants off us in international exams.

Conclusion: Premise 1 explains premise 2.

Additional conclusion: If U.S. teachers assigned more homework, our students would perform better.

Every step of this syllogism is either flawed or simply false. We've already seen that premise 1 is no longer true, if indeed it ever was (see p. 8). Premise 2 has been debunked by a number of analysts and for a number of different reasons.[48] Even if both premises were accurate, however, the conclusions don't necessarily follow; this is another example of confusing correlation with causation.

But there is now empirical evidence, not just logic, to challenge the conclusions. Two researchers looked at TIMSS data from 1994 and 1999 to compare practices in fifty countries. When they published their findings in 2005, they could scarcely conceal their surprise:

> Not only did we fail to find any positive relationships, [but] the overall correlations between national average student achievement and national averages in the frequency, total amount, and percentage of teachers who used homework in grading are all *negative!* If these data can be extrapolated to other subjects—a research topic that warrants immediate study, in our opinion—then countries that try to improve their standing in the world rankings of student achievement by raising the amount of homework might actually be undermining their own success. . . . More homework may actually undermine national achievement.[49]

In a separate analysis of the 1999 TIMSS results that looked at twenty-seven U.S. states or districts as well as thirty-seven other countries, meanwhile, "there was little relationship between the amount of homework assigned and students' performance."[50] And the overall conclusion was also supported by TIMSS data showing that "Japanese junior high school students performed at the top but did not study as much as their peers in other countries."[51]

8. Incidental research raises further doubts about homework. Reviews of homework studies tend to overlook investigations that are primarily focused on other topics but just happen to look at homework, among several other variables. Here are two examples:

First, a pair of Harvard scientists queried almost two thousand students enrolled in college physics courses in order to figure out whether any features of their high school physics courses were now of use to them. At first they found a very small relationship between the amount of homework students had in high school and how well they were currently doing. Once the researchers controlled for other variables, such as the type of courses kids had taken, that relationship disappeared. The same researchers then embarked on a similar study of a much larger population of students in college science classes and found the same thing: Homework simply didn't help.[52]

Second, back in the late 1970s, New Jersey educator Ruth Tschudin identified about three hundred "A+ teachers" on the basis of recommendations, awards, or media coverage. She then set out to compare their classroom practices to those of a matched group of other teachers. Among her findings: The exceptional teachers not only tended to give less homework but also were likely to give students more choices about their assignments.

It's interesting to speculate on why this might be true. Are better teachers more apt to question the conventional wisdom in general? More likely to notice that homework isn't doing much good? More responsive to its negative effects on children and families? More likely to summon the gumption to act on what they've noticed? Or perhaps the researchers who reviewed the TIMMS data put their finger on it when they wrote, "It may be the poorest teachers who assign the most homework [because] effective teachers may cover all the material in class."[53] (Imagine that quotation enlarged and posted in a school's main office.)

This analysis rings true for Steve Phelps, who teaches math at a high school near Cincinnati. "In all honesty," he says, "the students are compelled to be in my class forty-eight minutes a day. If I can't get done in forty-eight minutes what I need to get done, then I really have no business intruding on their family time."[54] But figuring out *how* to get it done isn't always easy. It certainly took time for Phil Lyons, the social studies teacher I mentioned earlier who figured out that homework was making students less interested in learning for its own sake, and then watched as many of them began to "seek out more knowledge" once he stopped giving them homework. At the beginning of Lyons's teaching career, he assigned a lot of homework "as a crutch, to compensate for poor lessons. . . . But as I mastered the material, homework ceased to be necessary. A no-homework policy is a challenge to me," he adds. "I am forced to create lessons that are so good that no further drilling is required when the lessons are completed."

Lyons has also conducted an informal investigation to gauge the impact of this shift. He gave less and less homework each year before finally eliminating it completely. And he reports that

each year my students have performed better on the AP economics test. The empirical data from my class combined with studies I've read convinced me. Homework is an obvious burden to students, but assigning, collecting, grading, and recording homework creates a tremendous amount of work for me as well. I would feel justified encroaching on students' free time and I'd be willing to do the grading if I saw tangible returns, but with no quantifiable benefit it makes no sense to impose on them or me.[55]

The results observed by a single teacher in an uncontrolled experiment are obviously not conclusive. Nor is the Harvard physics study. Nor is Tschudin's survey of terrific teachers. But when all these observations are combined with the surprising results of national and international exams, and when these in turn are viewed in the context of research literature that makes a weak, correlational case for homework in high school—and offers absolutely no support for homework in elementary school—it gradually becomes clear that we've been sold a bill of goods.

People who never bought it will not be surprised, of course. "I have a good education and a decent job despite the fact that I didn't spend half my adolescence doing homework," said a mother of four children whose concern about excessive homework eventually led to her becoming an activist on the issue.[56] On the other hand, some will find these results not only unexpected but hard to believe, if only because common sense tells them that homework *should* help. But just as a careful look at the research overturns the canard that "studies show homework raises achievement," so a careful look at popular beliefs about learning will challenge the reasons that lead us to expect we will find unequivocal research support in the first place. The absence of supporting data actually makes sense in retrospect, as we'll see in Chapter 6 when we examine the idea that homework "reinforces" what was learned in class, along with other declarations that are too readily accepted on faith.

It's true that we don't have clear evidence to prove beyond a reasonable doubt that homework *doesn't* help students learn. Indeed, it's hard to imagine what that evidence might look like—beyond repeated findings that homework often isn't even associated with higher achievement. To borrow a concept from the law, however, the burden of proof here doesn't rest with critics to demonstrate that homework doesn't help. It rests with supporters to show that it *does*, and specifically to show that its advantages are sufficiently powerful and pervasive to justify taking up children's (and parents' and teachers') time, and to compensate for the distinct disadvantages discussed in Chapter 1. When a principal admits that homework is "taking away some of the years of adolescence and child-hood" but then says that requiring it from the earliest grades "give[s] us an edge in standardized testing," we have to wonder what kind of educator—indeed, what kind of human being—is willing to accept that trade-off even if the latter premise were true.[57]

Most proponents, of course, aren't saying that all homework is always good in all respects for all kids—just as critics couldn't defend the proposition that no homework is ever good in any way for any child. The prevailing view—which, even if not stated explicitly, seems to be the premise lurking behind our willingness to accept the practice of assigning homework to students on a regular basis—might be summarized as "Most homework is probably good for most kids." I've been arguing, in effect, that even that relatively moderate position is not supported by the evidence. I've been arguing that any possible gains are both minimal and far from universal, limited to certain ages and to certain (dubious) outcome measures. What's more, even studies that seem to show an overall benefit don't prove that more homework—or any homework, for that matter—has such an effect for most students. Put differently, the research offers no reason to believe that students in high-quality classrooms whose teachers give little or no homework would be at a disadvantage as regards any meaningful learning.

But is there some other benefit, something other than academic learning, that might be cited in homework's defense? We turn now to that question.

CHAPTER 3

Does Homework Provide Nonacademic Benefits?

Twan DECADES AGO, I was investigating the topic of competition and discovered something interesting about how its proponents defend the idea of setting people against each other in a race to be number one. The data suggested that, contrary to American myth, competition tends to hold people back from doing their best work, particularly if what they're doing requires creativity. Study after study has found that when we're involved in some sort of contest we end up not doing as well on most tasks as we would in the absence of competition. Indeed, a cooperative arrangement, in which we work *with* others rather than against them or apart from them, is often the most productive of all.

In response to this surprising evidence, however, I noticed that many people who are firmly committed to the idea that competition is a good thing simply stop talking about achievement. Instead, they insist that there must be other benefits for the individuals involved. Rather than rethinking the value of an arrangement in which one person must fail in order for others to succeed, they smoothly shift to the claim that competition "builds character."[1]

Something very similar happens in discussions of homework. If it can't be shown that filling children's backpacks and evenings with school assignments is likely to help them learn better, many people try to defend homework on other grounds instead. Rather than beginning with the question, What does it make sense to do with kids? they ask, What reasons can we come up with to justify homework, which we're determined to assign in any case?

One such justification is that it "gives parents insights into a school's philosophy, curriculum, and objectives."[2] Homework is said to facilitate communication between school and home, if not a genuine dialogue then at least an opportunity for parents to see what their kids are being taught. It's said to be a window into the classroom. A pamphlet produced by the National Education Association and the National PTA asserts that homework is "the link between schools and home that shows what children are studying."[3] Not just *a* link—*the* link.

But if the goal is to give parents information about classroom practices, why would we need to compel students to do schoolwork at home every night? Couldn't they just take home assignments that they'd completed during class and explain what they'd done? If more was needed, why not have teachers send occasional descriptive memos and sample lesson plans to parents—or invite them to visit classrooms to learn more about what's happening there? Conferences and phone calls, meanwhile, could provide ample information about what (and how well) their own children were doing. Any combination of these mechanisms would likely be more effective at keeping parents in the loop than homework is, and without placing a burden on the students and their families.[4]

"Helping children with their homework is also supposed to be a way that parents demonstrate their interest in a child's schoolwork," says Kalman Heller, a Boston-area psychologist. However, "the same thing can be done much more effectively by having discussions about what a child is learning in school and by parents modeling the value of learning in their lives and in shared activities with their children. 'What are you discussing in Social Studies these days?' is far better than questions that focus primarily on grades and homework."[5]

Sometimes homework is defended as a way of showing parents *how* their children are doing these assignments. Homework is supposed to offer parents insights into the way their kids' minds work. One California mother wrote to me that she was told

> schools assign homework so that parents can see "how their children are learning." But this has put me in a bind: Do I require that my child do the homework only when I can watch, so I can see how she is learning? Or do I "allow" her to do it on her own [even though parents at our school are] required to sign that they have checked the homework and it is "complete and correct." My daughter was kept in for recess because I did not catch a spelling mistake and a missing period at the end of a sentence.

In general terms, as I noted in Chapter 1, parents may understandably feel that they can't win since conflicting messages are sent about how involved they should be in what their children are doing. But this dilemma becomes even more frustrating when parents are expected to be actively involved (to enforce the teacher's agenda) at the same time that homework is supposed to be a way for them to sit back and observe how their children are learning. In any case, if there's little evidence that homework *helps* kids learn better, it's hard to justify making kids do it, particularly if there are other ways to inform parents about what's happening at school.

Looking for Proof

So what does that leave as a rationale? The most common nonacademic justification for homework is that it, like competition, has character-building properties. Specifically, it's said to help students "take responsibility for school work, . . . to build 'study skills' through homework assignments to develop students' perseverance, ability to follow directions, neatness and completeness, and overall level of responsibility."[6] Others have asserted that homework promotes "self-discipline"[7] as well as "initiative" and "independence."[8]

When parents and educators were asked in a survey which reason(s) for giving homework they endorsed, the first choice of both groups had nothing to do with enhancing academic skills or understanding. Instead, they picked "develops children's initiative and responsibility."[9] The proposition that making children do homework would in fact lead them to acquire these characteristics—let's group them under the heading "good work habits"—is asserted endlessly and accepted uncritically even by otherwise thoughtful teachers and parents. In a study that probed for beliefs about the effects of homework, both elementary and secondary teachers were at least as sure that it helped students "gain study skills" or do better with "time management" as they were that it helped students learn.[10]

But as with claims about academic effects, we should ask to see what empirical support exists for this hypothesis before requiring children to sacrifice their free time or other activities. We would want either a study that randomly assigned students to classrooms with and without homework (but which were otherwise similar) or one that looked at existing classrooms featuring a lot of (as compared to a little or no) homework and then employed statistical controls to hold other factors constant. That would give us some insight into whether students in the former classrooms exhibit better work habits than those in the latter and, if so, how much of that difference is due to the homework.

So *does* homework have such an effect? No one has a clue. As far as I can tell, no experiment of either type has ever been conducted to investigate common claims about responsibility, self-discipline, and so on. To that extent, no evidence exists to support those claims.

At first I was reluctant to believe that this could be true. So many people, including researchers, sounded so sure of themselves when defending homework along these lines that I assumed studies must have been done that I hadn't found. Indeed, I came across academic articles that made such claims, but the sources they cited contained no empirical data. (I'll have more to say about that in the next chapter.) Harris Cooper wrote in 1989 that "no studies [have] looked at non-academic outcomes like study habits."[11] I asked him in 2005 whether anything had been published since then. He was able to come up with only two studies, and they looked not at work habits but at the relation between homework and students' conduct. (The two studies reached different conclusions, by the way.)[12]

Finally, I checked the entry on homework in the authoritative *Encyclopedia of Educational Research* and found the following summary statement: "Of all the research questions asked about homework, the paramount one has always focused on the relationship between homework and academic achievement." Whether homework has any effect on "objectives other than test marks and course grades—such as developing discipline and independence, extending understanding, or strengthening a positive attitude to learning—cannot be stated."[13]

That last sentence suggests—and my own review of the data corroborates—that what's missing from the research literature can be grouped in three clusters:

First, as I noted earlier, we don't know whether homework provides any meaningful intellectual benefits—any effects beyond what's reflected in standardized test scores and teachers' grades.

Second, we have almost no empirical evidence showing how homework affects the way students come to regard school, their teachers, themselves, or even the idea of homework itself. One exception: Cooper and his colleagues asked about seven hundred students of different ages whether they thought homework helped them to learn. There was no relationship between how much homework the older students were assigned and how they felt about this. But the more assignments the younger students (up to fifth grade) had to do, the more negative their attitudes were.[14]

Finally, to return to the focus of this chapter, there is no research to support the belief that homework helps students to develop any of the characteristics that appear under the heading of work habits. Thus, if we were guided by the demand for "evidence based" or "scientifically validated" education policies that we hear so often these days, it would be impossible to use any nonacademic justifications for assigning homework.

Rethinking the Logic

Some claims seem persuasive even in the absence of data. For example, we know certain things are true because they make intuitive sense or are confirmed by our personal experience. Can we argue that this applies here, and therefore the lack of research need not trouble us where homework is concerned?

Consider the idea that doing homework promotes "responsibility." Such a claim might seem plausible until we stop to ask what it is, exactly, for which students are actually responsible. Almost never are they permitted to decide whether to have homework, or how much, or what kind. Instead, their choices are limited to such peripheral questions as when to do what they've been required to do. This is, it must be conceded, a rather pale version of responsibility.

Still, if homework taught children how to budget their time well, that would be something. But this is a hard case to make for two reasons. First, the choice of when to do their homework is typically made for students by their parents, who insist that they finish it before doing something they find enjoyable. One mother remarked to me that what her kids' assignments are really testing is *her* proficiency at time management. Of course we might reply that she, and other parents, could back off and leave kids on their own to finish their homework (or not). But this is neither caring[15] nor practical. The consequences are unpleasant for parent and child alike if the assignment is discovered undone just before bedtime or early the next morning. In fact, if it remains undone, parents can usually count on hearing from the teacher, which would suggest that a hands-off policy on the part of parents really isn't expected or desired. It's understandable, then, that most parents are accustomed to saying, "You need to get your homework out of the way before you . . ." What's not so understandable is that they would turn around and defend homework on the grounds that it helps children to develop responsibility or become more independent.

Second, even if a parent did refrain from becoming involved, that doesn't mean homework assignments in themselves can *teach* children responsibility. The idea that they can, however, is remarkably tenacious. A sixth grade teacher recently told me how her students sometimes get no homework but at other times "may be responsible for homework over weekends or vacations and possibly three weeks straight." This policy, she declared, "requires a student to develop a sophisticated sense of organization, and in itself, this is beneficial." The premise here seems to be that (the teacher's) requiring a sophisticated sense of organization is tantamount to (the child's) developing it. In reality, if students lack this capacity, the primary effect of homework would be to make them feel anxious and incompetent. Few of us today believe that tossing kids into the deep end of a pool teaches them how to swim. Why, then, do we believe that giving children a set of tasks to do in a limited amount of time somehow provides them with the wherewithal to accomplish this?

Apart from whether homework is *sufficient* for promoting such skills, there's the question of whether it's even *necessary*. How good someone is at budgeting time would seem to be a function of two variables. The first is age: Most twelve-year-olds are better than most seven-year-olds regardless of how much homework they've been assigned. It's both naive and unhelpful to expect younger children to defer gratification or know how to engage in long-term planning.

The second variable is personality. Plenty of people who didn't have much homework when they were young turn out to be quite adept at independent thinking and completing tasks on a schedule. Plenty of people who had loads of homework are lousy at these things. And incidentally, one way children *may* get better at devising and carrying out plans, seeing tasks through to completion, and so on, is by doing chores and participating in other activities that are part of family life. Yet, as authors Etta Kralovec and John Buell have observed, there's less time for them to do this because homework gets in the way.[16]

It's equally dubious to think that the act of assigning homework is necessary to improve students' "study skills." Assuming that this phrase refers to the ability to formulate questions, locate information, and organize one's thoughts, what reason is there to believe that these capabilities can't be developed during the six or seven hours a day, five days a week, that children spend in school? It seems peculiar to claim that homework is a school's sole tool, or even best tool, for supporting any of these character-related attributes. The premise that homework is necessary to improve study skills becomes persuasive only if that phrase is defined so narrowly that the whole argument becomes circular: Homework is useful to help kids get better at doing homework. As I'll argue in Chapter 8, that kind of reasoning is used to justify other activities, too, and it ought to be questioned wherever it appears.

Even if one were to insist that homework does provide such benefits, moreover, how often would it need to be assigned in order to help students develop the requisite work habits and skills? A few times a month, perhaps? Clearly, these arguments for homework, even if true, wouldn't justify the practice of assigning it day after day after day. It seems more likely that these nonacademic considerations are invoked to justify a practice that some people favor for other reasons.

The proposition that homework has nonacademic advantages becomes even less credible in light of the psychological literature dealing with motivation, child development, and education.[17] One insight derived from that literature is that children, like adults, fare better in just about every way when they have some control over the events that affect them—when they feel like "origins" in their lives rather than "pawns," as one researcher put it. The benefits of experiencing a sense of autonomy range from better physical health to bet- ter emotional adjustment, and, in the case of students, also include greater academic self-confidence, which is associated with more successful learning. Apart from the practical benefits of being able to make choices, one could argue from a moral perspective that all people ought to have some control over their own lives. There are limits, of course—notably with respect to age—but even children should be able to make decisions about matters that concern them except when there is a compelling reason to deny them that right.[18]

Consider, then, the fact that preschoolers often request homework, "either real or pretend, in an effort to emulate their older siblings," as one researcher reports. When they start school, they may still "appear excited by the idea of homework, but it takes a remarkably short period of time before many are disillusioned."[19] So what changed? The quality of what they've been given to do, perhaps, but mostly the fact that the homework is now assigned to them rather than chosen by them. Indeed, it rarely occurs to parents to ask, "What role did the kids have in deciding what sort of homework they'd be doing, or whether homework was appropriate at all for a given lesson?" Teachers, too, even in most self-styled progressive schools, generally take for granted that students will have virtually nothing to say about most of what they do, or with whom they'll do it, or how long it should take, or how it will be evaluated. To understand the human need for autonomy—and the consequences of thwarting that need—is to understand why homework, at least as it's typically assigned, is likely to be as unproductive for kids as it is unwelcome by them.

The effect of choice, or its absence, speaks to an even more basic point that's often overlooked in such discussions. We want children to know how to do certain things, but that doesn't mean much if they don't want to do them. Homework proponents typically focus on skills, on whether kids *can* do long division, or write a competent book report, or figure out how much of a lengthy project they'll have to do each night in order to meet a deadline. But assigning homework doesn't help them acquire the desire to do those things. In fact, any number of features of that homework—its lack of intrinsic interest, its inappropriate difficulty level, its having been assigned without any input from students, its encroachment upon time during which the child had hoped to do other things— may actually *reduce* that desire. From our point of view, homework may be fully justified. But our point of view isn't what matters most when the question is what its effect will be on children.

When our kids complain about constant, compulsory homework, some of us respond with compassion: "Honey, I know you don't like it, but . . ." What follows that "but" is either an effort to defend the homework or an assertion of its inevitability (which suggests we're unable to defend it). We try to be understanding, but our message is clear: How the child experiences the assignment ultimately doesn't matter. "My son cries about homework every other day, and I have to tell him he has to do it," says the mother of an eight-year-old.[20] Other adults, meanwhile, are unsympathetic, confident that children's concerns can safely be ignored. The only problem with homework in their view is that kids don't get enough of it.[21] We need to raise our expectations, push a generation of coddled kids to work harder—during school and after school. They don't like it? Tough cookies. Sometimes you have to do things you don't like.

The first thing that strikes me about these two reactions, the gentle and the harsh, is that they differ in tone but not really in substance. In the final analysis, both fail to take children's unhappiness seriously and both are therefore disrespectful. Even more important, if we fail to appreciate the significance of children's reactions, how those reactions color the way they think about learning and about themselves, we're not just being rude. We're being foolish. The evidence demonstrates that we can make students do things they don't want to, but we can't make them *want* to do those things. And whatever we may think about the fact that they don't want to do them, people of any age are less likely to derive value from doing what they experience as unpleasant or simply worthless. Sure, a child's body may benefit from nutritious foods even if swallowed reluctantly. But reluctance in regard to an action is directly relevant in determining whether it ends up having a positive effect on attitudes and values.

Thus, an effort to make kids into hard workers by compelling them to work hard—to instill good work habits in them by sheer force or cleverness—reflects a stunning ignorance about how human beings function in the real world. People are active meaning makers. They are not passive receptacles into which knowledge, or skills, or dispositions can be poured. To help children acquire responsibility, or independence, or any other characteristic requires us to work *with* them, as opposed to doing things (like homework) *to* them. It requires us to attend to what they want, what they need, and how they see things. The usual defenses of homework seem uninformed by these considerations. To that extent, these defenses are as lacking in credibility as in supportive data.

Reconsidering the Values

To this point, I've been assuming that the work habits in question are desirable and have confined myself to asking whether there's reason to believe that homework is required—or even particularly effective—at helping kids to acquire them. But let's take a closer look at the value of these characteristics, beginning with the idea of making children more *independent*. Our culture prizes the capacity to do things on one's own. We often assess children's development according to how little help they need to do something— a perspective by no means shared worldwide, incidentally. That we may have gotten carried away with our emphasis on individualism—that the importance of self-sufficiency may have come to eclipse other values (such as relationship and community)—has been suggested by any number of thinkers. It may be appropriate to ask, then, whether we really need to give students assignments to take home in order to advance this agenda of self-sufficiency. Is learning in most classrooms so collaborative that it is necessary to demand independent effort at night? (Before answering, keep in mind that the usual word for collaboration among students during school is "cheating.")

It seems more reasonable to propose that what's missing from American schools are opportunities to help kids learn to cooperate effectively so they'll become proficient at dividing up tasks and exchanging information, building on other people's ideas, gently challenging one another, listening respectfully, and understanding points of view other than their own—in short, to be part of well-functioning teams and to find value in collaboration. If that makes sense, then homework is hardly going to help. While the occasional assignment may involve a group project, the vast majority are intended to be done alone. Even a teacher who wanted to encourage cooperative learning would be unlikely to look to homework to achieve that goal because it takes considerably more effort for students to get together after school than during it.

Homework does, however, lend itself to getting help from a parent. On many assignments, a child may end up learning more from receiving that help than by doing the task alone.[22] Yet parents are constantly cautioned about becoming too involved. There is a difference, as I described in Chapter 1, between helping the child to figure things out, and taking over and doing the homework *for* the child so the product will be perfect. But even the former sort of involvement is often discouraged in the name of promoting "independence," and that should lead us to ask whether the primary purpose of homework is to help children become more enthusiastic and proficient learners, or to set up a situation where we can judge how good students are at doing things alone—and, perhaps, to teach the value of solitary effort.

Related to independence is the idea of helping children acquire *responsibility*. If that word is defined as "making decisions on one's own," then I've argued that homework (at least the way it's usually assigned and completed) does little to help kids acquire this characteristic. But often the word is used in an entirely different sense. The psychiatrist William Glasser observed some time ago that many educators "teach thoughtless conformity to school rules and call the conforming child 'responsible.'"[23] Listen carefully to some homework proponents and it becomes apparent that this is the kind of responsibility they hope and believe will be taught. One researcher, for example, conducted an experiment to "investigate children's understanding of their responsibility for homework and to clarify the role teachers and parents play in encouraging this developing understanding." But in her study the children's "understanding" of their "responsibility" turned out to mean their uncritical acceptance of what they were told to do.[24]

If that's what we intend by the word *responsibility*, then homework may be quite effective after all. Indeed, as educator Patricia Hinchey points out, "Schools are much too good at teaching people to do as they're told. . . . We need to question the practice of assigning students homework every night primarily so that they learn to practice unquestioning obedience at the expense of their own time and interests."[25]

Even more, we need to question the tendency to camouflage that agenda by using language intended to deflect objections. Few proponents of homework describe their goal as eliciting "unquestioning obedience." It's much more palatable to talk about responsibility or even "volition," which one homework researcher emphasizes is useful to "maintain students' intentions to accomplish academic goals in the face of competing (such as socioemotional) goals and other distractions" and to "provide quicker access to priorities that might not be among one's own."[26] This is a rather stilted way of saying that we need to figure out how children's own goals and preferences can be overridden rather than taken seriously. Moreover, we are discouraged from asking whether an adult's specific "academic goals" and priorities—or a given homework assignment—is of any value. That doesn't matter. The task is to get students to summon the will to do whatever they're assigned.

Homework is also said to teach children *self-discipline*—and, again, the phrase is more complicated than it might appear. For one thing, it's possible to discipline oneself too severely, to deny oneself pleasure and pursue one's obligations with an unhealthy urgency and a degree of organization that borders on compulsiveness. Some children who look like success stories—every parent's dream of a dedicated student—may in reality be anxious, driven, motivated by a perpetual need to feel better about themselves rather than by anything resembling curiosity. These youngsters don't need to be goaded or threatened into studying, so their motivation might be said to be internal. However, it surely isn't intrinsic.[27] Many of them are workaholics in training.

Because self-discipline (or internal motivation) is not always healthy, the ostensible role of homework in leading children to acquire that characteristic wouldn't necessarily mean that homework was a good thing. We'd have to know more. Surely we wouldn't want to take the position—as so many people give the impression of doing—that as long as kids are working hard on their assignments, managing their time well, and getting positive feedback from their teachers, it doesn't matter whether they're doing so joylessly. Indeed, it would make sense to revisit our basic objectives, to stop asking, "How do we make our kids more self-disciplined?" in favor of a question such as, "How can we help our kids to be psychologically healthy?" Of course we want them to look beyond instant gratification, but we also want them to experience real pleasure—in general and from learning in particular. Moreover, we'd want to help them develop outside interests so all their waking hours aren't devoted to work, either now or as adults.

Such reservations about an unqualified endorsement of self-discipline don't in themselves argue against the idea of homework, but they should give us pause about casually invoking the notion of self-discipline as an argument *for* homework. Moreover, even when it's not taken to extremes, self-discipline may not play as integral a role in many activities as is generally assumed. The essayist Annie Dillard once pointed out that writing doesn't depend on discipline in the way that many people believe it does. "You don't do it from will power; you do it from an abiding passion." In fact, she continues, it's rather like being a parent. "If you have a little baby crying in the middle of the night, and if you depend only on willpower to get you out of bed to feed the baby, that baby will starve. You do it out of love." For writing as for caring, "willpower is a weak idea; love is strong."[28]

But surely, some will object, lots of people don't share Dillard's delight in getting words to fit together in just the right way. True, but her insight reminds us that one of our primary obligations is to do what we can to *spark* a love of writing and thinking, a desire to figure things out.

Another objection: No matter how successful we are at promoting that desire, there are still going to be many things in life that must be done even though they're not particularly pleasant. Again, true. But this is a troubling justification for turning school—including what students are required to do after school—into a regimen to train students to put up with stuff that's unappealing. The veneration of self-discipline should lead us to inquire why so many aspects of formal education would require a grit-your-teeth-and-bear-it attitude.

More than once, after arguing for reforms that would make schooling more engaging for children, I have been huffily informed that life isn't always interesting and kids had better learn to deal with that fact. The implication of this response seems to be that the goal of education is not to nourish children's excitement about learning but to get them acclimated to doing mind-numbing, if not downright unpleasant, chores. The author John Holt once remarked that if people really felt that life was "nothing but drudgery, an endless list of dreary duties," one would hope they might "say, in effect, 'I have somehow missed the chance to put much joy and meaning into my own life; please educate my children so that they will do better.'"[29]

In any case, the "effort to teach self-discipline by continually imposing tasks" for them to complete at home often rests on a false dichotomy, as the writer John Buell pointed out: a "world of self-indulgence on the one hand, where the child is relieved of every possible burden and disappointment the parent can manage, and a world where the child is expected perpetually to measure up to extraordinarily difficult cognitive and moral challenges," on the other. It's important to point out that those who resist the latter do not necessarily support the former. Moreover, Buell argues that "self-discipline does not mean primarily learning that life is tough and that one must generally do what one is told. It means learning to manage freedom. . . [by having] gradually expanding opportunities. . . [to] be responsible for free time."[30]

The refreshing idea that it's at least as important for children to learn to manage freedom as it is for them to learn how to handle more assignments is missing from any hearty defenses of homework I've come across. So is a more nuanced understanding of self-discipline that would challenge the simplistic tendency to contrast it with absolute self-indulgence. For example, the conservative *National Review* published an essay a few years ago that strongly supported the practice of giving homework on the grounds that its most important lesson is "personal responsibility and self-discipline. Homework is practice for life."[31] In fact, the title of the essay was "Training for Life." But what aspect of life? The point evidently is not to train children to practice making meaningful decisions, or become part of a democratic society, or learn to think critically. Rather, what's being prescribed are lessons in doing what one is told and learning to work hard regardless of whether the work is worth doing.

What comes to mind here is the timeless Latin question *Cui bono?*—Whose interests are served? Who benefits when people are taught not to question the value of what they have been told to do but simply to toil away at it—and to regard this as virtuous? Follow this query where it leads and what initially looked like uncontroversial claims on behalf of homework turn out to reveal a very specific, very debatable set of cultural values.

In fact, we may sniff out an economic component to this defense, too. Among the reasons homework is seen to be useful is that it develops "work-related skills that can transfer to adult occupations."[32] So perhaps all the talk about homework's value at promoting good work habits is actually less about what children need than about what their future employers need. Perhaps the assertion that homework is "practice for life" is a partial truth: It's really practice for a life spent working in corporations. And perhaps it's not just about teaching *skills* that may be useful to a future employer; it's about inculcating *norms*, helping to produce "workers who are used to, and will not complain about, the long working day."[33]

Anyone who mentions the nonacademic benefits of homework is reminding us that academic achievement is not the only purpose of school or the only thing that matters about children. That is surely a welcome perspective. But if all those benefits turn out to be so many variations on the Protestant work ethic—taking responsibility for planning and finishing assignments, acquiring the necessary self-discipline to spend time on unappealing tasks, learning how to study hard and succeed on one's own—then we really haven't moved very far beyond academics after all. Even if this defense of homework doesn't hinge on helping kids to excel at math or reading, it's still about acquiring skills that will ultimately make them more productive academically (and perhaps economically).

What if we were concerned about children as whole human beings, though, not merely as achievers or producers? How would truly nonacademic considerations bear upon the question of homework? Concerns about an excess of self-discipline, as I've already mentioned, may remind us of very different goals, such as emotional health and well-roundedness. The more seriously we take those goals, the less likely we should be to accept a regimen of daily homework.

When I give lectures or workshops, I like to begin by asking parents (or teachers) in the audience to think about their long-term objectives for their children (or students)—what characteristics they'd like these kids to have for the rest of their lives. Having conducted this exercise scores of times all over North America, I can report with some confidence that even educators tend to be chiefly interested in nonacademic qualities. They're focused on the kind of people, not only the kind of learners, that their students will grow up to be. And while my question occasionally elicits the sort of characteristics that homework is supposed to help develop, most of the long-term goals I hear are not about "work habits." Both parents and teachers are more likely to say they want children to be happy, honest, caring, ethical, sensitive, passionate, socially responsible, and appreciative. (I'm copying these items off the list that was created the last time I asked this question, a few days ago. But the lists don't vary much from one group to the next, regardless of the demographic characteristics of the people in the audience. And that, of course, is part of my point.)

Earlier, I started with the nonacademic attributes that homework is said to promote, and I asked whether it really did so. Then I considered whether those attributes are always desirable. What I'm doing now is beginning with the nonacademic attributes that most parents and teachers care about and then asking whether homework is likely to facilitate their acquisition. All else being equal, does making kids do academic assignments when they get home from school seem likely to help them become happy, honest, caring, ethical, and all the rest of it? At best, homework will have no impact on these crucial qualities. At worst, the net effect will be negative, particularly when we consider other activities and interactions in which children might have had more time to take part. As a little boy comments to a backpack-laden classmate in a *New Yorker* cartoon, "No one's last words were 'I wish I'd done more homework.'"

One characteristic that often shows up on those lists of long-term goals is something like "curious" or "lifelong learner." Psychologists sometimes call it an intrinsic motivation to learn. For many of us, this is our single most important objective for our kids, at least with respect to school. Unhappily, as I argued in Chapter 1, this is often one of the most salient casualties of homework: "Most of what homework is doing is driving kids *away* from learning," says education professor Harvey Daniels.[34] To that extent, even if homework really did provide other important benefits, we'd have to weigh them against this overwhelming disadvantage. If there was reason to *doubt* the existence of those other benefits, then the effect on kids' love of learning would be decisive in our thinking about the issue.

A third grade teacher in Washington remembers being asked by a parent what her goal was in assigning homework. That simple question prompted a great deal of reflection and finally resulted in her decision to eliminate all homework with the exception of asking students to read books of their own choosing. "I want students to be decision makers, and when it comes from them it is more meaningful and will have lasting effects." The result: Many of her students now invent and complete their own academic projects "because they are so motivated to do so when the boundaries are removed. And many parents comment that they have never seen their child so positive about school."[35]

In sum, the usual claims that homework provides nonacademic benefits turn out to be dubious and unsubstantiated. Peel back the conventional labels and it's not clear how advantageous the process would be even if it did work as advertised. To talk about "independence," "taking responsibility," and "time management skills" may be a fancy way of saying that children must labor in solitude to complete mandatory assignments in such a way that they can quickly get through something they experience as pointless drudgery. Once we consider other goals and values, particularly if we regard them as more important than work habits, the conclusion that ineluctably follows is this: If we're going to evaluate homework on the basis of nonacademic considerations, those considerations not only fail to provide a convincing case for homework, but argue rather convincingly against it.

PART II

Six Reasons Homework Persists (Despite What the Data Say)

CHAPTER 4

"Studies Show . . ."—
Or Do They?

RESEARCH GENERALLY DOESN'T substantiate the belief that children need to do homework. Neither academic nor nonacademic justifications are supported by the available evidence. Yet homework is nearly universal and rarely questioned; indeed, some people insist that kids should get even more of it.

How to reconcile these two sets of facts is the puzzle that the remainder of this book will attempt to solve. To understand our collective attachment to the idea of making children spend time on school assignments at home, we'll need to look beyond what's in their backpacks. Homework, I'll argue, is a field on which much larger disputes are played out, including those involving standardized testing, the characteristics of good pedagogy, the nature and purposes of education, our attitudes toward research, and the ways we raise and regard children. Homework is an intriguing topic in its own right, but it also can be seen as a kind of case study, a way of illuminating some of our culture's basic values.

At the end of the book, I'll draw from the practices of educators who have challenged the conventional wisdom in order to propose a different way of thinking about the subject. But first, in this chapter and the five that follow, I want to offer half a dozen reasons to explain why homework is so widely accepted despite what the data say.

The first two reasons are generic, by which I mean they describe the way we tend to approach any number of topics. Specifically, it's common to find:

- A disregard for research findings, sometimes even on the part of researchers
- A reluctance to ask challenging questions about common practices and institutions

The remaining reasons help to explain why homework in particular is so readily accepted. They include:

- Fundamental misconceptions about the nature of learning
- An emphasis on competitiveness and "tougher standards" in education
- The belief that any practices students will encounter later, however unproductive, should be introduced earlier by way of preparation
- A basic distrust of children and how they choose to spend their time

Doubts About Data

Why, and under what circumstances, we should look to research before making decisions is a question far too complex to be settled here. Clearly, though, the *type* of decision is relevant; many choices don't require that we consult studies at all. Moreover, even when scientific findings are relevant, there's a difference between consulting them and using them as our sole guide. In education, it may make sense to attend to personal experience, too, as well as insights derived from other fields of study, such as philosophy, history, and literature. Scientism—the assumption that all true knowledge is scientific—may be as dangerous as an absolute aversion to, or ignorance of, the scientific method.

How we make use of data is also important. We need to distinguish well-conducted from poorly conducted research, and to understand what the outcome variables are in a given investigation. For example, if someone announces that studies have shown traditional classroom discipline techniques are "effective," our immediate question should be, "Effective at what?" Promoting meaningful learning and perhaps concern for others? Or eliciting short-term obedience? Empirical findings can come from rigorously conducted scientific studies but still be of limited value; everything depends on the objectives that informed the research.

Even well-conducted studies with reasonable criteria for evaluating the success of an intervention have to be applied with caution for the simple reason that on-average findings, however reliable and valid, may not apply to every student. "Our current 'scientific' method focuses almost exclusively on identifying what works best generally," education researcher Richard Allington points out. But "children differ. Therein lies what worries me about 'evidence-based' policy making in education. Good teaching, effective teaching, is not just about using whatever science says 'usually' works best. It is all about finding out what works best for the individual child and the group of children in front of you."[1]

Nevertheless, what is most worrisome about those who make and carry out education policy is not an overreliance on scientific investigations but a profound indifference to what those investigations have found. That indifference is particularly troubling (which is to say, the need for supporting data is particularly acute) when we're talking about policies with potentially serious disadvantages. When that's *not* the case, it might be fine to say, "I can't prove that this idea will be helpful, but I believe there's good reason to think it will be—and there don't seem to be any compelling arguments to the contrary." On such a basis, a principal might decide, for example, to schedule activities in which older and younger students spend time together, the point being to foster a sense of community in the school. Or a teacher might decide to allow extra time for class meetings so children can have more experience making decisions and solving problems together. Even if there aren't any studies to justify such changes, there's no reason not to give them a try.

But homework is very different. The potential downside, in terms of stress, lost time for other activities, and family conflict is considerable. And if a plausible argument can be advanced (in the absence of data) that homework might be beneficial, just such an argument could also be made that it probably won't be. Here's a case, then, where data matter—and where we ought to insist on having those data before doing something that affects the vast majority of children on a daily basis.[2]

Yet those data aren't there, and few people seem to mind. Indeed, as I mentioned earlier, most of the explosive growth in homework over the past decade or two has taken place with younger children, even though this is the age-group for which studies most clearly fail to show any positive effect. It would be difficult to imagine more compelling evidence of the irrelevance of evidence.

To be sure, homework isn't the only example of an education policy that continues, and even expands, despite a conspicuous absence of research support—or despite the presence of research proving that it's a terrible idea. Consider the practice of forcing students to repeat a grade. The evidence clearly shows that holding children back a year because they're experiencing academic difficulties is about the worst possible course of action with respect to their academic success, their psychological well-being, and their likelihood of eventually graduating. However, for reasons of ideological commitment or political expedience, many policy makers and pundits invoke the specter of "social promotion" and demand that children be retained in a grade despite the proven disadvantages of that strategy. In fact, this practice has grown in popularity "during the very time period that research has revealed its negative effects on those retained."[3]

Research makes a difference only if we know it exists, understand it correctly, and take it seriously. On many topics, even the first of these three conditions isn't met. The most obvious answer to the question, "If the data say x, why are so many people doing y?" is that those data are published in obscure journals. But sometimes this explanation doesn't apply. Sometimes people who make policy do have access to research; they just have no interest in learning what it shows. Or maybe they know what it shows but don't care, perhaps because they don't understand research reports or because they're reluctant to trust them. That's bad enough. But even more troubling is the practice of invoking or ignoring research selectively, depending on whether it supports ideas one happens to like.

One painful example is some officials' tendency to demand "scientifically validated" or "research-based" education policies (particularly with regard to how children are taught to read) but then to carefully define these terms so that only certain forms of instruction can meet the criteria. Worse, these same officials may simultaneously pursue other agendas—such as draconian requirements for do-or-die standardized testing—for which there is no supporting evidence at all.[4] Or they may commission a study but then refuse to release it if the results fail to support the preferred conclusion.[5] In all of these examples, science is used to lend legitimacy to ideas that have already been accepted for other reasons, and that, of course, is not really science at all.

If there isn't any good research to support a favored policy, either research suddenly becomes irrelevant or an impression is created that the data *do* support the policy. Thus, many writers, both scholarly and popular, vaguely claim that "studies show" a given practice (say, homework) is effective, the point being to give the appearance that their personal preferences enjoy scientific support. Rarely, if ever, are they called upon to defend such pronouncements and name the studies. Meanwhile, other writers, including some researchers, misrepresent not just what "the data" say, but what specific studies have found.

When Researchers Mislead

It's been said that much of academic scholarship actually consists of routine clerical work. Thus, when a published assertion is followed by a parenthetical note to "see" certain studies, it doesn't require any special talent to accept the invitation: Head over to the library, dig out those studies, and see what they say. That's what I did several years ago after coming across the following sentence in a book by E. D. Hirsch, Jr. (known for the What Every N[th] Grader Should Know series): "Research has clearly shown that students learn more when grades are given." An accompanying footnote contained five citations. Given the existence of a considerable body of evidence showing that grades have precisely the opposite effect, I was curious to see what research Hirsch had found. It turned out that his references didn't support his claim at all.[6]

I had that experience in mind while combing the literature on homework. One of the more prominent books I came across, which has been extremely popular among teachers and administrators, is called *Classroom Instruction That Works: Research-Based Strategies for Increasing Student Achievement* by Robert Marzano, Debra Pickering, and Jane Pollock.[7] The subtitle caught my attention, as did the fact that a full chapter was devoted to arguing for the importance of homework. The authors acknowledged that a prominent research review provided scant support for the practice of giving homework to elementary school students. But they then declared that "a number of studies" published in recent years have shown that "homework does produce beneficial results for students in grades as low as 2nd grade." This statement was followed by five citations, all of which I managed to track down. Here's what I found.

Study 1 was limited to middle- and high school students; no younger children were even included in the investigation.[8] Study 2 looked at students of different ages but found no positive effect for the younger children—only a negative effect on their attitudes. (This is the same Cooper et al. study that I mentioned on pages 33 and 53–54.)[9] Study 3, conducted in the 1970s, listed a number of practices employed by teachers whose students scored well on standardized tests. Among them was a tendency to assign more homework than their colleagues did, but the researchers made no attempt to determine what contribution, if any, was made by the homework; in fact, they cautioned that other, unnamed factors might have been more significant than any of those on the list.[10] Study 4 measured how much time a group of students spent on the homework they were assigned but didn't try to determine whether it was beneficial to assign more (or, for that matter, any at all). Even so, the researchers' main conclusion was that "high amounts of homework time did not guarantee high performance."[11] Finally, the subjects of study 5 consisted of exactly six children with learning disabilities in a classroom featuring rigidly scripted lessons. The researcher sought to find out whether sending them home with more worksheets would yield better results on a five-minute test of rote memory. Even under these contrived conditions, the results were mostly negative.[12]

I was frankly stunned by the extent of misrepresentation here. It wasn't just that one or two of the cited studies offered weak support for the proposition. Rather, none of them offered *any* support. The claim advanced vigorously by Marzano and his colleagues—

that homework provides academic benefits for younger children—
actually had no empirical backing at all. But readers who took
them at their word, perhaps impressed by the inclusion of five citations, would never know that.

Had this occurred only in a single book, I probably wouldn't
bother to mention it. But when I went in search of evidence regarding the nonacademic effects of homework, I found more misrepresentation. In a scholarly article, Janine Bempechat, an enthusiastic
defender of the "motivational" advantages of homework, wrote,
"Overall, the research suggests that assigning homework in the early
school years is beneficial more for the valuable motivational skills it
serves to foster in the long term, than for short-term school grades."

This way of putting things seems to suggest that the absence of
academic benefits is tantamount to the presence of nonacademic
benefits: If homework doesn't help students to learn better, then it
must help them to develop good work habits. (The possibility that
it does neither is apparently beyond the realm of consideration.)
However, Bempechat offered four citations in support of her
claim.[13] Again I dug up the articles. It turned out that none of her
sources contained *any* empirical demonstration of such benefits or
even references to other studies that contained any.

One of the four citations Bempechat included was to an article
by Joyce Epstein and Frances Van Voorhis which, apart from providing no data on the issue in question, made an interesting claim
of its own: "Good teachers assign more homework (Corno
1996)."[14] Would you be surprised to learn that the article by Corno
that they reference actually says no such thing? In fact, it actually
includes this statement: "The best teachers vary their use of homework according to students' interests and capabilities. . . . The
sheer amount of homework teachers assign has little to no relation
to any objective indicator of educational accomplishment."[15]

Meanwhile, another well-known pair of scholars, Brian Gill and
Steven Schlossman, whose specialty is tracking the history of

homework attitudes and practices over the decades, assert in one of their monographs that "homework. . . can inculcate habits of self-discipline and independent study." Then they cite a 1960 article by Avram Goldstein.[16] I returned to the stacks and discovered that Goldstein had reviewed seventeen studies dealing with homework's effects on achievement test scores. Only in his conclusion, after he had finished summarizing the results of all those studies, did he remark that many people hold the "opinion" that homework can have a positive effect on study habits and self-discipline. He then cited several essays in which that unsubstantiated opinion had been voiced.

Results Versus Conclusions

Misrepresenting what other people's research shows is bad enough. Even more remarkably, though, some scholars give an incomplete or inaccurate account of their own data. Over the years, I've noticed that researchers may be so committed to a given agenda that they ignore (or at least minimize the importance of) what their investigations have turned up if it wasn't the outcome they apparently had been hoping for. Their conclusions and prescriptions, in other words, are sometimes strikingly at variance with their results.

This phenomenon was already common enough back in 1962 that the psychologist Harry Harlow, best known for his terry cloth monkey experiments, offered a satirical set of instructions for researchers who were preparing to publish their findings. "Whereas there are firm rules and morals concerning the collection and reporting of data which should be placed in the Results [section]," he reminded them, "these rules no longer are in force when one comes to the Discussion. Anything goes!"[17]

I learned this lesson in the 1980s, while sifting through research about television viewing and how it affects children. Jerry and

Dorothy Singer, a husband-and-wife team who published extensively on the subject, turned up some unexpected (and evidently unwelcome) evidence that watching TV doesn't always have a negative effect and may even be associated with desirable outcomes. Children who watched a lot, for example, were more enthusiastic in school than their peers who watched less. In another study, preschoolers who logged more hours in front of the set tended to display more of an artistic orientation and speak longer sentences than other children. The Singers always mentioned such findings very quickly and then swept the results out of sight. By contrast, any results that supported an anti-TV view were enthusiastically repeated in the discussion section of the paper and then again in their subsequent publications.

Take the question of whether television has an adverse impact on children's imagination—a claim for which the Singers' work is frequently cited. In a 1984 study, they described several tests they had performed, of which two showed a very weak negative relationship between viewing and imagination—so weak as to be practically meaningless until facts about the children's family were entered into the equation. Another test showed that children who watched a lot of TV were *more* imaginative than their peers. Yet the Singers concluded their article by emphasizing the negative result and, in a later paper, declared unequivocally that "heavy television viewing preempts active play practice and the healthy use of the imagination." Anyone who skipped the results section of their papers and read only the conclusions would have gotten a mighty skewed view of their actual findings.[18]

There are other illustrations of this practice, too, of course,[19] but let's return to homework. As we've already seen (p. 26), an influential review of research published in the mid-1980s by Rosanne Paschal, Thomas Weinstein, and Herbert Walberg concluded with a ringing statement about positive achievement effects even though, as another educator discovered, the studies they looked at didn't support that conclusion at all. Around the same time, one education expert went so far as to write, "A careful reading of the review articles tends to create a mistrust of homework researchers. It appears that the conclusions they have reached are sometimes nearly independent of the data they collected."[20]

It's worth exploring whether that disturbing assessment applies to the work of Harris Cooper. His reviews of the research are the most ambitious and the most recent, and he is regarded as the country's leading expert on the subject (and consequently is quoted in virtually every newspaper and magazine article about homework), so it makes sense to look closely at what he says and whether it squares with what his research reviews, and his own studies, have actually found.

Cooper laments that "the role of research in forming the homework attitudes and practices of teachers, parents, and policymakers has been minimal" and particularly criticizes those who "cite isolated studies either to support or refute its value." [21] Indeed, he makes a point of evaluating other people's recommendations in light of the research literature.

His detailed summary of that literature, as we've already seen, includes the crucial acknowledgment that "there is no evidence that any amount of homework improves the academic performance of elementary students."[22] Yet when it comes time to offer advice, Cooper is adamant that younger children should be required to do homework. In fact, he urges school districts to "adopt a policy that requires some homework to be assigned at all grade levels" and to include in that policy "a succinct statement indicating that homework is a cost-effective technique that should have a positive effect on student achievement."[23]

Perhaps homework "should" have such an effect, but Cooper knows there's no evidence that it does. What he and a group of colleagues say in light of that fact is most revealing: "It seems safe to conclude that the benefits of homework for young children should not be evaluated based solely upon homework's immediate effects on grades or achievement test scores."[24] This response suggests a determination to find some justification for defending the practice of giving homework to all students. If research on academic effects fails to deliver the goods, then we'll just have to look elsewhere. In fact, the implication seems to be that the failure to raise achievement levels doesn't even matter because other criteria are actually more important after all.

And what are those other criteria? "Homework for young children should help them develop good study habits, foster positive attitudes toward school, and communicate to students the idea that learning takes place at home as well as at school."[25] Let's put aside the last of these three putative benefits, which is almost comically circular—making kids do academic assignments at home will teach them that they're going to have to learn (academic content) at home—and consider the other two: positive attitudes and good study habits. Cooper hasn't reported, and I haven't found, any evidence that homework leads to an improvement in students' attitudes. (At the elementary level, in fact, he discovered that exactly the opposite was true.) That leaves only one possible reason to assign homework, but unfortunately Cooper admitted four paragraphs earlier in that same article that "no studies looked at nonacademic outcomes like study habits."[26]

In his 2001 book, Cooper wrestles with the question again: "If homework has no noticeable effect on achievement in elementary school grades, why assign any at all? [Timothy] Keith's comments on grade level and parent involvement hint at what I think is the primary rationale. In earlier grades, students can be given homework assignments meant not to produce dramatic gains in achievement [he should have said *any* gains in achievement] but, rather, to promote good attitudes and study habits." He adds, "Of course, there is as yet no research evidence to support or refute whether the recommended types of homework for elementary school children actually have the intended effects."[27]

This all-important qualification is missing in an article Cooper published that same year. In the conclusion, he and a colleague wrote, "We have also reviewed the research and popular literature that suggests homework can have beneficial effects on young children well beyond immediate achievement and the development of study skills. It can help children recognize that learning can occur at home as well as at school. Homework can foster independent learning and responsible character traits." The implication here is that research to back up this claim not only exists but was discussed in that very article. In fact, it doesn't and it wasn't.[28]

In most of Cooper's statements on the issue, including comments offered to reporters, the message that comes through clearly is that the preeminent researcher in the field believes—presumably on the basis of his research—that young children should be doing homework.[29] What does not come across is the message that no data have ever been found to justify this recommendation.

You have to dig down pretty deep in his most scholarly book on the topic to discover how Cooper justifies a prescription that's conspicuously inconsistent with the research he has analyzed. In his original review—but not in any of his subsequent writings—he admits that a list of "suggested [homework policy] guidelines would be quite short if they were based only on conclusions that can be drawn firmly from past research." Since the data he has reviewed don't permit the homework-for-all recommendation that he evidently is intent on offering, he therefore has chosen to set the bar much lower: "My recommendations are grounded in research in that none of them contradicts the conclusions of my review."[30] _what!_ That's a sentence worth reading twice. No studies show any benefit to assigning homework in elementary school, but because few show any *harm*, Cooper is free to say it should be done, and then to assert that this opinion is "grounded in research."[31] Of course, many studies have looked for a benefit but failed to find it; almost no studies have bothered to investigate homework's negative effects.

Cooper is also credited with the "ten-minute rule," which many schools have adopted. It says that homework should "last about as long as ten minutes multiplied by the student's grade level."[32] The practical effect of this recommendation is often to limit the length of assignments, since many teachers assign far more than that amount; ironically, Cooper is sometimes cast in the role of a moderating influence. But, again, there doesn't seem to be any research backing for this catchy formula, particularly as applied in elementary school. Cooper found that "more homework assigned by teachers each night was associated with less positive attitudes on the part of students," but that doesn't support the practice of giving "shorter but more frequent assignments" in the younger grades, as he suggests it does.[33] Neither this finding nor any others seems to justify the practice of giving any homework at all to children in elementary school.

A careful reading of Cooper's own studies—as opposed to his research reviews—reveals further examples of his determination to massage the numbers until they yield something—anything—on which to construct a defense of homework for younger children. (The fact that even these strenuous exertions ultimately fail to produce much of substance underscores how weak the case really is.) When you compare the results section to the conclusion section of these publications, the image that comes to mind is of a magician frantically waving a wand over an empty black hat and then describing the outlines of a rabbit that he swears sort of appeared.[34]

By the way, I'm not the only reader to conclude that Cooper's conclusions are way out ahead of the data. The entry on homework in the *Encyclopedia of Educational Research* takes him to task for "his somewhat overstated conclusion" (an unusually pointed criticism in a monograph of this kind) that "the more homework high school students do, the better their achievement." After all, "Cooper has no data whatsoever to describe what actually happens beyond 10 hours [of homework] per week."[35]

Decades ago, an article in an education journal concluded with the following observation: "Fair assessment of the values of homework has been hampered by a tendency for authors of experimental research to frame their conclusions in terms that favor preconceived notions."[36] Ironically, this complaint reflected the writer's belief that researchers ended up with a view of homework that was more *negative* than their data warranted. Whether or not that was really true of studies published in the 1930s, precisely the opposite now seems to be the case.

I have three reasons for illuminating these discrepancies between a given researcher's results and his prescriptions, or between the findings attributed to other sources and what those sources actually said. First, I think they cast into sharp relief how the appearance of empirical support for the effectiveness of homework may be just that—appearance. Second, they remind us of the importance of being skeptical readers in general. After all, what turns out to be true of claims about homework may be true of claims about other topics, too.

Finally, citations that don't really prove what they're said to prove, or conclusions that don't match the data that preceded them, reveal a fundamental lack of respect for research. Elsewhere, that disrespect shows up as an indifference to what studies show or a cynical willingness to cite studies only when doing so serves a certain agenda. All of these actions help to explain an otherwise baffling enthusiasm for a practice that enjoys little empirical support. What I'm arguing, in other words, is that such enthusiasm may simply reflect the assumption that empirical support isn't all that important. The message is: We *know* homework is good for kids, and we're not going to let the facts get in our way.

CHAPTER 5

The Questions
Left Unasked

ONE REASON WE don't ask challenging questions about homework is that we don't ask challenging questions about most things. Homework continues to be championed by policy makers, assigned by teachers, and accepted by parents in part because of our cultural aversion to digging out hidden premises, pressing for justification, and opposing practices for which justification is lacking.

Too many of us sound like Robert Frost's neighbor, the man who "will not go behind his father's saying." Too many of us, when pressed about some habit or belief we've adopted, are apt to reply, "Well, that's just the way I was raised," as if it were impossible to critically examine the values one was taught. Too many of us, including some who work in the field of education, seem to have lost our capacity to be outraged by the outrageous; when handed foolish and destructive mandates, we respond by asking for guidance on how best to carry them out.

Even when we do regard something as objectionable, that doesn't mean we will object to it. Indeed, we're apt to see the situation as being like the weather—something you just learn to live with. We may not "accept" (that is, believe) everything we're told by public officials and professionals, but in the other sense of that word, we tend to accept (that is, put up with) what they do.

Indeed, there's no shortage of cynicism about authority figures and powerful institutions. But cynicism, unlike vibrant, reasoned skepticism, actually contributes to passivity. People who write off all politicians as "a bunch of liars" are unlikely to become politically active, just as those who say you can "prove anything with statistics" are unwilling to distinguish between better and worse research. For that matter, the statement "everything's bad for you these days" can be used to rationalize eating junk food. These are shrugs, not positions. Whereas the skeptic thinks and doubts and in so doing affirms a vision of the way things ought to be, the cynic affirms nothing, takes no action, and ends up perpetuating arrangements that make our lives worse. (Those arrangements, in a neat self-fulfilling prophecy, then confirm the cynical conclusion that no one can make a difference.)

Whether or not it's accompanied by cynicism, passivity is a habit acquired early. From our first days in school we are carefully instructed in what has been called the "hidden curriculum": how to do what we're told and stay out of trouble. There are rewards, both tangible and symbolic, for those who behave properly and penalties for those who don't. As students, we're trained to sit still, listen to what the teacher says, run our highlighters across whatever words in the book we'll be required to commit to memory. Pretty soon, we become less likely to ask (or even wonder) whether what we're being taught really makes sense. We just want to know whether it's going to be on the test.

I remember hearing about a college instructor who implored his students on the first day of class to think critically about all he would tell them rather than just mindlessly copying down his lectures in their notebooks. As he spoke, students were obediently writing, "Don't just copy down lectures." I myself caught a whiff of this sensibility when, as a brand-new teacher, I pinned a yellow button to my shirt that said QUESTION AUTHORITY. Alas, this concept was so unfamiliar to the students that some of them assumed the phrase was a descriptive label rather than an exhortation. One girl wanted to know who had appointed me the school's authority on questions.

When we find ourselves unhappy with some practice or policy, we're encouraged to focus on incidental aspects of what's going on, to ask questions about the details of implementation—how something will get done, or by whom, or on what schedule—but not whether it should be done at all. The more we attend to secondary concerns, the more the primary issues—the overarching structures and underlying premises—are strengthened. We're led to avoid the radical questions. I use that adjective in its original sense: *Radical* comes from the Latin word for root. It's partly because we spend our time worrying about the tendrils that the weed continues to grow. Noam Chomsky put it this way:

> The smart way to keep people passive and obedient is to strictly limit the spectrum of acceptable opinion, but allow very lively debate within that spectrum—even encourage the more critical and dissident views. That gives people the sense that there's free thinking going on, while all the time the presuppositions of the system are being reinforced by the limits put on the range of the debate.[1]

There are many institutions in our culture that point us in this direction, but not all are identified as such. Consider parenting magazines. To spend time with these publications is to realize that their purpose is not just to teach us how to socialize our children. Rather, they're about the business of socializing *us*—to accept the status quo. You'll find articles about how to teach kids the basics of good sportsmanship on the playing field but none that raise questions about the desirability (or inevitability) of competitive games. You'll be treated to advice on how to help your child get better grades—or what to do about a poor grade—but you'll look in vain for an inquiry into whether there are alternatives to grades, or whether the curriculum is worthwhile, or how parents, if they organized themselves, might be able to change essential features of our educational system. These magazines ultimately teach parents to take the important things for granted and deal with reality as they find it.

On the other hand, there is seldom any *need* to discourage us from posing more probing questions. It never occurs to most of us to ask them—or even to inquire into other aspects of our lives. Discontent is siphoned off to minor matters, with the effect that our institutions are left to function unimpeded. We've already been conditioned to accept most of what is done to our children at school, for example, and so we confine our critical energies to the periphery. Sometimes I entertain myself by speculating about how ingrained this pattern really is. If a school administrator were to announce that, starting next week, students would be made to stand outside in the rain and memorize the phone book, I suspect we parents would promptly speak up. . . to ask whether the Yellow Pages were included. Or perhaps we'd want to know how much of their grade this activity will count for. One of the more outspoken moms might even demand to know whether her child would be permitted to wear a raincoat.

Our education system, meanwhile, is busily avoiding important topics in its own right. For every question that's asked in this field, other, more vital questions are never raised. Educators weigh different techniques of "behavior management" but rarely examine the imperative to focus on behavior—observable actions—rather than on reasons and needs and the children who have them. Teachers think about what classroom rules they ought to introduce but are unlikely to ask why they're doing so unilaterally, why students aren't participating in such decisions. It's probably not a coincidence that most schools of education require prospective teachers to take a course called Methods, but there is no course called Goals.

More: Teachers are invited to consider how often they call on students to answer questions, whether they're allowing enough time for a response to be formulated, maybe even whether they are unconsciously calling on more boys than girls. But they are assuredly *not* prompted to think about why they are calling on students in the first place. Why should the teacher's questions, as opposed to the kids', drive the lesson? What would happen if the students didn't raise their hands—and had to figure out together how to avoid interrupting one another? What if some of the power was shared and classrooms became more democratic? It's partly because of the earnest attention to evaluating techniques for leading a traditional classroom discussion that more profound questions are excluded.

It can be simultaneously exhilarating and unsettling to be reminded how much we take for granted. Several years ago, I was exploring the criteria used for college admission. My thesis was that it's silly to ask whether grades are more useful than test scores because both are terribly flawed as predictors of future academic performance. Grades and tests in high school give us a clue only about grades and tests in college; they tell us almost nothing about intellectual engagement, depth of thinking, or what happens when college is over. And then I happened to come across an offhand observation made decades earlier by the psychologist David McClelland. Rather than asking which criteria best predict success in higher education, he wondered why colleges were looking for the most qualified students in the first place. "One would think that the purpose of education is precisely to improve the performance of those who are not doing very well," he mused. "If the colleges were interested in proving that they could educate people, high-scoring students might be poor bets because they would be less likely to show improvement in performance."[2]

A breath of fresh air is invigorating but it can also make you shiver a little. How much harm are we doing—or at least allowing to be done—when we fail to ask the right questions and look at the big picture? We like to congratulate people who "think outside the box," but we get nervous if the thinker in question does this too often or too well, particularly if we happen to call that box home. Sometimes it seems that the effusiveness with which we esteem the appearance of independent thought is directly proportional to the displeasure with which we greet its reality. And even when gadflies are celebrated, the box itself stays the same. This ensures that we will continue to need more people to think outside it.

Accepting Homework

Bearing all this in mind, we approach what may be the single most intriguing and disturbing question about homework, which is "why so many feel cursed, and are yet so willing to be imposed on."[3] Parents anxiously grill teachers about homework policies, but they mostly ask about the details of the assignments their children will be made to do. If homework is a given, it's certainly understandable that one would want to make sure it's being done "correctly." But this begs the question of whether, and why, it *should* be a given. The willingness not to ask provides another explanation for how a practice can persist even if it hurts more than helps.

For their part, teachers regularly witness how many children are made miserable by homework and how many resist doing it. Some respond with sympathy and respect. Others reach for bribes and threats to compel students to turn in the assignments; indeed, they may insist these inducements are necessary: "If the kids weren't being graded, they'd never do it!" Even if true, this is less an argument for grades and other coercive tactics than an invitation to reconsider the value of those assignments. Or so one might think. However, teachers had to do homework when *they* were students, and they've likely been expected to give it at every school where they've worked. The idea that homework must be assigned is the premise, not the conclusion—and it's a premise that's rarely examined by educators.

Unlike parents and teachers, scholars are a step removed from the classroom and therefore have the luxury of pursuing potentially uncomfortable areas of investigation. But few do. Instead they are more likely to ask, How much time should students spend on homework? and even to regard this as "the single most general and fundamental, yet most complex and controversial question" about the topic.[4] Whether students need to spend any time on it at all would seem to be a much more fundamental question, but it is apparently outside the bounds of acceptable inquiry. A secondary topic in the academic literature concerns which strategies will succeed in "improving homework completion" rates, which is simply assumed to be desirable.[5] The point of departure in one monograph, for example, was that it is a sign of maturity for students to complete any assignment they're given. Younger children, we are told, simply don't grasp "that homework might help develop important personal attributes or responsible academic behavior."[6] Success is defined as acquiescence; the value of the task—let alone of homework per se—is not at issue.[7]

Why homework continues to be assigned despite the absence of supporting evidence is almost never a topic of empirical investigation. But even more remarkable is an unwillingness to take seriously the possibility of rethinking homework, even by re-searchers who have reported evidence that would seem to invite just such a reconsideration. The authors of a pamphlet published some years ago by a mainstream education organization con-ceded that the available research raised serious doubts about the value of homework. After reporting these data, they asked, rhetorically, "Do we dare suggest that we have reached a point when we should consider doing without homework altogether? Maybe, just maybe, we should. However, it is not our intent to offer a diatribe against homework."[8] Having thus conflated a substantive position (the abolition of homework) with a style of argumentation (which of course could characterize any view-point), they retreat to the safety of offering suggestions for how homework should be assigned and done.

Exhibit B here might be the 2005 cross-cultural study showing that homework isn't even associated with, let alone a contributor to, higher achievement (p. 43). After reviewing the evidence, these authors, too, opt for a question both rhetorical and loaded: "Should national educational policy makers just join the 'abolish home-work' bandwagon? No."[9] It is by caricaturing this option that they justify declining to consider it. (*What* bandwagon? One can count on one's fingers the number of contemporary writers who have taken this position. Furthermore, why reframe a no-homework scenario as "joining a bandwagon" even if one did exist? The in-tent seems to be to sway readers without offering reasons, to create the impression that there's something inherently suspect about the absence of homework.)

A reliance on rhetorical devices—loaded language, straw men, and false dichotomies—is even more flagrant among writers who are enthusiastic fans of homework. We are called upon by one group of researchers to reject "the claims of some educators" (none of whom is named, naturally) "that hard work is somehow inimical to know-how and creativity."[10] Another scholar makes her case by insisting that "all children, rich and poor, need to be pushed, not pitied"—as if these two options exhausted the possibilities.[11] A teacher asserts that parents who don't support homework just "don't value education."[12] In short, if homework cannot be defended on its merits, one merely has to imply that the people who oppose it are against hard work or indifferent to educating children.

When we turn from researchers to policy groups, we are again more likely to find cheerleaders than thoughtful critics. The major document on the subject issued jointly by the National PTA and the National Education Association, for example, concedes that children often complain about homework, but it never considers the possibility that their complaints may be justified. Parents are exhorted to "show your children that you think homework is important" (regardless of whether it is, or even whether one really believes this is true) and to praise them for compliance.[13]

Health professionals, meanwhile, have begun raising concerns about the weight of children's backpacks and then recommending. . . exercises to strengthen their backs! This was also the tack taken by *People* magazine: An article about families struggling to cope with excessive homework was accompanied by a sidebar that offered some "ways to minimize the strain on young backs"—for example, by choosing "a [back]pack with padded shoulder straps."[14] This sort of response, as one writer has remarked, is "a classic case of treating the symptom and not the disease. . . . The real questions are: 'What is in that backpack, who put it there, and why?'" Once you think about these underlying issues, you realize that "it's not just your kids' backs that are aching. They are also aching for some free, unstructured time to think, to play, to be kids."[15]

The *People* article reminds us that the popular press does occasionally—cyclically—take note of how much homework children have to do, and how varied and virulent are its effects. But such inquiries are rarely penetrating and their conclusions almost never rock the boat. One such article in a North Carolina newspaper ran under the headline "Too Much of a Good Thing?" Evidently, the notion that homework might not be a good thing at all is beyond the scope of imagination.[16]

Time magazine published a cover essay in 2003 entitled "The Homework Ate My Family." It opened with affecting and even alarming stories of homework's harms. Several pages later, however, it closed with a finger-wagging declaration that "both parents and students must be willing to embrace the 'work' component of homework—to recognize the quiet satisfaction that comes from practice and drill."[17] Likewise an essay on the Family Education Network's website: "Yes, homework is sometimes dull, or too easy, or too difficult. That doesn't mean that it shouldn't be taken seriously."[18] (One wonders what *would* have to be true before we'd be justified in not taking something seriously.)

A freelance writer contacted me not long ago to describe an article she was planning to write for a parenting magazine. Its thesis was that parents today have become too involved with their children's homework. I responded that the real problem may not be that parents are doing the assignments for their kids so much as that many of the assignments simply aren't worth doing. In fact, I added, focusing on the degree of parental involvement might distract readers from the more important question of whether homework is truly necessary. The writer was unconvinced—not about the substance of my argument, which she didn't dispute, but about whether this was worth writing about. Her position seemed to be that it doesn't matter whether homework is good or bad for kids. As long as it continues to be assigned, the role of experts and journalists is to help people learn how to deal with it. The bigger questions might be appropriate for an education periodical, she allowed, but certainly not for a parenting magazine.

Nor, apparently, are these questions seen as appropriate by most medical and mental health professionals. When a child resists doing homework—or complying with other demands—their job is to get the child back on track. Very rarely is there any inquiry into the value of the homework or the reasonableness of the demands. One prominent example of this sensibility is the pediatrician and author Mel Levine, who invites his readers to think about differences in learning styles and redefines what appears to be laziness as a "neurodevelopmental dysfunction." His approach is welcomed by thoughtful parents and educators who appreciate the message that all children don't learn the same way.

But Levine's advice for dealing with kids who don't do what they've been told reads like a heavy-handed parody of early-twentieth-century scientific management—except that he wants us to chart the "work output" of six-year-olds. Parents "need to take on the sometimes adversarial and perverse authoritarian role of taskmaster," he tells us. They should "set up and enforce consistent work times" and limit the hours that children spend on purely relaxing activities, which are "likely to be detrimental to output." Levine offers helpful examples of logs, charts, and bar graphs that should be posted in our homes so we can keep track of kids' productive output. Meanwhile, of all the questions one might imagine asking about the way our children are educated, his is, "How can schools instill habits of quality output? Our educational institutions need to be arenas that encourage, train for, and reward productivity."[19]

Someone who looks at children and sees (insufficiently productive) workers is unlikely to raise questions about the structural imperatives of schooling—what kids are made to do, and why, and whether it is of any value to the kids themselves. Levine offers case studies of children who don't do their homework, but never once examines the content of the assignments to determine whether they're likely to be beneficial, let alone what basis there is for believing that homework in general is necessary. Our goal, as parents and teachers, is merely to maximize kids' "output," to make them more efficient at carrying out any instructions they've been given.

This effort to turn us into quality-control supervisors to enforce a crude work ethic in living rooms and classrooms might be expected from the local chamber of commerce, but again, notice that it comes to us from an expert regarded as progressive and refreshingly nonjudgmental. (Indeed, Levine has been criticized by some traditionalists for failing to insist on "high standards" with struggling children.) This is the marvel of American discourse: how much liberals and conservatives actually share, how many critical issues they agree not to raise. The status quo, with respect to homework and so much else, has nothing to fear from either the old-school, tough-love disciplinarian or the soft-hearted, jargon-wielding counselor. They offer different prescriptions but share the same goal, which is compliance.[20]

Levine joins countless authors of magazine and newspaper articles, school websites, PTA pamphlets, government brochures, and even a publication for parents with children in Montessori schools in providing advice about how homework ought to be done.[21] The specifics are repeated endlessly, and with little variation: Students should be given clear directions about what homework they must do, and how, and when; teachers should communicate frequently with parents to let them know what is expected for each assignment; children should have well-lighted and quiet places designated for homework; and so on.

This advice, which is almost never held up for critical reflection, is problematic in three respects. First, as I've been contending throughout this chapter, paying careful attention to the details of assigning and completing homework discourages all concerned from posing more meaningful questions. Second, it's not clear that there's any evidence to show these particular suggestions even help. If you think about it, a psychologist commented, "for children who are not doing their homework well or consistently, time and place are almost never the issue."[22] Indeed, at least one study has found that "having a regular place for homework is not highly associated with achievement" or, for that matter, with any other behavioral variable.[23] Finally, an emphasis on establishing a proper homework routine is less innocuous than it seems because it allows us to conclude that any difficulties families face are their own fault. If kids aren't getting anything out of their homework or parents find themselves dreading the whole experience, they have only themselves to blame: They failed to follow the directions properly.[24] *cou'2L*

Sometimes parents are invited to talk to teachers about homework, provided that their concerns are "appropriate." The same is true of formal opportunities for offering feedback. A list of sample survey questions offered to principals by the central office in one Colorado school district is typical. Parents were asked to indicate whether they agreed or disagreed with the following statements: "My child understands how to do his/her homework"; "Teachers at this school give me useful suggestions about how to help my child with schoolwork"; "Homework assignments allow me to see what my student is being taught and how he/she is learning"; and "The amount of homework my child receives is (choose one): too much/just right/too little."

The most striking feature of such a list is what isn't on it. Such a questionnaire seems designed to illustrate Chomsky's point about encouraging lively discussion within a narrow spectrum of acceptable opinion, the better to reinforce the key presuppositions of the system. Parents' feedback is earnestly sought. . . on these questions only. So, too, for the popular articles that criticize homework or the parents who speak out: The focus is generally limited to how *much* is being assigned. I'm sympathetic to this concern, but I'm more struck by how it misses much of what matters. We sometimes forget that not everything that's destructive when done to excess is innocuous when done in moderation. Sometimes the problem is with what's being done, or at least the way it's being done, rather than just with how much of it is being done.

The more we are invited to think in Goldilocks terms (too much, too little, or just right?), the less likely we become to step back and ask the questions that count: What reason is there to think that any quantity of the kind of homework our kids are getting is really worth doing? What evidence exists to show that daily homework, regardless of its nature, is necessary for children to become better thinkers? Why did students have no chance to participate in deciding which of their assignments ought to be taken home?

And: What if there was no homework at all?

CHAPTER 6

What We Haven't
Learned About Learning

W HEN SOME PEOPLE are deeply attached to an idea, they may ignore or misrepresent contrary research—or even avoid asking the kinds of questions that could cast doubt on that idea. Such responses, which I explored in the last two chapters, help us to understand how it's possible for unproductive practices to persist indefinitely. In a way, though, these explanations just set the problem back a step. They leave us wondering why so many people are inclined to accept the value of such practices in the first place.

With respect to homework, which is widely thought to help students learn better, part of the answer may involve misconceptions about learning itself. These erroneous assumptions about how children come to acquire knowledge and make sense of ideas are responsible for a number of educational policies whose appeal is greatest for those who understand the least about education. Standardized testing is one example: The less one knows about how real classrooms function, and about how to figure out which students are having trouble, the more likely one will be to regard test scores as important. Support for homework, I've come to believe,

similarly benefits from ignorance about cognitive science, pedagogy, and child development. To learn more about these fields is to
realize that what may seem like common sense actually doesn't
make much sense at all.

Time

To begin with, let's consider the assumption that homework ought
to be useful just because it gives students more time to master a
given topic or skill. Plenty of pundits rely on this premise when
they call for extending the school day—or the school year. Indeed,
homework itself can be seen as a way of prolonging the school day
on the cheap. After-school assignments ratchet up the amount of
time students spend on academic topics by an hour or two. Ergo,
higher achievement.

Unfortunately, this reasoning turns out to be woefully simplistic.
Back "when experimental psychologists mainly studied words and
nonsense syllables, it was thought that learning inevitably de-
pended upon time," a group of educational psychologists explained. But "subsequent research suggests that this belief is false."[1]

Why? Let's begin by conceding that the statement "People need
time to learn things" is true. The problem is that it's a trivial truth
that doesn't tell us much of practical value. On the other hand, the
assertion "More time usually leads to better learning" is considerably more interesting. It's also inaccurate, however, because there
are enough cases where more time *doesn't* lead to better learning.
In the real world, the loose connection between these two variables
doesn't mean much. When the *Economist* editorialized in favor of
assigning more homework, it justified this position on the grounds
that "other things being equal, the more you study, the more you
know."[2] The trouble is that other things are rarely equal.

It's hard to deny, for example, that lots of kids spend time in
school looking at books or listening to lectures without getting

much out of the experience. Would *more* of what the experts call "time on task" (ToT) be likely to make a difference? The answer to that question is so obvious that ToT proponents were forced some years ago to revise their original proposition. In the amended version, learning was said to improve in proportion to the quantity of *engaged* time on task. But how do we help kids become engaged with what they're doing? There's been quite a lot written on creating classrooms that promote student engagement. These ideas pull us in a variety of directions, some more promising than others. But time is, at best, only one consideration among many. More to the point, compelling students to do more school assignments at home is not especially likely to maximize engaged time. The upshot is that the idea of ToT, if it is to be of any use at all, has to be refined in such a way that time itself is no longer the dominant concept— and the practice of assigning homework isn't supported at all.

Let's look at the research more closely. The amount of time a student spends on a task "is not so consistently related to achievement as it may seem," one scholar concluded from her review of several studies on the subject. "Time is a necessary, but not sufficient, condition for learning. Learning takes time, but providing time does not in itself ensure that learning will take place. More time *may* result in more learning—if [lack of] adequate time was the major cause of the problem in the first place. If other factors were the real cause, then providing more time will not be an effective strategy."[3]

Undoubtedly there are teachers who would argue that the main problem is indeed a lack of time—particularly these days, when they are pressured to align their instruction to an increasingly elaborate standardized curriculum imposed by distant authorities. However, the main consequence of the fact that class time is finite is how little can be done *with* homework. If you multiply how long it takes for a teacher to read and respond meaningfully to each student's assignment by the number of students in the class, you can see why teachers who assign regular homework are usually unable to review students' efforts in any detail. Worse, time constraints create a powerful pressure not only to assign the same tasks to every child in class but to assign the least constructive sort of tasks—the kind that can be checked rapidly.

Nevertheless, does lack of class time justify the assignment of homework? Let's answer that question with another: How much time *would* be sufficient so that teachers who rely on this justification could announce that homework was no longer necessary? My guess is that there would never be enough, and homework would continue to be assigned no matter how many hours were available to teachers during the day.[4] If that's true, then something other than a lack of time must explain the decision to make students do homework on a regular basis. Furthermore, the learning difficulties experienced by many of those students won't be solved—*aren't* being solved—by giving them more tasks to take home.

Let's come at the question from another direction. Instead of asking, Does more time for academics help? maybe we should ask, Does more time for academics help more than other things we could do instead? A Stanford University study compared four different reforms: peer tutoring, smaller classes, increased use of computers, and adding an hour of instruction each day. The result: "On a cost-effectiveness basis, the time intervention was found to rank at the bottom with respect to improving student performance in mathematics and third out of the four [in reading]."[5]

Carole Ames, dean of the college of education at Michigan State University, points out that it isn't "quantitative changes in behavior" (such as requiring students to spend more hours in front of books or worksheets) that help children to learn better. Rather, it's "qualitative changes in the ways students view themselves in relation to the task, engage in the process of learning, and then respond to the learning activities and situation."[6] In turn, these attitudes and responses on the part of students emerge from the way teach-

ers think about learning and, as a result, the ways they've organized their classrooms. If the goal is to figure out how best to cover
a set curriculum—to fill students with facts—then it might seem
appropriate to try to maximize ToT, such as by assigning homework. But that's unlikely to have a positive effect on the critical
variables that Ames identifies. Perhaps it makes sense to see education as being less about how much the teacher covers and more
about what the students can be helped to *dis*cover. More time won't
do a thing to bring about that shift.

On an even more basic level, to think about providing more
time for students to learn something is to sidestep the question of
whether that something is worth learning. Suppose that extra
hours after school really did make it more likely that children
would be able to commit a list of dates or definitions to memory. If
there isn't a good reason to make students memorize something
they're likely to forget anyway (and which they can always look up
if necessary), then the apparent advantage of more time wouldn't
mean very much. Of course, this invites us to ask what *is* worth
learning, and how that should be decided. But my point is that a
conversation on so crucial a topic is less likely to take place when
we're focused on trying to maximize the amount of time spent on
the tasks that comprise the current curriculum.

In fact, the nature of the task helps to determine the relationship
between time and achievement. It turns out that *more hours are
least likely to produce better outcomes when understanding or creativity is involved*. "How much is learned by rote is a direct function of
time and effort," acknowledges literacy expert Frank Smith. "But
when the learning is meaningful we learn much faster. . . . Having
to spend long periods of time in repetitive efforts to learn specific
things is a sign that learning is not taking place, that we are not in
a productive learning situation."[7]

Sure enough, researchers have found that when children are
taught to read by focusing on the *meaning* of the text (rather than

primarily on phonetic skills), their learning does "not depend on amount of instructional time."[8] In math, too, even the new and improved concept of "engaged" ToT is directly correlated to achievement only if both the activities and the measure of achievement are focused on rote recall. By contrast, there is no "linear positive relationship for higher level mathematics activities, including mathematical applications and problem solving."[9]

For many different reasons, then, the idea that homework should be beneficial by virtue of giving students more time to spend on their studies proves to be a lot less straightforward or persuasive than it appears at first glance. Alas, that single glance is all it normally receives.

Practice

Closely related to the notion that more time yields more learning is the belief, widely held by both parents and teachers, that homework is useful because it affords an opportunity for students to practice the skills they've been taught. This, of course, is a defense of a certain kind of assignment—the kind that involves practice. (The premise that time on task predicts achievement, meanwhile, is used to justify the very idea of homework.) But because such a large proportion of homework *is* practice oriented,[10] we should evaluate this claim carefully.

There's obviously some truth to the idea that practice is connected to proficiency. People who do something a lot often get better at doing it. But once again we find ourselves with a proposition that turns out to be true in a far more limited sense, with more qualifications and caveats attached, than may have seemed to be the case.

Giving students homework that involves drill and practice is often said to "reinforce" the skills they've been taught in class. This verb is tossed around casually, as if it were sufficient to clinch the case. But what exactly is meant here? Unless it's assumed that practice is reinforcing by definition, one would have to demonstrate that good results are indeed likely to follow from mere repetition. And it's not at all clear that this is true, except under very limited circumstances. For example, it wouldn't make sense to say "Keep practicing until you understand" because practicing doesn't create understanding—just as giving kids a deadline doesn't teach time-management skills. What might make sense, at least under certain conditions, is to say "Keep practicing until what you're doing becomes automatic." But what kinds of proficiencies lend themselves to this sort of improvement?

The answer is behavioral responses. Expertise in tennis requires lots of practice; it's hard to improve your swing without spending a lot of time on the court. You learn to pull back and follow through with just the right movement so the ball lands where you want, and eventually you can do this without even thinking about it. But to cite an example like that to justify homework is an example of what philosophers call begging the question. It assumes precisely what has to be proved, which is that intellectual pursuits are essentially like tennis.

The assumption that the two activities are analogous is an outgrowth of a doctrine known as behaviorism, widely associated with John B. Watson, B. F. Skinner, and their followers. On this view, all that matters are behaviors that can be seen and measured, and "man is an animal different from other animals only in the types of behavior he displays," as Watson announced on the first page of his best-known book.[11] Thus, it makes perfect sense that most of the principles of learning that emerge from the work of behaviorists were developed on lab animals. Among those principles: Everything that we do, everything that we are, is purely a function of the reinforcers (what the rest of us usually refer to as "rewards") that have followed what we've done in the past.

When teachers and parents talk about using homework to "reinforce" the material students have learned—or, more accurately, the material they were taught, which they may or may not have learned—the term isn't being used in this technical sense. But that doesn't matter. Whether they realize it or not, they're buying in to the same attenuated view of learning that emphasizes drill and practice because their focus is on producing a behavior. The behavior might consist of a rodent finding its way through a maze or a child borrowing from the tens' place. For a behaviorist, these actions are different only in degree, and the same theory applies equally well to both. Thus, to justify sending students home with a worksheet full of practice problems on the grounds that it reinforces skills is to say that what matters is not understanding but behavior.

In the 1920s and 1930s, when Watson was formulating his theory that would come to dominate the way we teach students (not to mention the way we raise children and manage employees), a much less famous researcher named William Brownell was challenging the drill-and-practice approach to mathematics that had already taken root. "If one is to be successful in quantitative thinking, one needs a fund of meanings, not a myriad of 'automatic responses,'" he wrote. "Drill does not develop meanings. Repetition does not lead to understandings." In fact, if "arithmetic becomes meaningful, it becomes so *in spite of* drill."[12]

An emphasis on making meaning is directly opposed to the view that learning consists of the acquisition of a collection of behaviors. Brownell's insights about math instruction have been expanded and enriched by a long line of experts who have come to realize that the behaviorist model is, if you'll excuse the expression, deeply superficial. Learning isn't just a matter of absorbing new information or acquiring automatic responses to stimuli. Rather, we human beings spend our entire lives constructing theories about how the world works, and then reconstructing them in light of new evidence. Not only educational theorists but "virtually all" cognitive researchers today "[sub]scribe to this constructive view of learning and knowledge."[13] The kind of teaching most consistent with it treats students as meaning makers and offers carefully calibrated challenges that help them to develop increasingly sophisticated theories. The point is for them to understand ideas from the inside out.[14]

This basic distinction between behavior and understanding—with its implications regarding practice homework—applies to every academic subject. Its relevance to math, however, is particularly intriguing—and somewhat unsettling in light of the fact that most of us still think in behaviorist terms. Mathematics is the subject in which practice homework seems to be most commonly prescribed, so this is as good a place as any to understand the limits of the whole idea.[15]

An emphasis on practice to reinforce skills proceeds naturally from the assumption that kids primarily need to learn "math facts": the ability to say "42" as soon as they hear the stimulus "6 times 7," and a familiarity with step-by-step procedures (sometimes called algorithms) for all kinds of problems—carrying numbers while subtracting, subtracting while dividing, reducing fractions to the lowest common denominator, and so forth. You do one problem after another until you've got it down cold. And, as Brownell pointed out, if you have trouble producing the right answer, that's "taken as evidence only of the need of further drill."[16]

In reality, it's the children who don't understand the underlying concepts who most need an approach to teaching that's geared to deep understanding. The more they're given algorithms and told exactly what to do, the farther behind they fall in terms of grasping these concepts. "Mindless mimicry mathematics," as the National Research Council calls it, is the norm in our schools, from single-digit addition in first grade to trigonometry in high school. Students may memorize the fact that 0.4 equals 4/10, or successfully follow a recipe to solve for *x*, but the traditional approach leaves them clueless about the significance of what they're doing. Without

any feel for the bigger picture, they tend to plug in numbers mechanically while applying the technique they've been taught. As a
result, they often can't take these methods and transfer them to
problems even slightly different from those they're used to. Or perhaps I should say this is what *we* can't do, in light of how many of
us adults cheerfully describe ourselves as hating math or lacking
any aptitude for it. (Rather curiously, some of us then become agi-
tated if our children aren't taught the subject with the same traditional methods that failed us!)

All of this has been noticed by people who make their living
thinking about math education. Several documents for reforming
the field, including, most notably, the standards disseminated by
the National Council of Teachers of Mathematics, have recommended that math classes revolve around making meaning rather
than memorizing rules. Students should be encouraged to write
and talk about their ideas, to understand the underlying concepts
and be able to put them into words.

There's a sharp contrast between math defined principally in
terms of skills and math defined principally in terms of understanding. (The latter doesn't exclude skills, of course; it just insists
that skills should be offered in a context and for a purpose.) But
even a classroom centered on understanding may not be enough.
Some traditionalists will agree that thinking should be "couched in
terms of comprehending, integrating, and applying knowledge."
But in their classrooms, the student's job is "comprehending how
the *teacher* has integrated or applied the ideas. . . and to reconstruct
the teacher's thinking on the next test."[17] This returns us to the
fundamental question of whether understanding is passively absorbed or actively constructed. The best classrooms not only are
characterized by more thinking than remembering; they also have
students doing much of the thinking.

Thus, children, with the teacher's support, may reinvent the idea
of ratios for themselves or recreate the marvelously consistent rela-

tion among the three sides of a right triangle (and discover its relevance to real-world design issues). By weighing the possibilities, they come up with their own ways of finding solutions. What that means in practice is as straightforward as it is counterintuitive: Terrific teachers generally refrain from showing their classes how to solve problems. Rather than demonstrating the "correct" procedure for subtracting 37 from 82, for example, second grade teachers might let the students (individually or in pairs) find ways to solve it, encouraging them to try various techniques, giving them ample time before calling them back together for a discussion so they can explain what they did, challenge each other's answers (in a friendly, supportive way), ask questions, reconsider their own approaches, and figure out what works—and why it works. Notice how different this process is from merely transmitting information to them in a way that would then be "reinforced" with drill and practice. Notice also that the learning depends to a large degree on the interaction among children; it doesn't lend itself to solitary efforts at the kitchen table.

Until you've watched this kind of teaching, the idea of trusting children to solve unfamiliar problems, or the idea that math is a creative enterprise involving invention, can be very hard to accept. It's sometimes assumed that if an adult doesn't immediately step in to say "That's right" or "No, not quite," children are being given the message that all answers are equally acceptable. In fact, exactly the opposite is true. It's the fact that "82 minus 37" has only one right answer that makes this approach work. "Children *will* eventually get to the truth if they think and debate long enough because, in [math], absolutely nothing is arbitrary," says Constance Kamii, who has devoted her career to explaining—and proving—the value of this sort of math education.[18]

By contrast, when students are simply told the most efficient way of getting the answer, they get in the habit of looking to the adult or the book instead of thinking things through. They become

Drive

less autonomous, more dependent. Stuck in the middle of a problem, they're less likely to try to figure out what makes *sense* to do
next and more likely to try to remember what they're *supposed to*
do next—what behavioral response they've been taught to produce. Lots of practice can help some students get better at remembering the correct response, but not to get better at—or even accustomed to—thinking. "In traditional math," says Kamii, "kids
are given rules that don't make sense to them, and repetition seems
to be necessary to memorize rules kids don't understand." She generally recommends steering clear of homework, "partly because
what kids do at school is enough, and repetition is neither necessary nor desirable," and partly because when parents try to help
their children with math assignments they tend to teach them what
they've been told are the "correct" ways to solve problems. Again,
this shuts down children's thinking.[19]

Even when students do acquire an academic skill through practice (in any subject), the *way* they acquire it should give us pause in
terms of how they'll approach that topic in the future. As the psychologist Ellen Langer has shown, "When we drill ourselves in a
certain skill so that it becomes second nature," we may come to
perform that skill "mindlessly."[20] Practicing some things until you
can practically do them in your sleep often interferes with flexibility and innovation. What can be done without thinking usually *is*
done without thinking, and that may lock people into patterns and
procedures that are less than ideal. Practice often leads to habit—
which is, by definition, a mindless repetition of behavior—but not
to understanding. And when understanding is absent, the ability to
use and apply the skill is very limited.

Even under those circumstances and for those topics where a reasonable case can be made that practicing does make sense, we're not entitled to conclude that homework of this type is appropriate for most
students in any given classroom. For starters, such assignments aren't

of any use for those who don't understand what they're doing. "Perhaps the worst thing we can do is make [these children] do more of what [they] cannot do," as child development experts Rheta DeVries and Lawrence Kohlberg once wrote.[21] Giving practice problems to students who lack understanding can have any of several effects:

- It may make them feel stupid. (Over and over again, they're reminded of what they can't do.)
- It may get them accustomed to doing things the wrong way, because what's really "reinforced" are mistaken assumptions.[22]
- It may teach them to fake it, perhaps by asking someone else for the correct answers, to conceal what they don't know.
- Finally, the whole exercise subtly teaches that math—or whatever subject they're doing—is something people aren't *expected* to understand.

At the same time, other students in the same class already have *Syllable* the skill down cold, so further practice for them is a waste of time. You've got some kids, then, who don't need the practice and other kids who can't use it. Even if we were willing to put aside more basic concerns about this kind of assignment, it's entirely possible that only a handful of students in any classroom at any given time would be likely to benefit from it. Thus, the nearly universal tendency to give the same assignment to everyone in the class,[23] while understandable in light of time constraints, is awfully hard to defend pedagogically.

This is exactly why a New York math teacher, who has taught students from second to eighth grade, told me that she has "never found homework helpful. Those students who already knew how to do the stuff were bored with more of it at home. Those students who didn't understand it made up their own ways to do things which were often wrong and repeated the practice, making it that much harder to get them to see it another way in class."[24]

An eighth grade English teacher in southern California arrived at the same conclusion:

> I very rarely give my students any kind of homework. I do not believe in homework, especially in a language arts class. Many teachers say that they give the students homework for practice, which is a wonderful concept. However, does every student in the class need the exact same amount of practice? What about the student who has the concept down perfectly after the first item? Why does she have to do the other thirty-nine items? How about the student who practices all forty problems wrong? What good did the homework assignment do her? I want my students to do their learning in my presence, so I can immediately correct them, or take them in a different direction, or push them further, or learn from them.[25]

Let's assume for the moment that practice really could help most kids. Even so, it still hasn't been shown that they need to do it at home. Proponents of homework simply assume that if practice is worthwhile, it must take place after school is over—in part because there's not enough time for students to write or solve problems during the day. But this raises the question of what students *should* be doing. Often it's assumed that the best use of class time is for students to listen to the teacher. Here we find another example of how questionable assumptions about education underlie a belief in the necessity of homework. There is good reason to move beyond the "transmission" model of learning—sometimes known as "sit 'n' git." (The writer George Leonard once defined lecturing as the "best way to get information from teacher's notebook to student's notebook without touching the student's mind.")[26] There's a good case to be made that if class time is limited, most of those hours may be better spent having students read and write, discuss and reflect.

Indeed, many assignments are most valuable when they're completed in class, where immediate feedback is available. Listen to the testimony of three teachers who address reading, writing, and math, respectively:

> In addition to reinforcement-type worksheets which I do not assign for homework I also do not assign reading to be done at home. Instead, I begin each day with an article (1–2 pages tops) that relates to the topics we're studying. Using just ten minutes a day, students end up reading over one hundred college-level articles in the course of the year. Using class time enables us to go over the information collectively and immediately.[27]

> I have to give students time to write in class. I've never walked into an art class where students aren't actually engaged in making art; imagine how silly art classes would become if the teacher expected students to work on all of their projects at home alone, leaving class time for lectures or slides. Of course we should expect students to write at home regularly. But assessment depends on observation, and if we do not allow students to write during class, we cannot observe their process or find the time to give them the responses and ask the questions that matter.[28]

> I like to see students thinking through math. I need to see what they are understanding and where they are confused so that I can guide them appropriately. This, I find, only works in class.[29]

The Learner's Point of View

Even if practice homework really did help some students to acquire a skill, any such benefit would have to be balanced against the effect it has on their *interest* in learning. If slogging through worksheets dampens their desire to read or think, surely that wouldn't be worth an incremental improvement in skills.

But let's take this a step further. Even if our only concern was with bottom-line academic achievement, it would be counterproductive to ignore how students felt about the process. Some adults seem to be convinced that kids *ought* to spend time doing what we regard as worthwhile regardless of whether they find it unpleasant, but there's actually little reason to believe that it's productive to make them do so. This is because excellence tends to follow interest.

As I mentioned earlier, advocates of homework are fond of pointing out that you don't get to be proficient at activities like tennis or basketball without spending an awful lot of time practicing. But even here, what matters most is the fact that the would-be athlete *wants* to be out on the court. Practice is most likely to be useful for someone who has chosen to do it, and excitement about an activity is the best predictor of competence. That's why one of the main challenges for a teacher is to help spark and sustain children's intrinsic motivation to play with words and numbers and ideas. Conversely, when an activity feels like drudgery, the quality of learning tends to suffer. The fact that so many children regard homework as something to finish as quickly as possible—or even as a significant source of stress— helps to explain why there's so little evidence that it offers any academic advantage even for those who obediently sit down and complete the tasks they've been assigned.[30]

That fact makes perfect sense in light of a fundamental insight that has emerged from the work of psychological theorists and researchers who have transcended behaviorism: What matters most is not a child's action; it's what underlies the action—her needs, goals, and attitudes.[31] It's not what she does that's going to prove beneficial (or not) in the long run; it's *why* she does it, what she was hoping to get out of it, whether it makes sense to her (and, if so, for what reason). Of course, it's much harder to measure these things than a variable like ToT. By the same token, it's easier to make students spend hours practicing a skill than it is to change their view of what they're learning, how they see themselves in relation to that task, how competent they think they are, and so on. But that doesn't alter the fact that the best predictor of results is how things appear *from the student's point of view*.

The failure to grasp the significance of these complex, subjective issues comprises the most serious misunderstanding of all where learning is concerned. Essays in favor of homework generally reflect a tendency to regard children as inert objects to be acted on: Make them practice and they'll get better. My argument isn't just that this viewpoint is disrespectful, or that it's a residue of an outdated stimulus-response psychology. I'm also suggesting it doesn't work. Children cannot be made to acquire skills. They aren't vending machines such that we put in more homework and get out more learning.

Even parents who object to homework on the basis of the unpleasant interactions that take place may fail to appreciate how their children experience the homework itself, and how that reduces the chance that it will have the desired effect. Similarly, even researchers who consider students' perspectives tend to do so in the context of reporting that homework elicits considerable resistance, but only because those darn kids don't understand that homework is good for them. Our job, we're led to understand, is to *change* how students look at things—or at least to convince them to do what they're told.[32]

But what if our goal was to understand rather than to convince? What if we made a serious effort to imagine—from the child's point of view—what homework feels like and what it actually teaches? Do all those assignments really impress upon kids the importance of responsibility, achievement, and hard work? Or are their real messages that learning has to be unpleasant, that my parents and teachers have formed an alliance against me, that I'm not trusted to decide what to do with my spare time? Perhaps we so rarely try to experience homework from the vantage point of those who have to do it because this exercise would end up revealing its futility.

I argued in Chapter 2 that a careful review of the data provides little support for the idea that homework is necessary to help students learn better. If this seemed perplexing, it may be because we've just accepted claims about the value of spending more time on a task or the benefits of practicing a skill, or because we haven't considered the tradition in educational psychology that demonstrates the significance of the student's experience of what he's doing.

Misconceptions about learning are pervasive in all sorts of neighborhoods, and they're held by parents and teachers alike. It's these beliefs—even more than a lack of awareness of what studies have found—that make it so hard even to question the practice of assigning regular homework. You can lead people to the research results and show them that there are no data to support the value of giving homework to students in elementary school, but it won't have any impact if they're convinced that practice makes perfect sense and more time naturally produces more learning. If, in other words, we assume homework is a necessary part of education, that may be because of how little we know about how children actually become educated. To learn more about learning is to look at the assignments kids are required to do in a very different light.

CHAPTER 7

The "Tougher Standards" Fad Hits Home

In the 1830s, Dr. [Pierre-Charles-Alexandre] Louis studied the effect of bloodletting, or bleeding—the standard treatment of the time—on pneumonia. The data showed that bleeding didn't work. . . but Dr. Louis rejected this as terrifying and absurd. So he made a recommendation: bleed earlier and bleed harder.[1]

Rigor Mortis

The colorful brochure called *Homework Tips for Parents* produced by George W. Bush's Department of Education offers a combination of familiar advice ("Make sure your child has a quiet, well-lit place to do homework"), unsubstantiated assertions presented as fact ("Homework. . . can foster positive character traits such as independence and responsibility"), and a request for parents to "be positive about homework" rather than thinking critically about its value.

But the context for this material is perhaps more telling than the content. The brochure opens with a two-paragraph history of the subject that explains how, in the 1980s, "homework again came back into favor as it came to be viewed as one way to stem a rising tide of mediocrity in American education. The push for more homework continued into the 1990s, fueled by rising academic standards." Then, on the final page, parents are presented with a ringing defense of the No Child Left Behind Act, which emphasizes mandatory annual testing and punitive consequences for struggling schools. In fact, the words "No Child Left Behind," along with the program's logo, appear on the pamphlet's cover.[2]

For some time now, the most enthusiastic proponents of homework have been policy makers who are committed to the "tougher standards" movement that has had American education in its grip for more than two decades. The matter-of-fact reference to "a rising tide of mediocrity" in the new federal brochure, for example, is an allusion to a 1983 report released by the Reagan administration, which is widely credited with (or blamed for) jump-starting that movement. After offering dire warnings about our failing schools, that report, entitled *A Nation at Risk*, presented a series of conservative policy prescriptions. Among them was a recommendation that more homework be assigned.

The same basic line has been repeated ever since: Our public schools are lousy and our kids are lazy,[3] so we need to demand higher standards, and one obvious way to do that is to assign greater quantities of homework. Thus, the same article in the *Economist* that announces homework is "as close as anything could be to a one-word solution to America's educational problems" anchors its enthusiasm in the conviction that our schools are "notoriously mediocre."[4] Whenever you come across a particularly savage attack on the state of public education, it's a safe bet that a call for more homework (among other get-tough messages) will be sounded as well. And vice versa.

While it may come as a surprise to those who depend solely on the popular press for information about such issues, the claim that school quality has plummeted since the good old days has been repeatedly and decisively debunked by researchers.[5] That's not to say there aren't serious problems with American education. There are. But those problems aren't new and they have more to do with deeply bred inequities (reflecting those of society more generally) and a failure to engage students as active learners and meaning makers. The kinds of solutions favored by people who shrilly denounce our "failing schools" and "falling standards" not only don't address these issues but almost seem designed to make things worse. The more we find ourselves in thrall to a cult of rigor, the more sterile and shallow our children's classrooms become, and the wider the chasm grows between schooling for the rich and schooling for the poor.

It's not a coincidence that many of the people who demand tougher standards are actively trying to privatize our schools— along with other democratic public institutions. The demand for more "accountability" and a defense of market-oriented solutions (such as vouchers) often issue from the same politicians and corporate executives, the same conservative think tanks and editorial pages. As one scholar observed, "We find public schools under attack not just because they are deemed ineffective, but because they are public."[6] Thus, the fact that policies advertised as attempts to improve public schooling often have exactly the opposite effect isn't so puzzling once you consider that the objective all along may have been to undermine its capacities and its reputation.[7]

Beyond the premise that public education is terrible, the tougher standards movement has been constructed on a number of other assumptions. One is that the best way to reform schools is by having top-down, one-size-fits-all mandates imposed by officials far away from local communities. This version of reform consists of doing things *to* educators and students rather than working *with* them, issuing demands rather than offering help. Another assumption is that the best way to force people to comply with those mandates, and more generally to evaluate the quality of education, is by making students fill in ovals with their number 2 pencils in wave after wave of standardized tests.

However dubious they may be, these assumptions are at least out there in the open where we can evaluate them. But there's another belief that's rarely made explicit, even though it's shared by many parents and educators as well as public officials. In brief, it holds that harder is tantamount to better.[8] What's mostly wrong with our schools, on this view, is that they've been "dumbed down"; salvation therefore lies in "raising the bar" and demanding "higher expectations" and more "rigor." Almost by definition, the best lessons (or exams or classes) are those that are really difficult for children.

As far as I can tell, the phrase "raising the bar" originated in the world of show horses, which may say quite a bit about how people who talk this way look at children. As for "rigor," a few years ago I heard about a principal who was asked by a parent in his school whether students would receive a "rigorous" education there. The principal hesitated and then said he couldn't be certain until he found the word's definition in a dictionary. The next day, he sought out the parent and gave his answer, which was, "Good Lord, no!" (Look up the word for yourself and see if its meaning suggests an approach likely to promote engagement with, or deep understanding of, ideas.)[9]

Of course, the tendency to equate harder with better isn't problematic just because of the language used to express this idea. It's not just the etymology of the term "raising the bar" that should provoke questions, for example; it's the fact that this phrase signals an agenda of doing the same thing we've always done in classrooms, except now with fewer students being likely to succeed. Almost a century ago, John Dewey reminded us that the value of what students do "resides in its connection with a stimulation of greater *thoughtfulness*, not in the greater strain it imposes."[10] Yet despite the rhetoric in which they're wrapped, most reforms these days seem geared primarily to making students work harder rather than enhancing the importance of what they—or their teachers—are doing.

One example is the growing popularity of Advanced Placement courses in high school, which often consist of an accelerated version of the worst forms of teaching. Largely because their primary purpose is to prepare students to do well on an exam, these courses are typically lecture based and textbook oriented. The prestigious National Research Council has been sharply critical of A.P. courses because their "coursework resemble[s] a test-preparation seminar rather than an in-depth academic experience." This may help to explain why a 2006 study discovered that they "don't provide much of an academic boost for students when they get to college." Some very fine high schools have eliminated these courses because they tend to be so poor.[11] But of course these schools are the exception. In most places, it's simply assumed that A.P. classes must be the best in the school simply because they're the *hardest* ones in the school.

If parents sometimes confuse rigor with quality, it may be because the system encourages and virtually codifies the conflation of these two ideas. We assume if our children are bored with the worksheets they're given, it must be because the assignments aren't "challenging" enough, rather than because of problems with worksheets per se and the view of pedagogy on which they're based. One newspaper columnist observed that "parents who have a choice often put their kids in more rigorous programs when all they really want is to increase the odds of having good teachers and sound curriculum."[12] Only occasionally does it become clear that harder wasn't really better after all. Part of the problem is that a class or school may end up being *too* hard; maximum difficulty isn't the same thing as optimal difficulty. But more important— and less widely noticed—is the fact that focusing primarily on the difficulty level distracts us from more important criteria by which education should be evaluated.

The number of policy makers who tingle with excitement over adjectives like "rigorous" and "challenging" (but seem indifferent to engagement and meaning) helps to explain the current effort to reform secondary education. There's no question that our high schools desperately need improvement. They're too large and impersonal, too authoritarian, too competitive, too segregated, too driven by grades and tests, too focused on forgettable facts and isolated skills. In light of all this, declarations that the main problem with the high school experience is that it's too *easy* might almost be amusing if the impact of this misanalysis—which includes harder courses for everyone and still more standardized testing—wasn't so devastating for so many kids.

Astonishingly, the tests are sometimes justified on the grounds that they will reveal which schools are inadequate so that officials can "determine who needs extra help," as George W. Bush has put it. There are at least three problems with this argument. First, it's doubtful that there's a single school anywhere in the country whose inadequacy is a secret that will be revealed only by the release of yet more standardized test results. Second, the track record of those who demand accountability and tougher standards has not been encouraging in terms of providing needed resources for the many schools and districts that have long been known to be struggling. In fact, many of the same people who claim that their motive for requiring more standardized tests is to learn which schools need help have also been arguing for some time against devoting more resources to education on the grounds that more money for the poorest schools won't help.[13]

Finally, the policies enacted in the name of higher standards have transformed classrooms, particularly those in urban school systems attended by minority students, into glorified test-preparation centers distinguished by heavily scripted lessons and endless practice tests. Second-rate schools have basically been turned into third-rate schools; whatever was left of decent teaching has been squeezed out. Many of the best teachers have left such schools after being forced to become test-prep technicians—which is yet another reason that talk about "raising standards" has actually lowered the quality of the schools. Dorothy Strickland, an African American professor at Rutgers University, has remarked that "skills-based instruction, the type to which most children of color are subjected, tends to foster low-level uniformity and subvert academic potential." As a direct result of the tougher standards movement, it is hard to find any other kind of instruction these days in most inner-city schools.[14] *Harcourt*

The ultimate example of the current intensification effort, though, is the high-stakes exit exams students must pass in order to *MCAS* graduate. We know from both research and real-world experience that the policy of denying diplomas on the basis of a single standardized test score has resulted in more students dropping out—or being pushed out. We also know that the burden has disproportionately fallen on poor kids, kids of color, kids whose first language isn't English, and kids with special needs.[15] Put plainly, this policy threatens to create nothing short of an educational ethnic *True* cleansing in America. And yet it continues, propped up with slogans like "accountability" and "raising the bar."

The Role of Homework

The tougher standards movement that brought us standardized testing is also responsible for more homework. It shouldn't be surprising, then, to find that the effects of the latter are as profoundly inequitable as those of the former. In the mid-1980s, an educator named Bill Barber commented that "to include 'more homework' on an agenda for educational reform is embarrassing; it implies that we are nothing but amateurs if the best we can muster up for students who are dropping out at alarming rates, students who can't read or write, is a recommendation that they ought to get more of the same thing."[16] Now, however, there has been a subtle change in this equation: It isn't merely that more homework has been proposed as a (foolish) way of dealing with a rising dropout rate and other problems; rather, homework is rooted in the very movement that has helped to *cause* those problems. And homework itself makes a substantial contribution.

Let's begin by noting that the evidence is mixed on whether the burden of homework falls most heavily on kids who are white or black, rich or poor, successful or struggling. Certainly in high school it seems that "more homework is expected of the more advanced students."[17] This may be because their politically savvy and assertive parents demand it, but it may also tell us something about the likelihood of compliance. One state education official remarked that "it's probably true that schools of higher socioeconomic status assign more homework," partly because teachers in those schools "have an expectation that it can get done."[18] Where it's less likely that homework will be completed, teachers may eventually stop giving as much. Then again, they may just ratchet up the threats—or assign simpler, practice-oriented homework instead.

Other data, though, tell a different story about which students get the most:

- In a study of more than 150 schools in three states, kindergarten and first grade teachers were found to "assign more homework in schools that had a high proportion of low-income students, students of color, and students performing below grade level." The homework in these classrooms was much more likely to be scripted and didactic, whereas more privileged children were more likely to get lessons that focused on problem solving and understanding.[19]

- Interviews with about a thousand mothers and elementary school children in the Chicago area found that black and Latino kids were spending an average of six to seven hours a week on homework, whereas white kids spent about four hours. Nevertheless, teachers in minority schools were more likely than those who taught white students to believe that even more should be assigned.[20]
- African American middle school students, also in Chicago, spent less time on homework than did suburban white students. However, the white students did more of their homework during school; the amount of time spent on these assignments outside of school ended up being about the same for both groups.[21]

There isn't a straightforward answer, then, to the question of which students get, or do, more homework. But what matters in any case is the impact of those assignments. Here, proponents face a serious dilemma. If, on the one hand, homework in general hasn't been shown to be beneficial, then there wouldn't be much reason to assign it to anyone. But if we accept, even provisionally, that homework *does* help—or that certain kinds of homework may help—then those benefits are likely to accrue disproportionately to the students who are already positioned for success in school. The "rich get richer" as they plow through their assignments, while their classmates fall farther behind. That expression may be true literally as well as figuratively. If homework helps anyone, it's the affluent. As Deborah Meier dryly observes, "If we sat around and deliberately tried to come up with a way to further enlarge the achievement gap, we might just invent homework."[22]

The reason isn't hard to figure out: "Students whose parents understand the homework and can help them with it at home have a major advantage over students whose parents are unable or unavailable to help."[23] Richard Rothstein, a leading expert on education and equity, takes this a step further:

> Homework would increase the achievement gap even if all parents were able to assist. Parents from different social classes supervise homework differently. Consistent with overall patterns of language use, middle-class parents—especially those whose own occupational habits require problem solving—are more likely to assist by posing questions that break large problems down into smaller ones and that help children figure out correct answers. Lower-class parents are more likely to guide children with direct instructions. Children from both classes may go to school with completed homework, but middle-class children are more likely to gain in intellectual power from the exercise than lower-class children.[24]

In short, there are pronounced disparities in the extent to which parents are available to help, how able they are to help, and what type of help they're likely to offer. Let's not forget, too, that there are similar disparities in the books, computers, and other resources accessible to children in different neighborhoods. The net effect is that assigning "more homework is likely to increase family background effects, thereby generating more inequality," assuming that homework has any effect at all.[25] That fact is rarely considered by people who are in the habit of describing homework as a way to raise standards, and who seem to assume that more homework is inherently preferable because it raises expectations that much higher.

The same is true of more *difficult* homework, which brings us back to the current infatuation with rigor. The "harder is better" premise isn't limited to what happens while students are sitting in the classroom. A high school English teacher in Clovis, California, told me recently that he finds himself not only questioning homework but also being "skeptical of education as a process where more work always amounts to a better (harder) class or experience. Many teachers base their egos on how painful/difficult their class is, and in turn create students who feel a sense of pride for their ability to endure the unpleasant. Homework, obviously, is a major component of this system."[26]

But even if homework didn't emerge from the same sensibility that drives the tougher standards movement, it is clearly a byproduct of that movement. Recall that the push to have children take home additional assignments is often justified by concerns that there isn't enough time to teach everything during school hours. If those concerns are legitimate, it's at least in part because of mandates to teach specific curriculum content and make sure that the material is increasingly rigorous (that is, difficult for students to master). As a suburban New York middle school principal put it, "The higher standards require more information, and we can't cover everything. What we're having to do is ask kids to do more at home."[27]

"At this point in American history," a *New York Times* reporter comments, nothing matters more than "performance on standardized tests. And as long as that is true, those backpacks are likely to be full each night starting in grade 1 and maybe earlier."[28] The only good news here is the possibility that children's loads may be lightened once criteria more reasonable than test scores are used to assess the quality of teaching and learning. In the meantime, schools with low test scores reason that their only hope for turning things around is to give kids more homework, while schools with high test scores are afraid to let up on the pressure since all that homework seems to be working.

Actually, it's far from clear that the latter is true—even if we accepted the premise that better test results mean better learning. If higher scores were associated with a heavier homework load, it would probably be due to the fact that both are correlated with higher socioeconomic status, not because assigning more home-work *caused* the test scores to rise. In fact, when wealth is held con-stant, the two may not even be related. For example, Piscataway, New Jersey, schools attracted national attention in 2000 for placing what were actually very modest limits on homework assignments. It did so partly in response to the fact that "homework in the dis-trict had steadily risen over the past seven years [while] standard-ized test scores [had] steadily declined."[29]

Although the evidence doesn't support the idea that homework leads to more effective learning or even to higher test scores, that often doesn't seem to matter. No independent evidence of success is required because homework has *symbolic* value. The fact that kids are made to work harder is in itself taken to be a sign of "higher standards," which may help to explain why many parents find it reassuring (and its absence disquieting). Moreover, it's a popular way to demonstrate a commitment to that objective because it's cheap and asks almost nothing of officials and relatively little of ed-ucators—at least compared to other, more meaningful changes that could be made.

The Chain of Assumptions

The demand to raise standards and further cement traditional teaching methods in place is renewed with fresh fervor every few decades. It's not always clear why this happens on the schedule it does, but one hypothesis can be ruled out immediately. It isn't ex-plained by any objective decline in student achievement, because there is no evidence that such a decline precedes each new call to raise the bar. Nor does the demand for more homework follow the release of new studies on the subject. "Current thinking at any given point in time seems more influenced by cultural and political philosophy than by new information," one researcher commented.[30]

Policy makers tend to take an aerial view, looking at education as an abstraction rather than weighing whether homework helps this child—or even this group of children—to become better thinkers. What's more, the focus is on the state of our economic system, and specifically how we're in danger of falling behind [insert name of current rival]. If we're going to triumph over other countries, we're going to have to send our children home with packets of worksheets.

Thus does a New Jersey principal defend ever greater quantities of homework even for very young children by shrugging, "This is what's demanded to stay competitive in a global market."[31] Thus in the 1990s did we find that California board of education president Yvonne Larsen, appointed by a Republican governor, and the state's superintendent of public instruction, Delaine Eastin, a Democrat, finally made common cause by issuing a joint statement that proclaimed, "Our children are competing in a global economy. The extra hours spent after school on homework in Europe and Asia are giving those children an extra boost into the 21st century."[32] Thus do we find newspapers around the country issuing interchangeable editorials featuring statements like this one: "Homework. . . is more important than ever. Americans are competing in a world market. While kids here are shirking their math and science homework, kids in China and India aren't. When all of them grow up, guess where the best jobs will go?"[33]

A little historical context is useful to put such talk in perspective. In economics and education, in technology and the military, we are constantly being told—often in hysterical tones—that some other country is either ahead of us or gaining on us, and we must mobilize to beat them. The United States is not one country among others; we're one country *against* others, and we must always be ahead of them. The fact that the Soviet Union launched a rocket in 1957 meant that our approach to science education was a humiliating failure and had to be revamped. In the 1980s, it was

Japan's manufacturing prowess that ignited the same combustible combination of (nationalistic) fervor and fear (of coming in second). Today we hear about a whole world of potential rivals who may show us up—and that can't be permitted. We must be king of the mountain again, and therefore we must assign more homework to our children.

Let's spell out each of the links in this chain of reasoning.

1. Our primary concern ought not to be with the intellectual proficiency of individual children but with aggregate measures of achievement. And that achievement can be measured with standardized tests.
2. International comparisons of the results of those tests reveal that the achievement of U.S. students is shockingly low.
3. Assigning more homework will make children learn better and therefore raise those scores.
4. Our educational system and our economic system are—and should be—linked. Descriptively, the quality of our schools determines the performance of our economy. Prescriptively, the primary purpose of education is to train future employees and pump up the economy.
5. What counts most with respect to economic as well as educational matters is competitiveness; our chief goal should be to do better than other countries.

If even one of these assumptions doesn't stand up to scrutiny, then the whole economic rationale for assigning plenty of homework falls apart. As it happens, I believe there is good reason to doubt *all* of these assumptions. I've already addressed the first three, so it should be sufficient to review those findings very briefly. First, we have to question the idea of acting *on* students to improve their achievement. Second, standardized tests tend to measure what matters least about intellectual prowess. Third, the idea that

U.S. students consistently come up short, even as measured by those tests, is a drastic oversimplification of a complex set of results (see pp. 205–206, note 48). (To this last point we might add that the enormous variation in scores *within* this country further complicates matters. Trying to summarize all our schools with a single number is rather like looking at an average pollution statistic for the United States to determine the cleanliness of "American air." The fact is that our top states do as well on international tests as the top countries, while our bottom states are down there with the lowest-scoring countries.)

Fourth, not only is there good reason in general to doubt the proposition that homework is academically beneficial, but cross-cultural data have decisively refuted the claim that countries whose students do more homework tend to be those with the best test scores. As you may recall, the latest study of math and science achievement data suggests that exactly the opposite is true (see p. 43).

Assumption number four, which I haven't yet considered, consists partly of the value judgment that education ought to be seen chiefly in economic terms. This is so widely accepted by politicians, columnists, and others that it's rarely even acknowledged to be controversial. Education *could* be viewed as a way to do what's best for each child, promoting his or her development, or as a way to create a just and democratic society. But these objectives are inevitably relegated to the margins if the main purpose of schools is to prepare children to be productive workers who will do their part to increase the profitability of their future employers. Every time education is described as an "investment" or schools are mentioned in terms of the "global economy," a loud alarm ought to go off, reminding us of the moral and practical implications of giving an answer in dollars to a question about schools. Such a response reveals something about how we look not only at learning but at children.[34]

The empirical part of the fourth assumption, meanwhile, is that
the state of our economy is in fact a function of how good a job our
schools are doing at preparing tomorrow's workers. This, too, is
usually taken on faith. But various strands of evidence have con-
verged to dispute it. First, at the level of the individual, "test scores
have only a small relation to workplace productivity when earn-
ings or supervisory ratings are used as criteria."[35] (Since homework
isn't reliably associated with test scores, and test scores aren't reliably associated with students' eventual job performance, the connection between homework and later productivity is doubly dubious.) Furthermore, the connection between education and the
economy also fails to pan out at the level of entire countries. Education analyst Gerald Bracey found thirty-eight nations whose
economies had been rated on the Current Competitiveness Index
calculated by the World Economic Forum and whose students' test
scores had been assessed for the Third International Mathematics
and Science Study. There was virtually no correlation between
countries' scores on the two lists.[36]

Corporate executives regularly complain, of course, about the ignorance and incompetence of American students and, by extension, about the schools from which these students have emerged.
Again, however, some historical perspective is helpful. "School
critics have always claimed, without apparent foundation, that
graduates were not adequately skilled for the occupational demands of the future," writes Richard Rothstein. "Businessmen and
policymakers have been making this charge with regularity since
the early 1900s."[37]

Bad schools make a tempting scapegoat when a corporation's financial results are disappointing, or when the economy as a whole
isn't doing well. (Notice that public schools almost never get any
credit during those periods when economic indicators are looking
up.) The fact is, though, that an employee's educational background is only one of many factors that determine his or her pro-

ductivity. Worker productivity, in turn, is only one of many factors that determine corporate profitability. And corporate profitability is only one of many factors that determine the state of the economy—particularly the employment picture. Does anyone seriously believe, for example, that the primary reason U.S. companies are shipping jobs by the millions to Mexico and Asia is because they believe those countries' schools are better, let alone because children there do more homework?

Or consider the reverse situation: When foreign companies (say, Japanese auto manufacturers) decide to build a plant in the United States, do they choose a location on the basis of educational considerations—or do they tend to pick Southern states with a low cost of living and an antiunion climate despite the fact that these states are not exactly known for the quality of their schools? (Furthermore, these site decisions have worked out reasonably well for their bottom line notwithstanding the alleged inferiority of schools in the area.)

As one pair of researchers has shown, *the availability of meaningful work is far more likely to influence the study habits of students than the other way around.*[38] Students could spend every waking hour filling out worksheets or studying for tests, but it still wouldn't result in the creation of more (or better, or higher-paying) jobs wherever they happen to live, nor would it appreciably affect interest rates, the demand for professionals versus service workers, the degree to which market power is concentrated in the hands of a few giant conglomerates, or almost any other economic variable.

Winning Versus Learning

When public officials and editorial writers across the political spectrum discuss the effect of education on the economy, they assume that our goal should be framed in terms of beating others rather than doing well. Just as quality is confused with rigor, so excellence is confused with "competitiveness."[39] And so we come to the fifth assumption in that chain on page 132.

When the topic is our economic system, or the phenomenon known as globalization, it's widely assumed that competition is unavoidable: For one enterprise (or country) to succeed, another must fail. Even if this were true (and it's not at all certain that it is),[40] why would the same zero-sum mentality persist when we're talking about education? Consider the sport of ranking the United States against other nations on standardized tests. Once we've debunked the myth that test scores drive economic success, what reason would we have to fret about our country's standing as measured by those scores? What sense does it make to focus on *relative* performance? After all, to say that our students are first or tenth on a list doesn't tell us whether they're doing well or poorly; it gives us no useful information about how much they know or how good our schools are. If all the countries did reasonably well in absolute terms, there would be no shame in (and perhaps no statistical significance to) being at the bottom. If all the countries did poorly, there would be no glory in being at the top. Exclamatory headlines about how "our" schools are doing compared to "theirs" suggest that we are less concerned with the quality of education than with whether we can chant, "We're number one!"

Consider an essay published in early 2006 that reported U.S. students are now doing better in mathematics than earlier generations did. Was the author moved by this fact to express relief or even delight? Not at all. In fact, he pronounced the current state of affairs "disturbing" because children in other countries are also doing well—and that, by definition, is bad news.[41] Much the same thing happened in the late 1990s, when a front-page *New York Times* article warned that "American high school graduation rates, for generations the highest in the world, have slipped below those of most industrialized countries." Actually, there was no slippage in absolute terms; on most measures, the United States was doing better than ever in the proportion of adults who finish school. But again it was taken for granted that we should be worried because other countries had made progress too, and we were no longer ahead of everybody else.[42]

When people panic at the prospect of America losing its edge over the rest of the world on some academic measure, experts are permitted to disagree about how best to solve that problem. There may even be room to dispute the urgency of the situation. But it is beyond the bounds of acceptable discourse to ask why the question of math competence or literacy is framed in competitive terms, the goal being for our kids to triumph over those who live elsewhere. Because this worldview pervades our culture—and because children internalize it so early[43]—we are unlikely to recognize that it is more rivalrous than rational.

Try to imagine a different way of looking at things. At a minimum, we could ignore the status of students in other countries and just focus on how those who live here are learning. This perspective isn't especially neighborly but at least we wouldn't be viewing the gains of children in other lands as a troubling development. Better yet, rather than defending whatever educational policies will ostensibly help our graduates to "compete," we could make decisions on the basis of what will help them develop the skills and disposition to *collaborate* effectively. Educators, too, might think in terms of working with—and learning from—their counterparts in other countries so that children everywhere will become more proficient and enthusiastic learners. Even beyond the moral justification for doing so, Janet Swenson at Michigan State University points out that "we'll all benefit from the best education we can provide to every child on the face of this planet. Do you care if it's a child in Africa who finds a cure for cancer rather than a child in your country?" she asks.[44]

When the goal is excellence rather than victory, it seems silly to spend time figuring out who's doing better than whom. In fact, we may be inclined not only to stop comparing standardized test scores but also to rethink the whole rationale for giving such tests in the first place. The only reason for assessment to be standardized is to facilitate ranking—not just of countries but of states, towns, and schools. If we simply want to know how well a student is learning, or how well a teacher is teaching, there are many rich, authentic, classroom-based forms of assessment that can give us a meaningful answer.[45] Only if your primary concern is to know who's beating whom do you need to give the same mass-produced tests under the same conditions. In the absence of that imperative to rank, it would not only be possible to get rid of such tests; it would also be desirable, seeing as how they help to foster a competitive orientation, one in which we are led to fear other children's success and celebrate their failure.

The pathological impulse to create artificial scarcity and turn learning (along with just about everything else) into a contest is at the heart of the tougher standards movement. That movement, in turn, helps to explain the assignment of homework in ever-greater quantities. If our primary objective was not winning but learning—helping kids to become deep thinkers who love exploring ideas—then education policy would play out very differently, and it might be possible to question the value of things like homework. But people are not likely to question premises or think carefully when they're in the middle of a race. The prospects for critical thought are particularly bleak if we're told the race never ends.

And here's what's even worse: Competitiveness isn't just a matter of nation being pitted against nation. The same tendency to regard others as rivals shows up closer to home—and brings us closer to solving the puzzle of why homework persists when it doesn't seem to do much good. If school administrators are preoccupied with how well their schools (or districts) are doing compared with others, then it's difficult for any of them to call an end to unnecessary homework until those elsewhere are ready to do so. The (il)logic is comparable to that of an arms race. Likewise, if parents are intent on pushing their children to outperform their peers—to get better grades, better test scores, more awards, admission to more prestigious colleges, and so on—then reversing course on homework raises the terrifying prospect of falling behind someone else's kid who's continuing to slave away.

Homework, of course, is only one example of what is being done to children in the name of positioning them to defeat their peers. While I was writing this chapter, someone sent me a newspaper story about parents who are hiring academic tutors for *two-year-olds*—another example of how yesterday's satire becomes today's reality. The one constant theme in every report of such excesses is that no matter how extreme the practice, no matter what the costs to children's emotional, social, ethical, or intellectual development, the article is sure to feature at least one person saying, somewhat defensively, "Well, it's a competitive world." The question begins to dawn: Is there anything we could do to children that people would be embarrassed to try to rationalize with that phrase?

The most extreme practices may not make the best examples, though, because they permit those of us in the mainstream to shake our heads with self-satisfied disapproval. Ultimately, less outrageous manifestations of competition may end up doing more harm because they are more generally accepted. One example is the subtle way kids are led to believe they must earn their parents' love by being impressive—in fact, more impressive than their peers. When children infer that attention and approval are conditional on their performance, the psychological effects can be dreadful indeed.[46]

Even with ordinary homework, a competitive dynamic may help to explain why so many of us feel trapped. Like school administrators, we may feel that until *other* parents see the light, we can't challenge the status quo—no matter how mutually destructive it may be. Parents "may feel in their hearts that their children have too much homework, but as long as everyone else is doing it, there's pressure to do it."[47] What we sometimes forget is that each of us is part of the "they" to which all those others will point in order to justify *their* actions. The result is that even changes that many of us come to regard as desirable may never happen. In the final analysis, even the winners end up losing. Or perhaps it would be more accurate to say that the only winners are the officials who can claim credit for demanding "high standards." The losers are the children, straining like beasts of burden to pull the adults to glory.

CHAPTER 8

Better Get Used to It

T HE ONLY KINDS of study skills that students would have to do homework to acquire, I argued earlier, are those useful for doing . . . more homework. If that's true, we would have a pretty good reason to reconsider the practice of giving such assignments. After all, why would we make children do something whose sole benefit was helping them to engage in that same activity—a practice without any value beyond itself?

Amazingly, though, the claim that homework prepares children for doing more homework is often accepted as a good argument for assigning it. As one researcher contends (without a hint of irony), "Students develop an aptitude for future homework from the regularities of homework ongoing." Another proponent approvingly quotes a fifth grader who says, "I'm going to have to do it in high school so it's good that I learn how now." And a parent reports that "first graders (and in some schools, even kindergartners) are expected to do homework regularly. We are told they need to establish good 'study habits,' or develop good 'time management skills' so that they can cope with the exorbitant amounts of homework they will have in high school."[1]

That particular parent clearly finds this rationale unpersuasive, but it seems to make sense to many others. Tom Little, a school principal in Oakland, California, who has doubts about the value of homework, comments that

> the great challenge comes in convincing parents that two to three hours of homework (or more) is not the ticket to success in life, academically or otherwise. As their kids get older (fifth to eighth grade), parents seem to expect that the kids will have loads of homework and that it is somehow reassuring to see their kids slaving away under the lamp. We have worked hard to bring the research on this to the parents, but I never feel that they are convinced. They hear the horror stories of kids who went off to some traditional high school and are suffering under the burden of four hours a night. "If only we had prepared them," as though doing homework was like lifting weights.[2]

Since even parents characterize these reports from high school as horror stories, why would they want their children to be subjected to something so horrible any earlier than necessary? The answer, distilled into one unlovely acronym, is BGUTI (rhymes with duty): Better get used to it.[3] This way of thinking pervades education and child rearing. It's a two-edged sword that can be used to attack practices one opposes as well as to promote practices one prefers. In response to a humane and respectful approach to education, some people are fond of objecting, "Yeah, but what's going to happen to these kids when they learn that life isn't like that?" (By this logic, we shouldn't raise our children lovingly because not everyone they meet will treat them that way.) Conversely, when it's pointed out that a certain policy is destructive, the response is to declare that children will eventually experience something similar, so they need to be prepared.

This kind of reasoning is especially popular where curriculum is concerned. Even if a lesson provides little intellectual benefit, students may have to suffer through it anyway because someone decided it will get them ready for what they're going to face in the next grade. Lilian Katz, a specialist in early childhood education, refers to this as "vertical relevance," and she contrasts it with the horizontal kind in which students' learning is meaningful to them at the time because it connects to some other aspect of their lives.[4]

Horizontal criteria for deciding what to teach are the exception in our schools. Vertical justifications, on the other hand, are employed at just about every grade level. Countless middle school teachers, for example, spend their days disgorging facts and skills not because this is the best way to promote learning, much less enthusiasm for learning, but solely because they've been told that their students will be expected to know this stuff when they get to high school. Even good teachers end up routinely engaging in bad instruction lest their kids be unprepared when more bad instruction comes their way.

The current "tougher standards" craze not only pressures educators to teach too much too early, but also makes use of a vertical rationale—in part because of its reliance on testing. Here, too, we find that "getting them ready" is accepted as sufficient reason for doing what would otherwise be seen as unreasonable. Child development experts are nearly unanimous in denouncing the use of standardized testing with young children.[5] One Iowa principal conceded that many teachers, too, consider it "insane" to subject first graders to a four-and-a-half-hour test. However, she adds, "they need to get used to it," an imperative that trumps all objections. But why wait until first grade? A principal in California used the same phrase to justify testing *kindergarteners*: "Our philosophy is, the sooner we start giving these students tests like the Stanford 9, the sooner they'll get used to it."[6]

BGUTI is regularly applied to other practices in education, too. The use of traditional grading has been found to result in a lower quality of learning, less interest in learning, and a preference for easier tasks. But the fact that students' efforts will be reduced to a letter or number in the future is seen as a good enough reason to give them grades in the present. Likewise, setting children against one another in contests, so that one can't succeed unless others fail, has demonstrably negative effects—on psychological health, relationships, intrinsic motivation, and achievement. In fact, it generally has those effects for winners and losers alike.[7] No matter: Young children must be made to compete because. . . well, you get the idea.

I realize that many readers regard these practices as defensible, if not desirable. They may believe that competitive struggle brings out the best in children, that grading students is a constructive form of evaluation, that standardized tests accurately assess the most important aspects of learning. I've challenged each of these premises elsewhere; here, I'm concerned only with people who admit that these practices may be damaging but defend them anyway—purely on BGUTI grounds.

It may well be that each of these things is unhealthy for children of all ages and even for adults. What's bad, or at least pointless, in elementary school may be equally unhelpful in high school—and beyond. But even if a given practice did make sense for older students, that doesn't mean it's appropriate for those who are younger. Almost by definition, the preparation defense ignores developmental differences—the fact that younger children lack certain cognitive and social proficiencies. It's a serious mistake to see young children mostly as future older children, nor should any child be seen as just an adult in the making. As John Dewey famously said, education is a process of living, not just a preparation for future living. BGUTI turns that adage on its head.

Perhaps the preparation argument fails even on its own terms by virtue of offering a skewed account of what life is like for adults.

Our culture is undeniably competitive, but cooperative skills are also valued in the workplace—and competitive schooling (spelling bees, awards assemblies, norm-referenced tests, class rank) discourages the development of those skills. Similarly, adults are more likely to be evaluated at work on the basis of how they actually do their job rather than by results on a paper-and-pencil test. Nor, for that matter, is there much after graduation to justify the practices of same-age groupings or fifty-minute periods. In short, we're not making schools for little kids more like "real life"; we're just making them more like schools for older kids.

What underlies BGUTI isn't just preparation, but preparation for experiences that are unappealing. It's partly because kids won't want to do homework later that we're supposed to start assigning it to them now. They need to acquire the self-discipline to slog through what they don't see as worthwhile. If homework hasn't been shown to help children learn better, then proponents have to fall back on the claim that it will help them become reconciled to doing things that aren't necessarily beneficial. In fact, Janine Bempechat (see p. 78) actually says at one point that it's too easy for students to delay gratification when they "have an intrinsic interest in the assignment. Yet it is precisely when intrinsic interest is low that students need to be able to fall back on a repertoire of beliefs and strategies that will see them through difficulty and setbacks."[8] The more unpleasant the homework, in other words, the more valuable it must be.

The fundamental choice we face as parents and teachers is whether our primary obligation is to help children love learning, or to get them accustomed to gratuitous unpleasantness so they can learn to deal with it. To cast a skeptical eye on the latter objective isn't to dispute the fact that children *will* face unpleasant experiences in their lives. Of course they will, and they'll have to do many things that are demanding. But what are we willing to do to them in order to teach them this? As one pair of educators remarked, "Perhaps being in school seven hours a day is demanding enough. And if it is not, having the school day encroach on what might otherwise be family time may not be the best solution."[9]

More to the point, people don't really get better at coping with unhappiness because they were deliberately made unhappy when they were young. In fact, it is experience with success and unconditional acceptance that helps one to deal constructively with later deprivation. Imposing competition or standardized tests or homework on children just because other people will do the same to them when they're older is about as sensible as saying that, because there are lots of carcinogens in the environment, we should feed kids as many cancer-causing agents as possible while they're small in order to get them ready.[10]

Some people insist that kids ought to have early experiences with whatever they're going to encounter later so they won't be blindsided by it. But how many such experiences would be necessary to achieve the desired effect? Suppose you acknowledged the lack of any data supporting the value of homework in elementary school but you believed that it was beneficial in high school. And suppose you were genuinely worried that if you waited until then to make kids bring home academic assignments, they would be so unfamiliar with the concept, so disoriented, that they'd be unable to cope. Even so, would we really have to introduce them to homework *years* ahead of time? And would we really have to assign it every single night, for weeks or even months on end?

Common sense suggests that if our goal was just to familiarize children with the idea of homework, it would probably be sufficient to give them a few assignments during the year immediately before high school. "The way to get ready to do hours of homework in ninth grade is not to do hours of homework in kindergarten," says Marilou Hyson of the National Association for the Education of Young Children.[11] Furthermore, we could prepare students, at least to some extent, by *discussing* with them what they're going to face later, rather than by *immersing* them in it. One need not make children compete in order to help them antici- pate—and think critically about—the pervasiveness of competition in American culture. Admittedly, the analogy is imperfect; one may have to experience the intrusiveness of doing schoolwork in the evening to really understand what homework feels like. But even here, thoughtful classroom conversations in middle school about how to plan for this may alleviate the need to make students start doing now what they're going to have to do later.

If the practices defended on BGUTI grounds really aren't nec- essary as pragmatic preparation, what lies behind the penchant for making younger children do something unnecessary and unpro- ductive? One sometimes catches a whiff of vinegary moralism— the assumption that whatever isn't enjoyable must be valuable for that very reason. From this vantage point, it isn't that homework turns out to be beneficial *even though* kids dislike it; rather, home- work is beneficial at least in part *because* kids dislike it. Never mind whether unappealing labor is useful, either now or later. It builds character; it's good for you. Homework is the modern cod liver oil, and we are invited to take grim satisfaction from the fact that children are made to do something unpleasant—and are ben- efiting from it, by definition.

Alternatively, getting kids used to doing what may not be of any intrinsic value may be another example of conservatism mas- querading as realism. When children spend years at something, they are more likely to see it as inevitable and less likely to realize that *things could be otherwise*. "You'd better get used to it" not only assumes that life is pretty unpleasant, but that we ought not to bother trying to change the conditions that make it so. Adults, meanwhile, are discouraged from working to improve our schools or other institutions, and instead set themselves the task of getting children ready for whatever is to come.

Thus, a middle school whose primary mission is to prepare students for a dysfunctional high school environment soon comes to resemble that high school. Not only does the middle school fail to live up to its potential, but an opportunity has been lost to create a constituency for better secondary education. (The same is true when kindergartens come to resemble bad first grade classrooms.) Eventually an entire generation learns to regard various phenomena as "the way things are" rather than as practices that happen to define our society at this moment in history. The result is that their critical sensibilities are stillborn and debatable policies are never debated. Perhaps this helps to explain why so many people seem content with asking incidental rather than integral questions.

Finally, there is a remarkable callousness lurking just under the surface here. The message children often get is, "Your objections don't count, your unhappiness doesn't matter. Suck it up." As a rule, the people who talk this way are usually on top, issuing directives, not on the bottom being directed. "Learn to live with it because there's more coming later" can be rationalized as being in the best interests of those on the receiving end, but it may just mean "Do it because I said so" and thereby perpetuates the power of those offering the advice. This is a way of socializing individuals to accept whatever they encounter in other environments.

The BGUTI defense puts me in mind of a Monty Python sketch that features getting hit on the head lessons. When the student recoils and cries out, the instructor says, "No, no, no. Hold your head like this, then go, 'Waaah!' Try it again" and gives him another smack. Presumably this is useful training. . . for getting hit on the head again. ("I'm going to be hit in high school, so it's good that I learn how now.")

Whatever the reason for it, though, there's no disputing the fact that, in the words of one teacher, "schools routinely assign homework that does not lead to real learning with the argument that young students need to get used to the workload."[12] And, sad to report, most of them probably will. Nothing about homework, no matter how aversive or pointless, will be surprising to kids by the time they're teenagers. By then, as one commentator remarks, they "won't even remember what it's like to spend an idle afternoon."[13] So if the objective is to acquaint students with the imperative to do what doesn't seem to make sense, then we must admit that homework, at least as it currently exists, is perfectly suited to this task. By the same token, the BGUTI principle is perfectly suited to ensuring that homework starts early in life and continues to be assigned, no matter what the data say about its effects.

CHAPTER 9

Idle Hands . . .

I like it when my kids get homework over the summer.
Keeps 'em out of trouble!

Comment posted on-line by anonymous parent

THERE'S ONE MORE reason that homework doesn't have to be valuable in order for teachers to keep assigning it and parents to keep accepting it. On some level, many of us just don't trust kids. We're suspicious of what they would do with more free time and we're doubtful that they'd learn anything if they weren't given very specific assignments. This outlook isn't shared by all proponents of homework, of course. But a rather dark view of children is threaded through enough discussions of the topic—and is sufficiently common in our culture—that it ought to be included in any list of explanations of homework's popularity.

Adolescents are routinely and unapologetically described with sweeping generalizations that we wouldn't think of applying to any other subset of the population. Many of these characterizations turn out to be greatly exaggerated, if not simply false, which suggests that teens are often made into scapegoats for pervasive social problems.[1] In fact, surveys of American adults consistently find what one newspaper report called "a stunning level of antagonism not just toward teen-agers but toward young children as well." Substantial majorities of our fellow citizens say they disapprove of kids of all ages, calling them rude, lazy, irresponsible, and lacking in basic values.[2]

Perhaps we've forgotten that our parents (or at least their contemporaries) said much the same about our generation; indeed, older people have been denigrating younger people for thousands of years. The following rant, for example, is widely attributed to the Greek poet Hesiod, who lived about twenty-seven hundred years ago: "I see no hope for the future of our people if they are dependent on the frivolous youth of today, for certainly all youth are reckless beyond words. When I was young, we were taught to be discreet and respectful of elders, but the present youth are exceedingly [disrespectful] and impatient of restraint."[3]

Is this attitude toward young people just one of many postures—along with specific parenting practices—that we uncritically reproduce from our families of origin? Do we feel the need to exert more control over kids than they're willing to put up with, and then blame them for their resistance? Does our view of children offer a glimpse of our view of human nature more generally? Do we react with disapproval because we envy children their youth, the fact that they have more life ahead of them than we do? Or do children reflect back to us (with disconcerting clarity) some of our own less appealing qualities? (As Piet Hein, the Danish poet and scientist, reminded us, "The errors hardest to condone/In other people are one's own.")

Whatever the reason for it, a distrust of young people is so widespread that we've come to take it for granted—and to lose sight of its relevance to common practices at home and at school. For example, the way we think about discipline seems to assume, as educational psychologist Marilyn Watson remarked, that Thomas Hobbes's famous characterization of life also applies to children:

They are nasty, brutish, and short.[4] That's why teachers are often told that if they don't take control of the classroom, the most likely result will be chaos. Such a dichotomous view implies that students, or perhaps people in general, will never act responsibly or considerately unless they are tightly regulated. Rather than being helped to reflect on how to conduct themselves, they must be told exactly what is expected of them.

Closely related, and equally revealing, is the assumption that children must be threatened with some sort of punitive consequence if they fail to comply. Requests and explanations don't suffice, on this view; reasonable expectations won't be honored unless kids fear that the disobedient will be made to suffer in some way. Because most traditional classroom management programs proceed from just these premises, it's reasonable to conclude that they are based on a fundamental mistrust of children's motives.

No less problematic is the tendency to praise children when they do something nice ("Good job!"). The tacit assumption here seems to be that anything generous they may have done was a fluke, and the only reason they would ever do it again is to receive an extrinsic reward, such as an adult's approval. To talk about the need to "reinforce" desirable behaviors is to imply that these behaviors would disappear in the absence of that reinforcement. Orthodox behaviorists believe this is true of everything, but a lot of people seem to think it's true specifically of helping, sharing, and caring. This, in turn, suggests that qualities like generosity are unnatural, that children left on their own are concerned only about themselves.[5]

The counterpart to the idea that children must be told exactly what to do—with rewards or punishments made contingent on their response—is that they must be told exactly what to *learn*. In my experience, there is a striking correlation between a negative view of children and a traditional approach to education in which virtually all the important decisions about what is to be learned are made by adults. Direct instruction takes precedence over exploration and discovery; students are led, step by step, through a list of facts and skills and are continuously evaluated on their mastery of an agenda that they had no part in creating. It's widely assumed that even older children can't—or shouldn't—participate in formulating their own questions or help to design their own investigations. All of this speaks not only to our view of learning but to our view of the learners.

In 1960, the management theorist Douglas McGregor proposed that workplaces differed depending on the core assumptions made by people with more power (managers) in regard to people with less power (employees). "Theory X" was his name for the belief that human beings basically don't like to work and workers therefore need to be controlled and coerced to do anything. "Theory Y," on the other hand, holds that when people have something worthwhile to do and are treated with respect, they enjoy being productive, take pride in their work, and actively seek out challenges and responsibilities.[6] My point, of course, is that Theory X describes many people's implicit view of children, if not of our entire species.

In reality, the data overwhelmingly support Theory Y. The idea that it's natural to do as little as possible is a relic of old-fashioned "tension-reduction" or homeostatic theories, which state that organisms always seek a state of rest. Few psychological ideas have been so thoroughly repudiated by empirical evidence.[7] Children in particular are naturally inclined to try to make sense of the world, to push themselves to do things just beyond their current level of competence. When they (or we) do slack off, that's not a reflection of human nature; it's a sign that something is amiss. Perhaps the individual feels threatened and has fallen back on a strategy of damage control. Perhaps extrinsic motivators have undermined interest in the task by reframing it as a tedious prerequisite to obtaining a reward. Perhaps the task itself is perceived as pointless and dull. Or perhaps the environment—a classroom, let's say—is a place where results, not intellectual exploration, are valued. In that case, students who cut corners aren't being lazy; they're being rational. By choosing the easiest possible task, they're just maximizing their chances of succeeding.

Thus, when schools give grades—or, worse, when honor rolls and other incentives are added to accentuate the significance of grades—students are discouraged from stretching themselves to see what they're capable of doing. Ironically, school officials and reformers complain bitterly about how kids today take the easy way out . . . even as they create an educational system that leads predictably to that very outcome.

A similar vicious circle operates at the level of specific school tasks. As one father of a high school student commented, the purpose of book reports and similar assignments is to make students prove that they've "actually read the book. And that's either rooted in a belief that the kids are too stupid and thick-witted to perceive that the book is good, or else it acknowledges that the book actually *isn't* good enough for the kids to want to read." These dreary assignments kill off whatever interest the kids might have had in reading, thereby confirming the teacher's original mistrust and belief that such assignments are necessary.[8]

Homework seems to rest on two distinct forms of distrust. The first is a general suspicion of kids that leads many adults to believe we need to fill up what would otherwise be free time lest those hours be wasted—or devoted to who knows what kind of mischief. Homework on this view is justified less because it will help them learn than because it will make sure they are constructively occupied. It is, quite literally, busywork—in the words of *The Music Man*'s Harold Hill, "a way to keep the young ones moral after school."

Several years ago, an article in the *National Review* derisively dismissed the concern that homework takes time away from potentially valuable after-school activities: "To any parent, it seems obvious that most teenagers would use their free time to watch TV, play video games, listen to music, talk on the phone, chat online, and go to the mall (or just take drugs and have sex)."[9] The educational researcher Herbert Walberg echoed this sentiment, insisting that if teenagers weren't doing homework, they'd just be sitting in front of the television or "work[ing] to earn money for cars, dating, and stylish clothes."[10]

The epigraph for this chapter reminds us, sadly, that even parents may share this view. Similarly, a Virginia mother explained why she's pleased that her thirteen-year-old daughter is forced to stay up late to finish her homework: "If you have too much time on your hands, you might get into the wrong crowd."[11] To state what should be obvious, if we don't trust our children to stay out of trouble, then trying to keep them busy is unlikely to accomplish this goal. Whatever our kids are doing says more about our relationship with them than it does about how much free time they have. In fact, a lack of trust in one's children is liable to create a self-fulfilling prophecy as they end up living down to those low expectations. If there are deeper issues that justify a parent's concerns, then these need to be addressed directly; they're not going to vanish under a pile of homework.

The authors of academic publications rarely offer straightforward expressions of distrust where children are concerned. But some take for granted that whatever kids might choose to do with their time is more problematic—or at least less important—than any school assignment they may be given. It is ultimately just as disrespectful to assume that anything else children are doing has little value, and therefore that it's always legitimate to figure out how to get them to do more homework instead.

One pair of researchers grumbled that "family schedules often interfered with consistent homework monitoring."[12] Evidently parents, too, have their priorities wrong and therefore can't be trusted. To some experts, it seems obvious that homework should take precedence over all family activities, and that parents' chief obligation is to make sure that their kids complete whatever assignments the schools send home. Here we find ourselves facing a basic value question of the kind raised in Chapter 1: Who should decide what children and families do with their time? Those who answer, in effect, "The schools—or the officials who make policy for the schools" seem to do so not only because of how much faith they have in homework but because of how little faith they have in kids (and sometimes parents).

To rethink the premise (that any child, given half a chance, will get up to no good) is to question the prescription (that children ought to be loaded down with assignments). Here's a reality check from a mother who also happens to be an attorney and an author:

> How would we be spending our time if we didn't have to slave over these piles of mind-numbing make-work? Maybe some kids would be vegging out in front of the television or exercising their thumbs on their Gameboys, but I would guess that's not what would be going on in my house, or in most others. Instead, we'd do the things we rarely have time for during the week, like go for bike rides or shoot hoops. My kids might even occasionally enjoy the opportunity to be bored. You remember boredom, don't you? That state where the imagination is forced to take over and create entertainment?[13]

The first kind of distrust, then, is a global one, dealing with kids' basic inclinations and what we fear they might do with their time. The second kind has to do with their motivation. A corollary of the belief that kids need homework to keep them busy is the belief that they need homework to make sure they keep learning. Mandatory assignments are seen as necessary because it's assumed that children are naturally lazy and will do as little as they can get away with if left to their own devices. Therefore, if we want them to do anything productive from 3:00 until bedtime, we'd better assign it to them.[14] And while we're at it, teachers had better check, and maybe even grade, those assignments the next morning—not to see what difficulties kids may have encountered but to make sure they've done what they were told.

In addition to questioning the validity of beliefs about motivation, it's also possible to directly challenge the claim that if students aren't doing homework, their minds aren't engaged. In fact, there is abundant evidence that children are constantly learning about the world around them. Some of that learning takes place in organized nonschool programs. Dark speculation about video games and drugs aside, we do know that homework leaves less time for children to take part in extracurricular activities. And we also know, from a growing body of research, that involvement in these activities provides clear benefits, particularly for "at-risk" children.[15] However, it shouldn't be necessary to offer instrumental justifications for extracurricular activities any more than music should have to be defended by citing its potential effect on math skills. If involvement in afternoon gymnastics or theater programs gives children pleasure and rounds out their lives, isn't that justification enough?

Other learning, meanwhile, takes place in unstructured activities, at home and in the community, alone and with friends, in the real world and on-line. The fact that this learning usually doesn't resemble traditional academic assignments is too quickly interpreted to mean it isn't real or important.

And some learning *is* academic but doesn't consist of traditional homework. Rather, it takes place as a natural extension of what children have done in school: projects that they choose and shape themselves. After abolishing traditional homework, the Kino School in Tucson, Arizona, discovered that students began to build on their classroom explorations, and they did so not in spite of the fact that no regular homework was assigned but *because* no regular homework was assigned. As Mary Jane Cera, the academic administrator at that school, explained to me, "Our goal as teachers is to make learning interesting enough that students often want to continue with a project in the evening." (The unavoidable implication is that if students *don't* want to do so, the problem may lie with the quality of classroom instruction. This possibility is almost never addressed in discussions of the topic; rather, students' lack of engagement with the curriculum is cited as evidence of the need for mandatory assignments.) Cera continued:

> Ideally, a student becomes caught up in a subject or a project and does not want to stop working on it. I think it's an ideal that we achieve pretty often—a student starts reading a book and can't put it down; students continue a discussion in the evening via instant messaging; band members get together to jam or rehearse; film crews film over the weekend or over the summer; a current events class leads to volunteering in a political campaign; parents are persuaded to buy an iguana. Our primary science classes usually involve common household supplies—cornstarch, soap, oil, drinking straws, balloons. We hear amazing stories about the messes kids can make when they want to show their parents what they did at school that day. . . . We recognize and respect that families have important things going on in their lives on weekends and evenings. On the other hand, schoolwork of interest and of one's own choosing that spills into the evening hours is enjoyable and emphasizes the concept that learning is ongoing.[16]

Will all students choose to engage in such projects? No. But that's not a good argument for forcing everyone to do homework (whose benefits, remember, are questionable) and thereby reduce the opportunity for at least some students to learn on their own.

In fact, let's confront our worst fears and consider the possibility that some children will simply goof off at least some of the time they're home. What if this is true? *We* need down time after work; why should kids have to be productive until they drop off to sleep? What if they want to hang out with their friends? What if they prefer to spend some time alone after being with other kids all day? The assumption that this is unacceptable should lead us to question the pitiless regimen of academic improvement to which so many people are so eager to subject them. And it may just say something about our basic view of children.

PART III

Restoring Sanity

CHAPTER 10

Rethinking Homework

"WHEN I TELL parents at our open house that I try not to give homework," says a fourth grade teacher in Wisconsin, "I almost always get applause."[1] Despite testimony like this, and all the comments from skeptics quoted throughout this book, the fact is that most parents tell pollsters they're satisfied with the amount of homework their children get, and some say they'd like to see even more.[2] Mind you, this doesn't mean parents are happy with the *kind* of homework their children are being asked to do; we don't know what most people think about that because I don't believe the question has ever been asked in a large-scale survey.

But even satisfaction in a quantitative sense is remarkable in light of what the data show—or don't show—about homework. Could it be that some parents accept the status quo because they don't realize the evidence fails to defend the assumptions on which their support is based? Would they change their minds if they knew there was no proof that homework improves children's work habits, or if they realized that homework isn't even correlated with, much less responsible for, higher achievement before high school? And what if they were invited to question the assertion that after-school assignments "reinforce" skills? What if they considered the possibility that homework's primary legacy (apart from stress and family conflict) may be to lessen their children's interest in learning?

Some people, of course, will challenge my interpretation of the research or will cite other reasons for continuing to believe that most homework is desirable. But what of readers who become— or have long been—skeptical? How can they defend what children are being asked to do? Will parents just smile weakly and say, "Homework generally varies between merely pointless and downright excruciating, but, look, the teachers are still assigning it, so we don't have any choice"? Will teachers be reduced to a similar justification? "Well, my administrators (and some parents) expect me to assign it, so *I* don't have any choice." Are those responses acceptable when we're talking about our children's well-being?

In this chapter, I want to outline a position—actually a constellation of suggestions—on homework. I'll start with an overall proposal that I think makes sense and then offer some related ideas that would represent improvements over what happens in most schools even if my primary suggestion isn't accepted. There is a balance to be struck here, between what is ideal and what is possible at a given time and place. To accept nothing less than the ideal may be impractical and even counterproductive. But to push for nothing more than the possible is to sell our kids short. (The latter error is by far the more common, as I argued in Chapter 5.) Where you choose to draw the line, and how hard you fight for what makes sense to you, will depend on how strongly you and your children feel about this issue, how many of your neighbors or colleagues can be persuaded to join you, and the open-mindedness of the people responsible for homework policies where you live.

Changing the Default

For the better part of a millennium, the word "default" has signified a failure to act. For the past century and a half, it has also had a financial meaning; one can default on one's loans. But it was only in the mid–1960s, according to the *Oxford English Dictionary*, that the word acquired a new definition from computer programmers: The default setting is the one that's selected automatically and must be actively overridden. This is an enormously useful concept, which is why the term quickly spread beyond the world of bits and bytes. Any situation that remains in effect until someone intervenes is the default.

At present, the default policy in almost all schools is to assign homework on a regular basis. Giving kids something to take home is the rule; the absence of homework is the exception. What this means, as I pointed out earlier, is that the primary commitment, both logically and chronologically, is to make sure students usually have schoolwork to do at home. Only secondarily do teachers figure out *what* to make them do on a given night.

This default makes sense only if homework itself—the very fact of having to do it, irrespective of its content—is beneficial. Even a cursory review of the evidence makes it impossible to defend this idea. One can disagree about the usefulness of individual assignments, the criteria for judging academic achievement, the value of drill and practice, the effect of homework on families, and many other issues. But it cannot be argued that homework by its very nature yields certain and compelling advantages, that it will have a positive effect regardless of its quantity or quality, for all children and in all circumstances. If that premise is insupportable, then so is the current default policy.

My primary recommendation, therefore, is that the default state should be no homework. Educators should have to opt in—that is, make a point of deciding to assign homework in a given instance—rather than opt out. As a matter of policy, those who defend homework as necessary or desirable need to show that its advantages outweigh its disadvantages. As a matter of classroom practice, students should be asked to take schoolwork home only when there's a reasonable likelihood that a particular assignment will be beneficial to most of them. Moreover, any assessment of potential effects should take into account the assignment's likely impact on their *interest* in learning and in the topic at hand.

The facts as I understand them don't lead me to the more straightforward prescription of banning all homework. Changing the default is a less extreme position, but it would nevertheless be revolutionary to say that assignments could be given only when they truly seemed important and worthwhile. I'll say more in a moment about what it might take to satisfy those criteria.

An expectation of no homework except under special circumstances is very different from the "homework policies" that many schools and districts have been adopting. First, asking teachers to be sure that a given assignment is likely to be beneficial is a way of encouraging mindful decision making at the classroom level. Typical homework policies, by contrast, shift power away from teachers, sacrificing at least some of their autonomy in order to have more consistency across classrooms. In fact, that's exactly why some people endorse these rules. *Time* magazine asserts that "in places that have instituted formal homework policies, a semblance of sanity has arrived." (This is followed in the next paragraph by a call for *national* standards.)[3] Without "an established homework policy," one pair of researchers warns, "practices tend to be based on individual teachers' beliefs rather than consensually agreed upon or research-based best practices."[4] The prospect of deciding by consensus and drawing from research sounds appealing, but there's little evidence that either plays much of a role in the development of district-wide policies. Furthermore, once homework rules are on the books, it's no easy matter to reconsider them. Their stipulations come to be seen as the way things must be done.

Consistency has its advantages, but I believe they are outweighed by the problems of specifying in advance the type or amount of homework for all students at a given grade level. Teachers ought to be able to exercise their judgment in determining how they want to deal with homework, taking account of the needs and preferences of the specific children in their classrooms, rather than having to conform to a fixed policy that has been imposed on them.

In some schools, teachers are required to announce ahead of time what the week's homework assignments will be, which by definition limits their flexibility and capacity to be responsive to changing circumstances.

Worse, teachers may be compelled to assign homework on the same schedule every week. This is a frank admission that such homework is not suggested by a given lesson, much less is it a response to what these kids need at a particular point in time. To decide *in advance* that homework in certain subjects will be assigned on certain days is to sacrifice thoughtful instruction on the altar of predictability. To announce that some sort of math homework will be assigned every Tuesday and Thursday throughout the year is a paradigmatic case of making kids accommodate to a one-size-fits-all policy rather than putting the kids first, treating them as individuals, and designing practices that benefit them.

The one redeeming feature of (some) homework policies is the limit they place on how much time students will be made to spend on their assignments. For example, the "ten minutes per grade level per night" rule, if taken seriously, is a step in the right direction, at least in districts where even more homework would be assigned. But even if this guideline was intended to curb excessive assignments for elementary school students, it's often treated as a floor rather than just a ceiling. The adage "an eye for an eye, a tooth for a tooth" was originally meant to place limits on revenge but eventually came to be seen as a demand for it. So the main effect of policies that suggest how much homework students should get is to ratify the expectation that *some* homework will be given on a regular basis, regardless of whether it's appropriate. The discussion is shifted from whether to how much. What may appear to be an enlightened, if modest, reform is actually a way of ensuring that homework for homework's sake continues to be the default.

Quantity

Changing the default to no homework would likely have two practical consequences: The number of assignments would decline and the quality of those assignments would rise. Both of these, I believe, represent significant improvements in our children's education. But it's worth addressing these two issues in their own right so that the current situation can be addressed before the default is reversed.

Let's begin with the question of how much homework students get. Parents who are critical of the status quo usually begin—and unfortunately often end—with this issue. They see how much time their children are spending on schoolwork instead of doing other things, they're troubled by the effects this is having, and they say, "Too much!" Some teachers, as we've seen, arrive at the same conclusion either because of their experiences as parents or because they've come to realize that large quantities of homework don't help kids to become more proficient or enthusiastic learners.

Teachers may also discover another problem: Some students simply don't do the homework, particularly when there's a lot of it.[5] The reasons for this vary widely: Kids don't know how to do it, or they're convinced they can't succeed at it, or something about their home environment (perhaps a simple lack of resources) presents a barrier, or they lack the time because of after-school commitments, or they just can't see the point. Regardless of the explanation, it's clear that a punitive response, such as giving a zero to such students or forcing them to miss recess, cannot help the situation. Other than affording the teacher the unpleasant satisfaction of having shown the kid who's boss, the only likely effect is to further damage the student's attitude toward homework, school, the teacher, and maybe even herself.

Meanwhile, to teach a lesson that's predicated on the (false) assumption that everyone in class completed an assignment the night before will leave some students mystified, alienated, and less likely to succeed. One high school English teacher in Arizona used to talk about her "frustration days." She "planned a lesson that was dependent on the students completing their homework only to find that half the class did not have time between band practice, soccer, dance, church and going between mom's and dad's houses." Her solution was to stop giving homework "unless it is absolutely necessary." Rather than feeling resentful about being compelled to change her practice, or concerned that the other students would lose out as a result of doing no homework, she has seen no problems with this policy. In fact, she reports, "I have found that students are actively engaged for the full [time] that I have them in class, that we discuss, learn, read, and grow together."[6]

Of course, many moms and dads push their children to finish all their homework even when the quantity seems excessive to the point of abusive. The official line in articles and brochures is that parents should "let the teacher know" if assignments have gotten out of hand. This sounds like a friendly and reassuring invitation until you think about the implications more carefully. First, notice that the students themselves—the people actually doing the homework—are almost never encouraged to speak up in their own behalf; a complaint is seen as legitimate only if it's made by an adult. *Of course* kids are going to be unhappy about having to do all that homework, we're told; the very predictability of that reaction is supposed to give us leave not to take it seriously.

Second, to say that parents can always speak to the teacher if there's a problem is particularly popular among pro-homework traditionalists, perhaps because the burden then falls on individual families to try to solve what is actually a systemic problem. Broader homework practices and assumptions need never be questioned as long as each family must act alone—and for the purpose of rescuing a single child rather than improving education more generally.[7]

Finally, consider what happens if parents finally do summon the courage to speak up, braving the risk that they will be seen as troublemakers, only to have the teacher respond defensively: I've been giving this much homework for years and no one else has complained! The problem is that your child doesn't apply herself! The problem is that she doesn't budget her time well enough! The problem is that *you're* not doing enough (or maybe you're doing too much)!

Some teachers, of course, would never dream of reacting that way. Indeed, they go out of their way to ask for feedback and then take it seriously. But they may be less likely than their colleagues to have gotten carried away with homework in the first place. They may have nursed doubts about its value and they respect the importance of family activities. Renee Goularte, who taught elementary school in California for more than ten years, told parents at the beginning of each year that "if homework ever interfered with any family activities or extracurricular activities such as music or sports, they were to please just write a note on the homework and I would waive it, and the same for any homework that students were struggling with." But this is a teacher who already found herself "assigning less and less homework over time, with a larger percentage of assigned homework being simply to read at home" or even to "do a good deed or help your parents with a household task."[8]

In many classrooms, assignments don't merely take a long time to complete—they take considerably longer than the teacher said they would.[9] Parents should not be shy about pointing this out.

And teachers, for their part, should formulate their estimates real-
istically rather than assuming "that children are geniuses and speed
typists," as one Massachusetts mom put it. "It's cheating to say this
is twenty minutes of homework if only your fastest kid can complete it in that time. You're disadvantaging the rest of the kids."[10]
Then, too, there may be a "difference between the *district's* stated
homework policies and the amount of homework students actually
have to do," in which case parents can begin by "asking simply that
the current homework policy be enforced."[11]

Ideally, educators should make and enforce limits to ensure that
homework is not excessive—and they should err on the side of
less rather than more. But if they don't, parents and children
should speak to the teacher. If it's possible to find other families
who feel the same way, then a group of people expressing their
concern respectfully but firmly will have more of an impact than
anyone on his or her own. If a discussion with the teacher doesn't
lead to changes, then it may be time to talk with the principal or a
district administrator. In the meantime, parents should do what
they feel is necessary to protect their children. "Set a time limit for
the homework and what's done is done and that's it," one psychologist urges.[12]

That's exactly what Artie Voigt finally resolved to do. "We set
definite time limits. We don't care what the school feels is appropriate. We have Voigt rules, which leave time for play and early
bedtime." He also believes part of his job as a parent is to protect
his child "from assignments that don't help her learn." It's probably
not a coincidence that Voigt is an educator as well as a parent; people who play both roles are more likely to understand the limited
value of homework—particularly when there's a great deal of it—
as well as to have the confidence to act on that understanding. Barbara Williams, who shares this distinction, recalls one evening
when, "with both of us in tears after two pages of math problems,
I finally told my third-grade son John to put the homework away.

In place of the classroom assignment, I chose a book and we read, I pulled out a notebook and John began a journal, and we enjoyed the rest of the evening. I took responsibility for the schoolwork not being done, and I know he learned."[13]

Quality

There is a relationship, albeit an imperfect one, between quantity and quality. To begin with, I've argued that changing the default to no homework would result in assignments that are both fewer and better. To come at this idea another way, classrooms where there's currently a lot of homework are often the same classrooms where the homework isn't particularly worthwhile. "I hear other teachers who say proudly, 'I assign an hour of homework a night,'" remarks one high school teacher. "What on earth are they assigning? It must be busywork that a bright student would despise and a poor student would simply refuse to do."[14] Everyone claims to hate busywork, of course, but that's exactly what students tend to get when there's a commitment to assign a large amount of homework on a regular basis—regardless of whether that commitment originates with the teacher or with the movement to "raise standards" that's imposed *on* teachers (and students). As the renowned high school reformer Ted Sizer sees it, "Just as 'tougher' courses often simply meant more to cover," so "'more homework' usually meant more mindless busy work."[15]

Still, even though quality and quantity are linked, we need to think separately about these two features. In particular, it's important that we not assume all is well just because kids are getting what we (or even they) decide is a reasonable amount of homework. Even if this is true, the assignments themselves may not be reasonable; they may not be worth even five minutes of our children's time. Too many first graders are forced to clip words from magazines that begin with a given letter of the alphabet. Too many fifth graders have to color in an endless list of factor pairs on graph paper. Too many eighth graders spend their evenings inching their way through dull, overstuffed, committee-written textbooks, one chapter at a time. Too many students of all ages are sent home with worksheets where the point is just to practice skills and memorize facts.

It's revealing to listen to teachers and researchers talk about the benefits of "shorter but more frequent assignments."[16] These, we're told, will be more manageable for younger children, less apt to cause anxiety, more likely to be completed. All of which may be true, but none of which tells us whether there is any educational value to these assignments. Even if kids *can* do them, why *should* they? We ought to be asking whether each example of homework will help students to think deeply about questions that matter. We ought to be asking what philosophy of teaching, what theory of learning, lies behind each assignment. Does it seem to assume that children are meaning makers—or empty vessels? Is learning regarded as a process that's mostly active or passive? Is it about wrestling with ideas or following directions? These dichotomies are oversimplified, of course, but they give a rough sense of what might be responsible for homework that is more or less intellectually valuable.[17] The same premises, of course, help to determine what students are doing *during* school: If they're saddled with busywork in the evenings, they've probably got busywork in the mornings, too. Homework is a problem in its own right, but in many cases it's also a symptom of more fundamental issues.

If there has to be homework, teachers should strive, and parents should push, to make it better. But I want to reiterate that until the default expectation has changed, better quality homework isn't enough. Good teachers can often manage to create reasonably good assignments. But that doesn't mean it's legitimate to make students do something at home on a regular basis even when there's no need. We should insist on homework that isn't merely defensible but truly justified.

Let me suggest three ways of thinking about that justification, which is to say, three kinds of assignments that it may be appropriate to give.

1. Activities naturally suited to the home. "Why can't they just do this at school?" is a reasonable question to ask—a question that *ought* to be asked—about most of what kids lug home in their backpacks. But it's a question that answers itself in the case of certain assignments, such as having children interview parents about their family history or asking parents to explain how *they* learned math (before the kids reciprocate). Similarly, it's logical to invite students to take something they're doing in class and continue it at home, such as performing an experiment in the kitchen—ideally of their own design—that may replicate a finding from an experiment they already conducted in the classroom. Among its many other advantages, such projects can help to create a connection between home and school. This, of course, is supposed to be a result of all homework, but it often doesn't happen, at least in any meaningful sense, when kids are just making a diorama or memorizing the correct spelling of a long list of words.

2. Family activities that we normally don't think of as homework. Among the most useful and satisfying activities that children can be doing at home, as the eminent educator Deborah Meier points out, are those in which they're "spending a lot of time in the company of grown-ups" and maybe also learning to plan or calculate or make meaning—by cooking, doing crossword puzzles, playing word games or card games or board games, reading out loud, or even watching good TV shows or looking for information on the Internet together.[18] As a rule of thumb, the more that traditional school assignments give way to these sorts of activities, the better for kids' social, emotional, and even intellectual development.

Adults may feel better about the academic value of these things if children are asked to keep a log of what they've done. If they're asked to reflect on the significance of, or their reactions to, a given activity, then a written account can spur more thinking and, of course, provide an opportunity for using language. But even when such records are kept, does cooking together or discussing a TV show really qualify as homework? This is mostly a semantic question. We can think of such activities as a richer, more organic form of homework, on the one hand, or as an alternative to homework (which one pair of educators prefers to call "home learning"), on the other.[19] Thus, our ultimate verdict on the value of homework may depend in part on how we choose to define the word: The broader the definition, the easier it is to rescue the concept, assuming we're inclined to do so. There may also be a tactical reason for referring to these family activities as homework. Teachers who see no value to traditional assignments often find their lives are made more difficult if they announce that they don't give any homework. At least some traditionalists may be mollified if the teachers explain that they just assign a different kind.[20]

3. Reading. Some of the most thoughtful elementary school teachers I meet tell me that the only homework they give is to ask children to read books of their own choosing. This is a satisfying policy, first, because sustained reading (of real books, not chunks of prose devoid of context) helps children to become more proficient readers. In fact, the research supporting that conclusion is as powerful as the research supporting homework is weak.[21] Second, authentic reading is one of the casualties of homework. For reading to be the only homework is advantageous both because of what kids are doing and what they're not doing. And if students have the chance to discuss what they've read with their classmates, that can make a good thing even better.

What if the children can't read yet? Erin Hyde teaches kindergarten and first grade, so her students' homework is simply "to be read to." She explains:

> The children bring home a book every night borrowed from school, have someone read it to them, and then bring the book back the next day. What I am trying to do is establish routines at home where families *will* read with their children every night. . . . [Yet] parents come to me and ask, "When is my child going to get homework?" Why isn't reading every night taken seriously? . . . And it aggravates me even more when parents come in and say (of a nearly five-year-old) "I had my child read this book to me." The goal of reading every night is *not* to teach your child how to learn to read. That can be my job. The point of reading every night is beginning a conversation, making connections, learning the *language* of books, and sharing a love of literature.[22]

Compelling as they are, the benefits of "free" reading are compromised if teachers stipulate that students must read a certain number of pages, or for a certain number of minutes, each evening. This is not an example of doing something constructive, an alternative to traditional assignments, and simply calling it homework to keep conservative parents and administrators happy. Rather, this is an example of turning something potentially positive *into* a traditional assignment and thereby reducing its value.

When students are told how *much* to read, they just "turn the pages" and "read to an assigned page number and stop," one teacher explains.[23] But when they're told how *long* to read, the results are not much better. A California mother wrote to me, "Our children are now expected to read 20 minutes a night, and record such on their homework sheet. What parents are discovering (surprise) is that those kids who used to sit down and read for pleasure—the kids who would get lost in a book and have to be told to put it down to eat/play/whatever—are now setting the timer, choosing the easiest books, and stopping when the timer dings. . . . Reading has become a chore, like brushing your teeth."[24]

One alternative to quantified requirements is to ask kids to write something about what they've read. But here we must tread carefully, particularly if our preeminent objective is to help them develop a lifelong love of books. Listen to Jim DeLuca, a middle school language arts teacher:

> The best way to make students hate reading is to make them prove to you that they have read. Some teachers use log sheets on which the students record their starting and finishing page for their reading time. Other teachers use book reports or other projects, which are all easily faked and require almost no reading at all. In many cases, such assignments make the students hate the book they have just read, no matter how they felt about it before the project. Students will become good readers when they read more. Students will read more when they enjoy reading. They will enjoy reading when they enjoy their reading material. They will enjoy their reading material when they are left to choose it themselves, and to delve into it on their own terms. I frequently have students ask me for help with their free-reading books, which I see as evidence that it is not necessary for me to make the students prove to me that they read.[25]

Another alternative, particularly in the case of younger children, is for the teacher to suggest some rough guidelines for how much reading should be done—which will vary depending on the child's proficiency—but to share these only with parents so the children can become immersed in the book rather than focusing on how much more there is to go. The goal is unself-conscious reading that is so enjoyable it doesn't feel like an assignment.

While parents may be asked to think about those guidelines from time to time, their main role shouldn't be to monitor compliance; rather, it's to welcome their children into the world of readers—what author Frank Smith calls the "literacy club." And that can be a pleasure rather than an obligation. "After long days at work and school, I don't want to spend my precious time with my kids badgering them about putting words in alphabetical order," says a Maryland mom. But she adds, "I would love to sit down and discuss a book they are reading."[26] This raises the interesting possibility that the all-too-familiar stresses and conflicts associated with homework can be ameliorated by having assignments that are not only shorter but better—including the kind that don't even bear much resemblance to what we've come to think of as homework.

Choice

One way to judge the quality of a classroom is by the extent to which students can participate in making choices about their learning. The best teachers know that children learn how to make good decisions by making decisions, not by following directions. As I argued earlier (pp. 57–58), students should have something to say about what they're going to learn and the circumstances under which they'll learn it, as well as how (and when) their learning will be evaluated, how the room will be set up, how conflicts will be resolved, and a lot more. What is true of education in general is true of homework in particular. At least two investigators have found that the most impressive teachers (as defined by various criteria) tend to involve students in decisions about assignments rather than simply telling them what they'll have to do at home.[27]

In some classrooms, kids are permitted to make choices only about peripheral matters, such as when a project will be due. (Unhappily, even this most basic sign of respect—asking the class to consider how much time they'll need—is the exception rather than the rule in U.S. schools.) Or students may be invited to choose one of several possible topics to investigate or write about. What really sets the best educators apart, though, is their willingness to discuss not just when or how or which, but whether. In a class meeting, they might ask students whether it would make sense for a given project to continue after school. Will we have enough time to revise these essays today, or should we polish them at home? Now that we've analyzed the water in the bathrooms here, would it be useful to take samples from our own kitchens and then compare the results? Should we interview our neighbors to see what plays they've always liked, and what they like about them? Since our discussion about whether to write letters to the school board about that new policy seems to have reached an impasse, how about if we all think about it tonight and scribble down some thoughts in preparation for further conversation?

A discussion about whether homework might be useful (and why) can be valuable in its own right—beyond what can be learned from the assignment itself. If opinions are varied, the question of what to do when everyone doesn't agree—take a vote? keep talking until we reach consensus? look for a compromise?—develops social skills as well as intellectual growth. And that growth occurs precisely because the teacher asked rather than told. Teachers who consult with their students on a regular basis would shake their heads vigorously if you suggested that kids will always say no to homework—or to anything else that requires effort. It's just not true, they'll tell you. When students are treated with respect, when the assignments are worth doing, most kids rise to the challenge and live up to our positive expectations.

If, on the other hand, students groan about or try to avoid homework, it's generally because they get too much of it, or because it's assigned thoughtlessly and continuously, or simply because they had nothing to say about it. The benefits of even high-quality assignments are limited if students played no role in formulating them. Such tasks seem less interesting and less legitimate in the students' eyes.

Complementing collective decision making is the opportunity for each student to make choices individually about his or her homework. At a minimum, schools can provide time during the day so that those who prefer to have their afternoons and evenings free for other activities will have a chance to finish (or at least start) an assignment before they get home. (Notice that this is very different from making students miss recess or lunch in order to complete their homework from the previous night.) At the Peninsula School in Menlo Park, California, for example, homework starts in fifth grade, "but the student always has the choice to do it during class time or at home," says Katy Dalgleish, the school's director. "By the time kids are in eighth grade, most have adopted personal habits about finishing work during school, or choosing free time at school and then doing the work at home. It is all about intentional personal choices, fostering and encouraging freedom and responsibility."[28]

Those goals are even more likely to be achieved if each student has some say about what to do, not only when to do it. In Japan, homework for older students rarely consists of a teacher-directed assignment, such as "read chapter 12 and do the even-numbered problems"; rather, there is an expectation that students will spend time "reviewing the day's lessons and anticipating the lessons for the following day."[29] In a program called Soundings offered in the Radnor Middle School near Philadelphia, students work on ambitious long-term projects of their own design and have the opportunity to continue their research and planning after school. "It is the student's responsibility to decide what he/she needs to accomplish at home," explains program director Mark Springer. "We view the work as ongoing and 'professional,' in that each student determines what to do and how much time to devote at home in order to complete tasks by the due dates they helped establish."[30]

The most open-ended arrangement would be a situation in which students are given no assignments and are therefore free to choose their own activities, which may continue or be sparked by what happened in class. Here there is a sense of ownership that tends to promote meaningful learning. That this really happens in the absence of traditional homework, and that its effects are re-markable, is confirmed by testimony from many different sources. We've already heard from individual teachers how elementary school students pursue their own projects (p. 68) and high school students "naturally seek out more knowledge" (p. 18) when re-leased from the burden of traditional homework. That's what the Kino School in Arizona has discovered (pp. 158–59), and so has the Open Classroom School in Salt Lake City, where "children regu-larly extend their school learning at home—reading their literature group book, researching information for a project, finding news-paper articles for a current events discussion, extending a project that was exciting in the classroom, and so on. However, since these activities involve children's ideas and choices rather than being teacher-assigned, the children do not see them as homework, even if they spend hours on them."[31]

Again, notice that the claim being made here isn't merely that the absence of conventional assignments doesn't *hurt*—in other words, that there aren't any intellectual costs associated with mini-mizing or abolishing homework. Rather, it's that this shift is asso-ciated with intellectual *benefits:* Kids are freed up to do more stuff that matters, that stirs their thinking, that both flows from and stimulates their interests, when homework doesn't get in the way.

CHAPTER 11

Making Change

TEACHERS WHO ARE wary, for substantive or political reasons, of adopting the ideas suggested in the preceding chapter
should realize that there are ways of edging toward them. It's not
an all-or-nothing proposition. One can begin by asking students
how they experience homework—perhaps by distributing anonymous questionnaires—and solicit their suggestions. The next step
might be to give students *some* say about the details of their homework, or *occasionally* include them in a discussion about whether to
assign homework at all for a given topic. (One teacher I know sets
as her goal to be "as democratic as I can stand.") As for the content
of what's assigned, it's possible to shift the balance incrementally
from worksheet drills to more thoughtful projects even if one isn't
inclined (yet) to eliminate the former altogether.

Even the abolition of homework can be the subject of an experiment before teachers commit themselves to it. A teacher with
more than thirty years of experience in Ohio and Florida schools
advises his colleagues to "at least stop giving homework every once
in a while to make sure it is doing what they think it is."[1] This
seems consistent with a spirit of scientific inquiry and open-mindedness: Teachers who believe that homework is beneficial should

be willing to test that assumption by finding out what life would be like without it. What are the effects of this moratorium on students' achievement, on their interest in learning, on their moods and the resulting climate of the classroom?

Here are a few other suggestions for making homework more constructive—or at least less destructive:

Design what you assign.   If teachers resolved to give only tasks that they themselves had devised—rather than prefabricated worksheets or exercises in textbooks—students would likely end up getting less homework and better homework. (These, of course, are exactly the same results that I indicated might follow from changing the default.) If it takes more time and thought to create an assignment, teachers are likely to be more selective about what they make students do.

One size doesn't fit all.   Even teachers unwilling to let each student decide which academic tasks, if any, to do at home should give serious consideration to individualizing the assignments in some way. Put aside considerations of quality or interest for the moment and just consider the question of difficulty level. In conventional classrooms, teachers face a dilemma. If they assign a task that every student can do on his or her own, many of them will find it too easy and therefore of little value. But if they assign a more difficult task, some kids will be over their heads and, again, will derive little if any benefit from the assignment. Indeed, they may come away feeling incompetent. They may also turn to their parents for help, which is at least as likely to generate frustration and conflict as real learning. And because some parents are more able than others to provide assistance, another result of hard homework is that it exacerbates the divide between the haves and the have-nots.

This dilemma is not a fact of life that we just have to live with; it's a function of the belief that twenty or thirty very different children should be given the same thing to do. Teachers ought to challenge that belief rather than struggle to find the perfect assignment (which probably doesn't exist). If the choice comes down to giving the same homework to everyone and giving no homework to anyone, the latter is preferable—and may be the wiser option for other reasons, too. But several different assignments—fitted to students' interests as well as their capabilities—make a lot more sense than one assignment for the whole class.

Bring in the parents. An elementary school teacher might say to parents, "Look, my experience as an educator supports what we know from research—that there's generally very little, if any, benefit to assigning homework. What's more, I think you and your children should be deciding how to spend your evenings; six or seven hours of academics—and of *me* telling your kid what to do—is enough for one day. However, if you strongly disagree and think your child should have homework, I'll be happy to work with him or her to come up with some." We'd have to hope that any parents inclined to take advantage of that offer would do so only after discussing the matter with their children. But even if these kids weren't thrilled at taking home assignments from which many of their peers were spared, such a classroom would still be an improvement over one where *every* child had to do something of questionable value just to placate a few gung-ho, "make 'em work!" parents.

Even teachers who are determined to give homework to everyone can invite parents and students to participate in thinking about how much, and what kind, will be assigned. This could be done by asking parents to offer their thoughts in writing or, better, during face-to-face conversations. The emphasis here would again be on shared decision making and individualization, but this time with moms and dads participating as well as kids.

Stop grading. If homework is going to be given, it's crucial that teachers shift away from a model in which assignments are checked off or graded, where the point is to enforce compliance, and toward a model in which students explain and explore with one another what they've done: what they liked and disliked about the book they read, what they're struggling with, what new questions they came up with, and so on. As the distinguished educator Martin Haberman put it, homework in the best classrooms "is not checked—it is shared."[2]

If there is going to be homework, in other words, everything about the experience—not only who decides and what's assigned, but also what happens the next morning—should be designed to promote two things: high-quality learning and the desire to keep learning. A place where students grind out assignments mostly so they'll receive credit for doing so is an anti-intellectual environment. If students conclude that there's no point in spending time on homework that isn't going to be collected or somehow recorded, that's not an argument for setting up extrinsic incentives and a climate of distrust; it's an indictment of the homework itself.

Even worse than checking off whether students have completed the homework is grading it. To the best of my knowledge, every study that has ever investigated how grades affect intrinsic motivation—the disposition to learn—has turned up bad news.[3] To grade homework is especially destructive because this tells students that the point of the exercise isn't to help them learn; it's to evaluate them on whether they've already succeeded. Nel Noddings, one of our most incisive educational theorists, emphasizes that "there should be no penalty for getting things wrong" on homework. When she was in the classroom, she "regularly told students, 'This is your opportunity to make mistakes and learn from them,' and I never graded homework."[4]

Address inequities. Many critics argue that homework has the effect of widening the divide between students from privileged and struggling families (see pp. 126–28). One way to address this situation (while still assigning homework) is to lengthen the school day slightly, at least for older students, in order to give them time to complete all their assignments before they leave for home, thereby making sure that all kids have access to the same resources.[5] Another proposal is to set up after-school centers in certain neighborhoods that offer help with homework as well as various cultural activities. The goal, says Richard Rothstein, is "to duplicate for disadvantaged pupils the home aid that middle-class children get" and thus "reduce the impact of social class on learning." These centers "will not eliminate the gap entirely," he adds, "but it is unconscionable for educators to exacerbate inequality by assigning homework without first ensuring such programs are in place."[6] If these proposals are rejected as unworkable, or if they turn out to be ineffective, then anyone for whom social justice is a priority shouldn't recoil from the prospect of eliminating homework altogether, particularly in light of the evidence concerning its effects. Getting rid of homework wouldn't do anything to remedy existing inequities, but at least it would prevent further harm.

Taking a Stand

Throughout this book I have offered observations and suggestions from teachers across the country who have come to doubt the value of homework. Some of them try to keep a low profile because they work at traditional schools and don't want to call attention to what they're doing. But I've been heartened by how many have taken the initiative to write to me, eager to add their testimony and unafraid to be quoted by name. Their willingness to take a stand should inspire educators who secretly share their skepticism about homework; the substance of their insights, meanwhile, should prompt others to reexamine the conventional wisdom.

In the current climate, it's noteworthy even to hear from elementary school teachers who have sworn off worksheets and who ask their students simply to read at home. But it's even more remarkable when high school teachers declare that the emperor of homework is wearing no clothes. I've already shared some comments by English and social studies teachers who say that it's not only possible but preferable to teach a first-rate course without any mandatory after-school assignments. Let me now add the voice of Leslie Frothingham, who teaches chemistry (and chairs the science department) at a high school in Vermont. "I know what they have to know to be scientists," she tells me. "I *did* science." Frothingham used to work as a molecular geneticist at the prestigious Dana Farber Cancer Institute in Boston, as well as at a neuroscience research company in Cambridge. It's not only her six years of experience in the classroom but her background in the field that leads her to "feel strongly about *not* assigning homework."

At the beginning of the year, she tells students "they'll be working hard but they won't be doing it outside of class unless they choose to. They get nervous. They're sort of thinking, 'We *have* to get homework!' It takes them awhile to get used to it, but they figure it out. They begin to take charge of their own learning, to enjoy it, to ask questions about how chemistry can really work in their lives. If you give them more responsibility and ownership for their own education, let them have choices about how they're going to do it, they rise to the occasion. Jamming homework down their throats isn't part of it.

"None of my students would say that chem is easy," Frothingham adds. "They have to learn how to balance equations; we practice in the classroom. They do some reading at night, but problem solving is something we do together. The kids tell me, 'If you give me problems to take home and I get stuck, I waste a hell of a lot of

time.'" By all indications, this no-homework approach is successful. Frothingham has yet to hear any complaints about her students
from the physics teacher who inherits them the following year, and
they seem to do quite well in college, too.

Just as some of the parents who have spoken out most strongly
against homework have a professional connection to the world of
education, so some of the teachers who have decided to eliminate
homework are also parents. Frothingham watched her two children struggle with enormous quantities of homework in a Montessori middle school, and the value of it never seemed clear to her.
"What other job is there where you work all day, come home, have ~Teaching~
dinner, then work all night," she asks, "unless you're some type A
attorney? It's not a good way to live one's life. You miss out on self-
reflection, community." Thus, when she became a teacher, she figured, "Well, here I am in a position of being able to do something
about it, at least in my classroom."

"At least in my classroom" is a phrase that invites one to ponder
how much more good could be done if a whole school challenged
the conventional wisdom by abolishing, minimizing, or redefining
homework. I've already mentioned several such schools; here are a
few more.

• At the Christa McAuliffe School in the Cupertino Union
School District in California, there is no homework through fourth
grade, and fifth graders, too, usually manage to complete their assignments during school. "The only time [students] might do
things at home would be if they are practicing for a speech or play
or working on a particular project in class and needed to go to the
library to bring books to add to their collection," says teacher Judith Barnes.

• The 2005–2006 school year saw the introduction of a new policy
in the elementary grades at the Sparhawk School in Amesbury, Massachusetts: no more than fifteen minutes of homework in third grade
and twenty-five minutes in fourth through sixth grades, three or four

times a week. There's also an emphasis on making sure the assignments aren't repetitive, skill-practicing tasks, and that they're based on children's interests.

Bethany Nelson, the administrator overseeing this policy, is interested in having children reflect on their homework: how much of the assignment they completed, what slowed them down, and what strategies might be more useful. She has always thought it odd that most schools give children homework and just assume they'll know how to plan for it. When she asked students in her school what strategies they used to get their homework done, a typical response was, "My parents scream at me." Nelson was struck by how much family conflict was associated with homework—but even more amazed that many parents nevertheless demanded that their kids continue to be made to do it.

Her overall assessment of homework—"I'd completely eliminate it until high school if it were up to me"—is based not only on her two decades in the classroom but on the experience of raising three children and "watching the joy just leach out of them." Over the years during which they attended different schools, Nelson maintains that she has "never seen a piece of homework at the elementary or middle school level that I felt moved my kids forward in their learning or [enhanced] their excitement over a subject. I've seen them come home excited about something they did in school, but I've never seen that response to homework." And it didn't help that students who didn't finish an assignment were often subjected to what amounted to a "public shaming" in class.

Furthermore, by the time they were in middle school, her children often labored over their homework for three hours or more a night. When she brought this to the teachers' attention, the response was that her child must not have been paying attention, which she knew was not true. Many parents, she eventually figured out, ended up doing a lot of their kids' homework for them simply because the assignments were so excessive. "If you accept that the sole possible advantage of homework at the earlier grades is that they're learning to do it themselves, to take responsibility, to plan their time, then why give so much that the parent has to help?" Nelson wonders.

Even though Sparhawk is a nontraditional school, a number of parents there have "had a really hard time" with the new homework limits; some have even made their children do more homework than the school assigns. But most of them adjusted to the change in expectations over the first few months, helped along by Nelson's having distributed articles that explain how homework is actually of little value, particularly in elementary school.

• There is no traditional homework at the Bellwether School in Williston, Vermont, except when children ask for it or "are so excited about a project that they continue to work on it at home," says Marta Beede, the school's top administrator. "We also encourage children to read at home—books that they have selected." She and her colleagues figure that kids "work really hard when they're at school. They're learning new things, negotiating social relationships. To then say they're going to have to work more when they get home doesn't seem to honor how much energy they were expending through the day." Also, Beede adds, there's the stress that homework puts on families. "If kids want to do something [at home], that's great." In fact, "they will ask for something to do fairly regularly, and our attitude is that if they're excited about the learning, let's go with it. But it feels too artificial to say, 'Here's what you have to do.'" The school's policy frees up time after school for children to pursue personal interests that they often end up sharing with their classmates.

• The Beacon Day School in Oakland, California, is unusual for the fact that its classes are in session for most of the year. This schedule offers families flexibility about attendance during any given month, and the additional hours in school also make it easier to convince parents that homework in the elementary grades is unnecessary. Some parents "from the puritanical school of no pain, no gain" remain wary, according to Thelma Farley, the school's principal, but most are reassured that their children do just fine without any homework in terms of both conventional academic achievement and their capacity to learn independently. It works out better, Farley contends, to have teachers rather than parents supervising children's learning.

• Students at the Wingra School in Madison, Wisconsin, "learn through thematic units of study that they help to design," according to director Diane Meier. "We are not a 'practice sheet' kind of school and we do not give homework. Our students have flexibility in determining how to use their time while at school, and they may take work home that they didn't finish."

• At the Golden Independent School in Golden, Colorado, "homework for homework's sake" is avoided, but if "something [students] are learning needs to be done at home, then that becomes their homework," says Erika Sueker, the school's director. They may ask their parents about (and write down) the family's Thanksgiving traditions, or practice their part for a musical performance, or "finish drawing the cover for a story because we want to meet the deadline for sending our classwork to the city council's local writing project." The guiding conviction is that anything done at home should be "useful activity that is part of participating in the school community, not a matter of practicing skills so that everyone can 'be on the same page' according to an arbitrary grade level or timeline—e.g. memorizing multiplication tables, doing worksheets. Sometimes homework involves working to meet a deadline," Sueker continues, "but only if the child had an active role in agreeing to or setting that deadline. Sometimes homework involves taking the responsibility to finish something because others in a group are depending upon that piece of a project being finished. Reading is always the default homework because it's a habit that we want educated citizens to have. Homework is done willingly and doesn't feel like 'homework,' because the child has an active, personal interest in accomplishing the task."

• Homework is among the traditional practices that have been rejected by a number of public charter schools. Conventional assignments are either rare or nonexistent at the Arts Based Elementary School in Winston-Salem, North Carolina, and both the Renaissance Arts Academy and the Pacifica Community School in Los Angeles. In Long Beach, California, educators at the New City School hold "a very strong belief that traditional homework (a bar- *vocab* rage of busywork and worksheets) cannot add value to our academic program." As a result, teacher Tanya Sullivan DeLeón reports, there is no homework through third grade, "nightly reading with student-selected literature responses for [grades] 3–5, and very limited and reasonable project-based stuff for [grades] 6–8. Nobody assigns homework on the weekends and we have a written homework policy that values the time that parents spend doing family activities in the home. . . . Over the years we have learned that you have to have a very strong academic program in order to ease some parents' 'natural' demand for homework."[7]

• Just as a commitment to homework for its own sake—often consisting of tedious drill-and-practice assignments[8]—isn't unique to the United States, so schools in other countries are beginning to challenge this policy. At Cargilfield, a school near Edinburgh, Scotland, headmaster John Elder observed that homework made students miserable and rebellious, which in turn slowed their academic progress. Since mandatory assignments have been eliminated, students have "become more responsible for what they choose to study away from school while sparing parents the anguish of having to help their children with intricate problems they themselves barely comprehend." The goal, Elder added, is to help "kids think for themselves" and "get on with the work that they know needs doing while not forcing them to do stuff they don't need to do."[9] One year after instituting this policy, Elder reported "a noticeable difference in the performance of pupils sitting entrance exams for senior schools. Exam marks in maths and the sciences have improved by as much as 20 percent."[10] In Wiltshire, England, St. John's School has likewise experimented with the elimination of traditional homework for eleven- and twelve-year-old students in favor of inviting them to decide how best to prepare for the next day's learning. "For each individual," says headmaster Patrick Hazlewood, "that can be the same or it could be different. Most importantly it is a question owned by the student, not imposed by the teacher." The result to date has been "high levels of interest and motivation" and a "quality of work beyond the child's normal level."[11]

Changing Minds

Disconcertingly, a number of schools that proudly describe themselves as "progressive" or "alternative" nevertheless assign traditional homework on a regular basis as soon as children reach third or fourth grade, and sometimes even earlier. It's equally discouraging to learn that other schools attempted to chart a different course but were then forced back into the mainstream. An elementary school in Oregon managed to abolish homework, only to have a new principal come in and promptly restore it. In central New Jersey, traditionally minded parents foiled an attempt by the founders of a new school to let children spend their evenings as they pleased. Some educators tell me the best they can do is limit the amount of homework kids get, or try to make it as thoughtful as possible.

Changing the default isn't easy, particularly in places where a commitment to the value of homework more nearly resembles religious dogma than scientific hypothesis. In fact, even the act of raising questions is sometimes unwelcome—as we saw with documents like the PTA/NEA position paper, which urges parents to "show your children that you think homework is important" (p. 95). Rather than encouraging adults to set an example of thinking for oneself, the message is to get with the program. "Some critics argue that homework is useless, even when students are diligent about doing it, and that it ought to be abandoned by the schools," one well-known education writer acknowledges. But "rather than debate the merits of homework," he says, "let us assume that as long as the schools assign it, parents ought to do all they can to reinforce it."[12] It's difficult to imagine a more precise statement of what it would mean for thinking people—and caring parents—to abdicate their responsibilities. To insist that we ought to support whatever policy happens to be in effect, even one that may be harmful, is profoundly disturbing advice in any context. Given that the subject here is education, the irony is positively painful.

Others, meanwhile, suggest that parents who are troubled by watching their children spend one evening after another on assignments of little value should avoid raising a fuss and instead supplement the homework with more interesting activities of their own invention. "If the school insists on having students memorize mountains of information about, say, Central Asia without giving them a sense of the place," parents could "bring out a book or rent a movie that brings the region to life," one expert proposes.[13] But this idea proves troubling as well. First of all, it raises serious equity concerns: Only some parents have the time, expertise, and resources to provide the kinds of enrichments for their children that would benefit *all* children; to avoid speaking out about the homework is to be complicit in widening that gap in the next generation. Second, a lot of homework isn't just inadequate—it's *harmful*. It leaves children with the idea that learning about faraway places (or poetry or math concepts) is dull and pointless, and it drains away their desire to explore ideas. As is true of many other educational issues, the benefits of adding good practices are limited unless we're also willing to work for the removal of bad ones.[14]

There's no getting around it: We ought to encourage one another
(and ourselves) to rethink basic assumptions about the inevitability
and desirability of homework. We ought to debate its merits and, if
we're persuaded that it does more harm than good, speak out against
it. Educators should talk about the issue with their colleagues as well
as with parents; parents should talk to their friends as well as to their
children's teachers. Sharing the data is one way to help that process
along, as Bethany Nelson at the Sparhawk School found. Likewise,
Ruth Lazarus, a social worker in the Chicago area, remarks, "Parents are often so anxious about the consequences of their children not
completing their homework that I would say this is the number one
source of stress for most families of school-age children I work with.
However, the research really does prove helpful in alleviating this
stress. Since the research doesn't demonstrate the value [of home-
work], families can often lighten up about it."[15]

Those who have always assumed homework is necessary may
not be receptive to having their ideas challenged—at least at first.
The prospect of questioning homework leads some people to react
in much the same way that creationists do "when you try to explain
evolution to them," says social studies teacher Phil Lyons. "Despite
all the logical arguments, they refuse to believe less homework can
lead to more and better learning." But he quickly adds that even
when we're talking about older students, and even in the sorts of
communities where high school is regarded mostly as a source of
credentials for the purpose of admission to selective colleges, people can be successfully invited to reconsider their assumptions:

> I've encountered a lot of hostility from parents who think their
> children are being shortchanged because they came home and
> said they didn't get any homework. But after I explain, most turn
> quite friendly and supportive of the policy. Adults freely admit
> that they can't remember anything about the election of 1876
> from their high school U.S. history class, and that other skills and

experiences were more important. Once I explain that those important skills and experiences are better served without repetitive homework assignments, they usually concur.[16]

Other parents, meanwhile, don't need to be convinced that homework is generally useless and stressful; they need to be convinced that speaking out about that fact is worthwhile. Here's Washington third grade teacher Kathy Oliver:

> What I have found is that most parents don't want the drudgery of homework but are afraid to let go of it because it's ATWTHBD (always the way things have been done). Last year I sent home a parent survey in January to see what the pulse was, and out of twenty-six parents, only two responded that they wished there was more homework, like memorizing times tables or spelling. I also have parents who tell me about fourth grade, two hours every night of homework, and how they hate it. One parent recently pulled her daughter from my school and put her [in] a different school because of it. I encouraged her to tell the principal, but she didn't. She said many other parents feel the same way but are afraid to "rock the boat."[17]

Katharine Samway had been one of those parents who accepted her assigned role "as surrogate teacher/controller. . . for the school," "a guardian of the educational status quo." Overseeing the homework ritual was "excruciatingly painful" for her child and herself. She had allowed "precious family time and psyche to be eroded, even destroyed on some nights" because she didn't "want to be criticized for not supporting my child in his education." But at last she had enough. "There have been too many evenings when I have allowed teacher-imposed obligations to supersede our family needs and interests." She found herself thinking, "You have our children for six hours, five days a week. Can't we have some time with them to do whatever we choose?" And so she resolved to say to her son, "'No, you can't do your homework until we have returned from the show/returned from the bike ride/finished the ball playing/read the book, the chapter, or the poem." If the schools' priorities were askew, that didn't mean she had to accept them. Family comes first, she decided. Children come first. *Real* learning comes first.[18]

By now you will not be astonished to learn that Katharine Samway is an educator as well as a mom. Her experience as a parent taught her the downside of homework—what it usurped. Her professional background told her there wasn't much of an upside; there was little to be lost by putting the poem or even the bike ride ahead of the assignment. Of course, courageous as her resolution was, what she was moved to do was only a stopgap measure that rescued her own son. But she chose to publish her reflections in an education journal, presumably in the hopes of helping her colleagues to rethink their practices.

If this book has established anything, it's that the forces responsible for stuffing homework into our children's backpacks are multiple and powerful. But we've overcome such forces before. We've exposed other beliefs as groundless, rescued other people who lacked the power to defend their own interests, changed other defaults. If homework persists because of a myth, we owe it to our kids—to all kids—to insist on a policy that's based on what's true and what makes sense.

NOTES

Chapter 1

1. Washburne. The idea that the school turns to the home for help with the mess that the school created was echoed years later by Martin Haberman. Unsuccessful teachers, he maintained, tend to hold "'uncooperative' parents responsible for not teaching the same lessons the teacher has been unable to teach during school hours" (p. 10).

2. Abrams.

3. I offer support for this argument in Kohn 1999b, pp. 5–9.

4. Winerip, p. 30.

5. For example, see Kralovec and Buell's book as well as articles by Begley (*Newsweek*); Lambert (*People*); Lord (*U.S. News & World Report*); and Ratnesar (*Time*).

6. Rosenberg (2004) cites the example of Scarsdale, New York.

7. Hofferth and Sandberg 2000; Hofferth, personal communication, January 2006. These young children reported spending 52 minutes a week studying in 1981 as compared with 118 minutes in 1997. (Originally, it had been reported that 55 [rather than 58] percent had homework in 1997, and that they did 128 [rather than 118] minutes of it a week. The new numbers reflect a recalculation performed by one of the researchers in 2006.)

8. Hofferth, personal communication, 2006.

9. Jacobson.

10. U.S. Department of Education, 2005. A much smaller study suggested that homework was already increasing for this age group in the early 1980s. "Mothers' estimates of the amount of homework done by Minneapolis fifth graders increased from an average of [4 hours, 12 minutes] per week in 1980 to

[5 hours, 4 minutes] in 1984" (Chen and Stevenson, p. 555). The Hofferth and Sandberg study, meanwhile, showed mixed results for nine- to twelve-year-olds. The proportion who reported that they did some studying dropped from 1981 (82 percent) to 1997 (62 percent) and then rebounded in 2002 (68 percent). But the total time that students in this age group spent studying edged up from 1981 (3 hours, 22 minutes a week) to 1997 (3 hours, 41 minutes) and then rose even more sharply in 2002 (4 hours, 20 minutes). High school students were not included in this research.

11. U.S. Department of Education 2005.

12. Campbell et al. If we look back half a century and restrict our inquiry to high school students, one pair of scholars says that variations in the amount of homework "have been relatively small, even in periods of major educational foment. . . . High school students in 1999 had approximately the same homework load as those in 1980, 1972, or 1948"—no more but certainly no less either (Gill and Schlossman 2003, p. 330).

13. Mullis et al., pp. 115, 119.

14. U. S. Department of Education 1998.

15. Baker and Letendre, p. 120.

16. See especially Loveless; Gill and Schlossman 2003.

17. Tsuneyoshi, pp. 373–75, 380. "That Japanese students are studying less than before, or at least less than children in other industrialized countries, is now widely quoted in Japan" (p. 373). For example, "the percentage of parents answering that the child studies 30 minutes or less per day was higher in Japan for every age category (7 to 9, 10 to 12, 13 to 15) that was studied. For the 7- to 9-year-old category especially, almost 60% of the Japanese answered that the child studied 30 minutes or less a day, compared to 26.8% of Americans and 10.3% of Koreans" (p. 374).

18. Natriello 1997, pp. 572–73.

19. McDermott et al., p. 391.

20. This father in Westchester County, New York, was quoted in Rosenberg 2004. One writer put it this way: "Sure, some students probably whipped out their perfectly organized assignment pad, did each task cheerfully and finished with time to spare for reading, television or play. We just don't know any" (Begley, p. 50).

21. Waldman.

22. Davenport.

23. Kouzma and Kennedy.

24. Grolnick et al.

25. Strauss.

26. Survey of fifth graders: Epstein, p. 13. Survey of parents: conducted by Public Agenda in 1998; for more information, see www.publicagenda.com/specials/parent/parent7.htm.

27. Levin et al. Third grade academic achievement was unaffected by the extent to which mothers helped with homework when the children were in first grade.

28. Noddings, p. 258.

29. Dudley-Marling.

30. VanDeWeghe, p. 76.

31. This seems to be true in England, too, judging by a study of family interactions conducted there. The researchers reported that "homework was spontaneously and frequently mentioned as a major factor in family relationships by the majority of respondents when they described their typical daily routines" (Solomon et al., p. 607).

32. Wingard.

33. AERA statement is quoted in Wildman, p. 204.

34. McReynolds, p. 10.

35. Personal communication from Erika Sueker, director of the Golden Independent School in Golden, CO, November 2005.

36. Dewey 1963, p. 48.

37. Meier in Scherer, p. 7.

38. Lyons, personal communication, December 2005.

39. For example, see *Punished by Rewards* (Kohn 1999a).

40. Wildman, p. 202.

41. Sonia Medrano, a third grade teacher in New York City. Personal communication, June 2005.

42. Kathleen Hennessy teaches in the Seattle public schools. Personal communication, January 2006.

43. Paul Kopp teaches seventh grade life science near Cleveland. Personal communication, January 2006.

44. Andrew Dominguez teaches high school English in Clovis, California. Personal communication, January 2006.

45. Leigh Peake, personal communication, December 2005.

46. "More a hindrance": mother of a fifth grader quoted in Strauss, p. A10. "Busywork": mother of a sixth grader quoted in Chenoweth. "Grown up in their rooms"; "missing out": mothers of four children in California and two children in Utah, respectively, both quoted in Lambert.

47. This finding from a Public Agenda survey is described in "Homework Hell."

48. Odum. Teachers also complained about "parents and children who place more importance on extracurricular activities than on academic work." They were talking, of course, about what happens after a full day of school.

49. One study distinguished between "parental support for autonomous student behavior" and "direct instructional involvement" by the parent. The former showed a positive relationship to student achievement; the latter, a negative relationship (Cooper et al. 2001, p. 197).

50. Renee Goularte, personal communication, November 2005.

51. Chen and Stevenson, p. 559.

52. Hui 2000.

Chapter 2

1. Cooper et al. 1998, p. 70.

2. This early study by Joseph Mayer Rice is cited in Gill and Schlossman 2004, p. 175.

3. Goldstein.

4. Austin.

5. Paschal et al.; Walberg et al.

6. Barber, p. 56. Two of the four studies reviewed by Paschal et al. found no benefit to homework. The third found benefits at two of three grade levels, but all of the students in this study who were assigned homework also received parental help. The last study found that students who were given math puzzles (unrelated to what was being taught in class) did as well as those who got traditional math homework.

7. Jongsma, p. 703.

8. There is reason to question whether this technique is really appropriate for a topic like homework, and thus whether the conclusions drawn from it would be valid. Meta-analyses may be useful for combining multiple studies of, say, the efficacy of a blood pressure medication, but not necessarily studies dealing with different aspects of complex human behavior. Mark Lepper, a research psychologist at Stanford University, has argued that "the purely statistical effect sizes used to compare studies in a meta-analysis completely and inappropriately ignore the crucial social context in which the conduct and interpretation of research in psychology takes place." The real-world significance of certain studies is lost, he maintains, when they are reduced to a common denominator. "The use of purely statistical measures of effect size" (overlooking what he calls the "psychological size of effects") "promotes a[n] illusion of comparability and quantitative precision that is subtly but deeply at odds with the values that define what makes a study or a finding interesting or important." This concern would

seem to apply in the case of distinctive investigations of homework. (Quotations from pp. 414, 415, 420.)

9. Cooper 1999a, 2001. The proportion of variance that can be attributed to homework is derived by squaring the average correlation found in the studies, which Cooper reports as +.19.

10. Trautwein and Köller, p. 119.

11. Cooper et al. 2006.

12. Trautwein and Köller, p. 131.

13. Hofferth and Sandberg, p. 306.

14. Cooper 1999a, p. 100. It's also theoretically possible that the relationship is reciprocal: Homework contributes to higher achievement, which then, in turn, predisposes those students to spend more time on it. But correlations between the two leave us unable to disentangle the two effects and determine which is stronger.

15. Cool and Keith. Interestingly, Herbert Walberg, an avid proponent of homework, discovered that claims of private school superiority over public schools proved similarly groundless once other variables were held constant in a reanalysis of the same "High School and Beyond" data set (Walberg and Shanahan).

16. For example, see Chen and Stevenson; Epstein; Georgiou; Gorges and Elliott; Schmitz and Skinner.

17. Epstein and Van Voorhis, pp. 183–84. Also see Walberg et al., pp. 76–77.

18. Muhlenbruck et al. In Cooper et al. 1998, "there was some evidence that teachers in grades 2 and 4 reported assigning more homework to classes with lower achievement, but students and parents reported that teachers assigned more homework to higher achieving students, especially when grades were the measure of achievement" (p. 80).

19. Cooper et al. 2006, p. 44.

20. Cooper et al. 2001, pp. 190–91.

21. Chen and Stevenson, p. 558.

22. "Several surveys have found that students consistently report their homework time to be higher than teachers' estimates" (Ziegler 1986, p. 21).

23. Ziegler 1992, p. 602. More recently, two homework researchers argued that "the empirical basis for addressing even the most basic questions such as 'Do homework assignments foster achievement?' is insufficient and contradictory" (Trautwein and Köller, p. 134).

24. Dressel, p. 6.

25. For a more detailed discussion about (and review of research regarding) the effects of grades, see Kohn 1999a, 1999b.

26. Cooper 1989a, p. 72. That difference shrank in the latest batch of studies (Cooper et al. 2006) but still trended in the same direction.

27. Cooper et al. 1998. The correlation was .17.

28. See Kohn 1999b and 2000, which include analysis and research to support the claims made in the following paragraphs.

29. Nevertheless, Cooper criticizes studies that use only one of these measures and argues in favor of those, like his own, that make use of both (see Cooper et al. 1998, p. 71). The problems with tests and grades are different and don't cancel each other out when the two variables are used at the same time.

30. Cooper 1989a, p. 99. On the other hand, a study reporting a modest correlation between achievement test scores and the amount of math homework assigned also found that "repetitive exercises" of the type intended to help students practice skills actually "had detrimental effects on learning" (Trautwein et al., p. 41).

31. Cooper 1999a, p. 72; 2001, p. 16. The studies he reviewed lasted anywhere from two to thirty weeks.

32. Natriello and McDill. "An additional hour of homework each night results in an increase in English [grade point average] of 0.130" (p. 27).

33. Tymms and Fitz-Gibbon. Quotation appears on p. 8. If anything, this summary understates the actual findings. When individual students' scores on the English A-level exams were examined, those who worked for more than seven hours a week in a particular subject "tended to get a third of a grade better than students of the same gender and ability who worked less than [two hours] a week, and if students with similar prior achievement are considered, the advantage only amounted to about a fifth of a grade." When the researchers compared classes rather than individuals—which is probably the more appropriate unit of analysis for a homework study—the average A-level grades in heavy-homework classes were no different than those in light-homework classes, once other variables were held constant (pp. 7–8).

34. Barber, p. 55.

35. Cooper 1989a, p. 109. Why this might be true is open to interpretation. Cooper (2001, p. 20) speculates that it's because younger children have limited attention spans and poor study skills, but this explanation proceeds from—and seems designed to rescue—the premise that the problem is not with the homework itself. Rather, it's the "cognitive limitations" of children that prevent them from taking advantage of the value that's assumed to inhere in homework. While it wouldn't be sufficient to substantiate this account, it would certainly be necessary to show that homework usually *is* valuable for older students. If there's any reason to doubt that claim, then we'd have to revisit some of our more fundamental assumptions about how and why students learn.

36. The unpublished study by C. Bents-Hill et al. is described in Cooper 2001, p. 26.

37. The four, in order, are Finstad; Townsend; Foyle; and Melroy.

38. When Cooper and his colleagues reviewed a new batch of studies in 2006, they once again found that "the mean correlation between time spent on homework and achievement was not significantly different from zero for elementary school students" (Cooper et al. 2006, p. 43).

39. Cooper 1989a, p. 100. The correlations were .02, .07, and .25, respectively.

40. Baker and Letendre, p. 118.

41. For example, see any number of writings by Herbert Walberg. Another possible reason that "elementary achievement is high" in Japan: Teachers there "are free from the pressure to teach to standardized tests" (Lewis, p. 201). Until students get to high school, there are no such tests in Japan.

42. See the table "Average Mathematics Scores by Students' Report on Time Spent Daily on Mathematics Homework at Grades 4, 8, and 12: 2000," available from the National Center for Education Statistics at http://nces.ed.gov/nationsreportcard/mathematics/results/homework.asp. As far as I can tell, no data on how 2004 NAEP math scores varied by homework completion have been published for nine- and thirteen-year-olds. Seventeen-year-olds were not asked to quantify the number of hours devoted to homework in 2004, but were asked whether they did homework "often," "sometimes," or "never," and here more homework was correlated with higher scores (U.S. Department of Education 2005, p. 63).

43. In 2000, fourth graders who reported doing more than an hour of homework a night got exactly the same score as those whose teachers assigned no homework at all. Those in the middle, who said they did thirty to sixty minutes a night, got slightly higher scores. See http://nces.ed.gov/nationsreportcard/reading/results/homework.asp. In 2004, those who weren't assigned any homework did about as well as those who got either less than one hour or one to two hours; students who were assigned more than two hours a night did worse than any of the other three groups. For older students, more homework was correlated with higher reading scores (U.S. Department of Education 2005, p. 50).

44. Ziegler 1992, p. 604.

45. Mullis et al. 1998, p. 114.

46. Chen and Stevenson, pp. 556–57.

47. Chen and Stevenson, p. 551.

48. Even at a first pass, TIMSS results suggest that the United States does poorly in relative terms only at the high school level, not with respect to the performance of younger students. But TIMSS results really don't support the proposition that our seniors are inferior. That's true, first, because, at least on the science test, the scores among most of the countries are actually pretty similar in absolute terms (Gibbs and Fox, p. 87). Second, the participating countries "had

such different patterns of participation and exclusion rates, school and student characteristics, and societal contexts that test score rankings are meaningless as an indicator of the quality of education" (Rotberg, p. 1031). Specifically, the students taking the test in many of the countries were older, richer, and drawn from a more selective pool than those in the United States. Third, when one pair of researchers carefully reviewed half a dozen different international achievement surveys conducted from 1991 to 2001, they found that "U.S. students have generally performed *above average* in comparisons with students in other industrialized nations" (Boe and Shin; quotation appears on p. 694). Also see the many publications on this subject by Gerald Bracey.

49. Baker and Letendre, pp. 127–28, 130. Emphasis in original.

50. Mullis et al. 2001, chap. 6.

51. Tsuneyoshi, p. 375.

52. Sadler and Tai; personal communication with Phil Sadler, August 2005. The larger study also found that students who took Advanced Placement science courses—and did well on the test—didn't fare much better in college science courses than those who didn't take the A.P. classes at all.

53. Baker and Letendre, p. 126.

54. Phelps, personal communication, March 2006.

55. Lyons, personal communication, December 2005.

56. Quoted in Lambert.

57. This New Jersey principal is quoted in Winerip, p. 28.

Chapter 3

1. In case you were wondering, neither logic nor evidence supports that defense of competition either. See Kohn 1992.

2. Strother, p. 423.

3. NEA and National PTA. Similarly, "teachers. . . say homework can help their students forge a stronger connection between home and school. 'It's a way to involve the parents in what's going on in the classroom,'" according to one elementary school teacher (quoted in Jacobson).

4. One writer turns this defense on its head, arguing that the elimination of homework, which is time-consuming for the whole family, could actually enhance parent–school contact (Buell, p. 126).

5. Heller.

6. Epstein, p. 5.

7. For example, see Amitai Etzioni, quoted in Strother, p. 425: "The role of homework is pivotal. First, not because it provides more hours to pump infor-

mation into pupils, but because it both encourages and measures the development of self-discipline and associated good working habits."

8. U.S. Department of Education, undated.

9. Savage. This reason was endorsed by 77 percent of parents and 87 percent
of educators. Separately, "helps build character and self-discipline" was endorsed by about two-thirds of both groups. The survey included responses from
1,480 parents and 242 teachers, principals, and superintendents.

10. Muhlenbruck et al., p. 307.

11. Cooper 1989b, p. 89. And again: "Better study habits, greater self-discipline and self-direction, better time organization, and more inquisitiveness and
independent problem-solving have all been offered as important positive outcomes of homework. Yet none has appeared in homework research" (1989a, p.
195). In an updated research review, Cooper (2001a, p. 18) referred to "the only
study I found that used study habits as a measured outcome of homework." But
that study just compared homework done at home to homework completed before school was over ("in-class supervised study"). No study measured the effects
of homework as such.

12. Vazsonyi and Pickering asked the students at a single high school how often
they'd used drugs or engaged in theft, vandalism, or various forms of school mis-
conduct, and found a negative correlation with how much time they said they
spent on homework each night. There was no attempt to demonstrate a causal relationship between the two. Epstein (1988) looked at elementary school students
and found no relationship between how much time each spent on homework and
how likely it was that the teacher identified him or her as a discipline problem. Epstein's finding that there was no association between these two variables was later
replicated by a huge national survey that turned up no relationship between the
behavior problems parents reported in their children and the amount of time those
children spent doing homework (Hofferth and Sandberg 2001, p. 305).

13. Ziegler 1992, p. 603.

14. Cooper et al. 1998.

15. While it's possible to overprotect children, it's also possible to err in the
other direction by withholding support. Doing nothing—in the name of teaching "natural consequences"—doesn't help children to budget their time better. It
teaches them that their parents could have been there for them but weren't.
(This is a topic I address at greater length in Kohn 2005a.) In any case, one survey found that "only 8 percent of American mothers thought [homework] was
solely the child's responsibility" (Chen and Stevenson, p. 559).

16. Kralovec and Buell, p. 13. Defenders of homework may respond that
while parents *could* help their children to acquire these skills through household

activities, not all do. But if this is what the defense of homework rests on, then it amounts to an assertion that parents can't be trusted to raise their kids correctly, so educators, who know better, should be permitted to assign tasks to be done after school to compensate for the inadequacy of parents.

17. I don't mean to suggest that all of the researchers on whose work I rely— Edward Deci, Richard Ryan, Carol Midgley, Carol Dweck, Carole Ames, John Nicholls, Ruth Butler, Martin Covington, and their respective colleagues and students, to name a few—agree with one another about every issue. There are meaningful differences, for example, between those identified with self-determination theory and those identified with attribution theory. Nor do I mean to imply that each of these researchers would agree with every aspect of my summary. But the various shades of differences would take us too far from the purpose of this book, and in any case I believe these distinctions are less significant than the gulf between this psychologically informed perspective taken as a whole, on the one hand, and the perspective that leads to the assertion of nonacademic benefits from homework, on the other.

18. For more, see Kohn 1993; 1999b, pp. 150–53.

19. Coutts, p. 182. One study of U.S., Chinese, and Japanese elementary students found that "fifth graders liked doing homework less than first graders" in all three countries (Chen and Stevenson, p. 557).

20. Hui 2003.

21. Thus the conservative education analyst Tom Loveless: "It's expected that kids are going to do some complaining about homework, but many need to do more" (quoted in Boser, p. 51).

22. This isn't always true, however. See p. 112.

23. Glasser, p. 22. "I once taught at a high school where the principal frequently exhorted students to 'take responsibility.' By this he meant only that they should turn in their friends who used drugs."

24. Warton; also see Corno 2000.

25. Hinchey, p. 16.

26. Corno 1994, pp. 232–33.

27. Ryan et al.

28. Dillard, p. 161.

29. Holt, p. 267.

30. Buell, pp. 141, 139–40.

31. Gartner.

32. Cooper 2004, p. 173.

33. Buell, p. 53. Also see Bowles and Gintis for a broader argument that schools are designed to prepare people for a life of essential passivity—socializ-

ing children to obey authority, to expect to be controlled with rewards and punishments for persevering at tasks they are compelled to complete—because that is what our economic system requires.

34. Personal communication, February 2006.

35. Kathy Oliver, a third grade teacher near Tacoma, Washington. Personal communication, February 2006.

Chapter 4

1. Allington 2005, pp. 462–63.

2. That it would be problematic to pursue this practice without supporting data is a point tacitly conceded by the number of people who hasten to assure us that research *does* support giving homework.

3. Natriello 1998, p. 15. Similarly, "Why is it that the stronger the research support for bilingual education" is, the "less support [we get] from policymakers?" asks James Crawford, the former executive director of the National Association for Bilingual Education (quoted in Zehr).

4. There is reason to doubt whether an approach consisting mostly of direct instruction in phonics skills accurately reflects the best available scientific findings—unless, of course, the term "scientific" is recast to exclude all data except those supporting this position. For more on this topic, see any of numerous writings by Richard Allington, Gerald Coles, Elaine Garan, and Stephen Krashen. Also see Kohn 1999b, pp. 217–24. As for an approach to school reform driven by standardized tests, the only evidence ever cited in support of that strategy consists of higher scores on the same tests that are used to enforce this agenda. There is considerable evidence to show that these scores can be made to rise even though meaningful learning, as assessed in other ways, does not improve at all (Allington 2000; Kohn 1999b, 2000). The fact that no independent corroboration exists to show that testing, preceded by a steady diet of test preparation, has any real positive effect means that our children are serving as involuntary subjects in a huge high-stakes experiment. A statement released by the U.S. Department of Education in 2002 declared: "We will change education to make it an evidence-based field" (p. 51). What actually seems to be taking place is a campaign to change evidence to make it correspond to a certain ideology.

5. It is always possible for officials to claim that they decided not to release a report for other reasons, of course. But a strong case can be made that ideological considerations played a role in at least two instances. The first was *Perspectives on Education in America*, better known as the Sandia Report, commissioned by the federal government in 1990. After an exhaustive study, the authors concluded,

"To our surprise, on nearly every measure, we found steady or slightly improving trends." But this was not the message that a Republican administration wanted to hear, given that its privatization agenda was predicated on the idea that American public schools are in terrible shape. The government refused to release the report, and it was eventually published in an academic journal. (For details, see Tanner.) The second example was a meta-analysis conducted by the National Literacy Panel that concluded bilingual education was superior to an English-only approach. In 2005, the Bush administration's Department of Education, which funded the study, declined to publish it when it was completed. The official explanation was that it didn't stand up well in peer review, even though "department officials had selected members of the panel and participated in all its meetings" (Zehr). These examples dealing with education policies may be symptomatic of a much wider and deeper phenomenon; see, for example, Chris Mooney's 2005 book, *The Republican War on Science*.

6. As I reported in Kohn 1999b, pp. 209–10, all five references in Hirsch's footnote were restricted to the use of pass–fail grading options, and all dealt exclusively with college students even though the focus of Hirsch's book, and the context of his claim about grades, was elementary and secondary education. Four of the five sources were more than twenty-five years old and two were unpublished reports and therefore impossible to verify. Of the three published references, one was just a commentary and another consisted of a survey of opinions of the instructors at one college. That left only one verifiable source with any real data. It found that undergraduates who took all their courses on a pass–fail basis would have gotten lower grades than those who didn't. But those researchers went on to conclude that "pass-fail grading might prove more beneficial if instituted earlier in the student's career, before grade motivation becomes an obstacle." In other words, the sole published study that Hirsch cites to support his sweeping statement about how the value of grades is "clearly shown" by research actually raises questions about the use of grades during the very school years addressed by his book. (This was far from the only example in Hirsch's book in which the research failed to substantiate the claim for which it was cited, by the way [Kohn 1999b, pp. 294–97 n. 4].)

7. Marzano et al.

8. Cooper et al. 1999. The primary purpose of the study was to assess the impact of involvement in extracurricular activities. But a correlation was found between time spent on homework by older students and the grades given to them by teachers.

9. Cooper et al. 1998.

10. Good et al. The first part of this book described a naturalistic study in which nine teachers whose students had high standardized math scores were compared to nine teachers whose students had lower scores. The former group gave more homework, but among many other differences, they also covered material more quickly and did more whole-class teaching. Many experts view these practices as problematic, which may indicate just how poor a measure of learning standardized test scores really are; they often make bad instruction appear to be successful. In any case, not only was there no evidence of homework's effects relative to other variables being studied, but the authors cautioned that "correlational findings do not lead to direct statements about behaviors teachers should utilize in classrooms." In fact, far from endorsing the use of homework, or any of the other practices on display, they continued, "We were well aware of the possibility that many factors other than the behaviors we had observed in high-achievement classrooms might be responsible for the higher achievement of students" (p. 29). The second part of the book described an experimental study in which upper-elementary teachers were asked to do a number of things differently, including altering the content, context, and amount of the homework they gave. They were asked to limit it to fifteen minutes a night and also change when and how it was assigned, how it was scored, what explanations would precede it, and so on. Not only was homework only one of many simultaneous interventions, but the point was to change the homework experience, not to compare homework with its absence, so it would be impossible to infer any benefit from giving it.

11. Gorges and Elliott; quotation appears on p. 28. The study involved third and fifth graders in two suburban schools. More time spent on homework turned out not to be beneficial in three respects: There were no meaningful effects among the fifth graders, where more homework had been assigned; the students who spent more time doing homework were the lower-achieving students; and the main impact of homework was on teachers' *perceptions* of children's competence, not on "actual subject-specific performance."

12. M. S. Rosenberg (1989). The problem, this researcher decided, was that the children didn't always do the homework, or do it correctly, or do it alone. (He also observed that practice homework was of no value for children who hadn't already learned the material during class.) In other words, his experiment too accurately matched the real world, where homework apparently provides little benefit. To remedy this, he set up a second experiment in which four children and their parents were pressed to follow his instructions to the letter. This time, drilling kids on spelling skills at home did improve quiz scores for three of the four students.

13. Bempechat; quotation appears on p. 193. These four citations are offered on the preceding page of her article (p. 192), as follows: "Those who have studied the effects of homework on academic achievement have discussed its non-academic benefits (Warton, 2001), its intermediary effects on motivation (Cooper et al., 1998), and its impact on the development of proximal student outcomes (Hoover-Dempsey et al., 2001) and general personal development (Epstein & Van Voorhis, 2001)." To be sure, all of these sources may have *discussed* these benefits, but none *found* that such benefits actually occur. The article by Hoover-Dempsey and colleagues, for example, actually looked at the effects of parental involvement in homework, not at whether homework is itself beneficial. Later in her essay (p. 194), Bempechat makes another assertion: "As previous research has shown, homework is a critical means of communicating standards and expectations (Natriello & McDill, 1986)." But what those authors actually discussed was whether setting high standards and expectations led students to spend more time on their homework. Nothing in their study permits the conclusion that homework itself is useful—let alone "critical"—for communicating those standards. It's disturbing to imagine future writers citing Bempechat's article in support of the assertion that homework helps students to develop responsibility, study skills, self-discipline, and so on. (Incidentally, I've written to her twice to ask her about these discrepancies, and have yet to receive a reply.)

14. Epstein and Van Voorhis, p. 181.

15. Corno 1996, p. 28.

16. Gill and Schlossman 2003, p. 333.

17. Harlow, p. 895. Thanks to Jerry Bracey for calling this article to my attention.

18. The Singers played the phantom citation game, too. For example, they repeatedly asserted that children who are heavy TV viewers, or who watch any fast-paced program, cannot absorb information effectively. By way of proof, their later papers cited their early papers, but the early papers contained the same assertions in place of data. In one monograph, they claimed that certain types of programming may make children hyperactive, citing as proof three works by other researchers. When I tracked down these sources, two didn't even mention hyperactivity and the third raised the claim only long enough to dismiss it as unsubstantiated. (Citations to the publications by the Singers are available on request. My own essay about television and children, which led me into this thicket, was eventually published as a chapter in Kohn 1998.)

19. One that has received some attention in education periodicals concerns discrepancies between the conclusions favoring direct instruction of phonics, which are contained in the widely circulated executive summary of the 1999 Na-

tional Reading Panel report, and the actual results of the studies described in the report itself (see, for example, Garan).

20. Ziegler 1986, p. 8.

21. Cooper 2001, p. xi; Cooper and Valentine, p. 144.

22. Cooper 1989a, p. 109.

23. Cooper 2001, p. 64.

24. Muhlenbruck et al., p. 315.

25. Cooper 1989b, p. 90.

26. Cooper 1989b, p. 89.

27. Cooper 2001, p. 58.

28. Cooper and Valentine, p. 151. The phrase "we also reviewed the research" apparently refers to an extended passage earlier in the essay that summarizes one of Cooper's previous articles: Muhlenbruck et al. But that article contains no data to support these claims.

29. For example, in the *Chicago Tribune*: "'Homework teaches children study and time-management skills,' [Cooper] said. . . . 'All kids should be doing homework'" (Napolitano). And a columnist for the *American School Board Journal* writes, "As you might expect, [Cooper] finds plenty of positive effects associated with homework, including improving students' study skills. . . developing their self-direction and responsibility" (Black, p. 49). One can certainly understand how she formed the impression that Cooper actually "finds" these effects.

30. Cooper 1989a, p. 175.

31. Cooper says that he intends to draw not only from the data but from the "tacit knowledge" (the quotation marks are his) that he acquired from reading publications on the subject that don't include any data, and also from "discussing homework issues with friends and colleagues" (1989a, p. 175). That seems reasonable, but only if one makes it clear which of the resulting opinions aren't substantiated by actual research.

32. Cooper 2001, p. 65. He also says that "general ranges for the frequency and duration of assignments" should be "influenced by community factors" (pp. 64–65). He doesn't explain what this means, but elsewhere he is quoted as suggesting that more homework might be given in a high-pressured suburban district—presumably just because parents are demanding it, not because it is in any way justified (see Winerip, p. 40).

33. Cooper 2001, p. 28, summarizing Cooper et al. 1998.

34. Example 1: The data reported by Cooper et al. 1998 offered a pretty compelling case that homework didn't do much for achievement regardless of how the results were carved up (see my summary on p. 33). But in the "Practical Implications" section of their conclusion (p. 82), the authors gave a very different im-

pression. "First, by examining complex models and distinguishing between homework assigned and homework completed, we were able to show that, as early as the second and fourth grades, the frequency of completed homework assignments predicts grades." In fact, what they found was a "nonsignificant trend" toward a correlation between how much of the assigned homework the students said they did and what grades their teachers gave them—a finding that arguably would have no practical significance even if had been statistically significant. The authors continue: "Further, to the extent that homework helps young students develop effective study habits"—and of course they provide no evidence that this happens to any extent—"our results suggest that homework in early grades can have a long-term developmental effect that reveals itself as an even stronger relationship between completion rates and grades when the student moves into secondary school. Thus, we suggest that the present study supports the assignment of homework in early grades, not necessarily for its immediate effects on achievement but rather for its potential long-term impact." This remarkable claim is based solely on the fact that the same correlation (between how much of the assigned homework kids claimed to do and what grades they ultimately received) *was* significant for older students. Given that teachers' grades generally reflect students' compliance with respect to a lot of things, it's amazing that there wasn't a strong correlation at all age levels. But there isn't a shred of evidence that the practice of assigning homework—which, remember, is what the authors are attempting to defend—has a beneficial "long-term impact" just because older kids get better grades for doing what they're told.

Example 2: In Muhlenbruck et al., Cooper and his associates announce in their conclusion that "homework appears to be assigned for different reasons in elementary school than in secondary school" (p. 315). This is evidently the outcome they were hoping to find in order to support the position that a lack of achievement effects for younger children shouldn't bother us because homework at that age is really just about teaching study skills and responsibility. But what the researchers actually investigated in this study was what teachers *believe* is beneficial to students of different ages, which, needless to say, doesn't prove that such benefits exist. Even those perceived differences, while statistically significant, were less than overwhelming. When asked whether they thought homework improved time-management skills, and when their responses ("very much," "some," or "not at all") were converted to a numeric scale, the average response of twenty-eight elementary teachers worked out to 2.86, whereas the average response of fifty-two high school teachers was 2.6. (The high school teachers were also slightly less enthusiastic about endorsing the idea that homework helped students to learn [2.6 vs. 2.78], which pretty much undercuts the whole premise that elementary school homework is uniquely intended for nonacademic purposes.) Other conclusions in this study, concerning possible explanations for the fact that homework is of no academic benefit to elementary school students, are similarly constructed on the basis of dubious and marginal results; see p. 314 and compare what's said there to what had been reported earlier.

35. Ziegler 1992, p. 604.

36. Goldstein, p. 222.

Chapter 5

1. Chomsky, p. 43.

2. McClelland, p. 2.

3. McDermott et al., p. 391.

4. Cooper and Valentine, p. 145. Likewise, the Bush administration's Department of Education states in a brochure for parents that "The most critical question about homework is 'How much homework should students do?'" (U.S. Department of Education 2003, p. 2).

5. Bryan and Burstein.

6. Corno 2000, p. 537.

7. This is not to say that researchers focus exclusively on children. They may lament not only that "some students do not do their work" but also that "some parents are not informed about or involved in their children's education; and some teachers do not design or use homework effectively" (Epstein and Van Voorhis, p. 191).

8. England and Flatley, pp. 8–9.

9. Baker and Letendre, p. 132. Their rationale is that "homework is only one facet of schooling, and. . . [therefore] is not a good target as a primary focus of reform." This would seem to be a plausible reason for deciding not to increase the homework load even if it *were* associated with higher achievement; after all, its impact would perforce be limited. But it's a curious explanation for why one shouldn't consider abolishing a practice that evidently doesn't help, particularly if that practice has substantial disadvantages.

10. Walberg et al., p. 78.

11. Bempechat, p. 195.

12. An elementary school teacher in Prince George's County, Maryland, is quoted in Odum.

13. National PTA and NEA.

14. Lambert.

15. Davenport.

16. Hui 2000.

17. Ratnesar.

18. Dorn.

19. Levine, pp. 150, 202–5, 210.

20. The tendency to adjust techniques of implementation while leaving the more important assumptions unchallenged shows up again when Levine suggests that we change the criteria for offering children rewards. These should be given "for an agreed-upon level of work output" (p. 200), we're told. The whole idea of using extrinsic inducements to control children is never called into question.

21. The advice column in the premier issue of what is billed as a magazine for Montessori families responds to the question "Yikes! My child is starting to get homework. What do I do?" not by suggesting that the reader ask the teacher or the school's director what justification exists for this practice—either in the research literature or in the writings of Maria Montessori—but instead by reciting the same "get used to it" rhetoric one might find in a Department of Education pamphlet: "Montessori homework is sometimes used to reinforce lessons taught in class as well as to teach good study habits. . . . First, make sure your child knows what the expectations are and what the schedule is for homework. . . . Second, establish a consistent time for homework to be completed quietly and calmly. . . . establish a work area. . . . utilize a homework bin," etc., etc. (Spring). Fortunately, many Montessori schools avoid traditional homework, at least for younger children.

22. Heller.

23. Epstein, p. 14.

24. On this point, also see Kralovec and Buell, p. 91.

Chapter 6

1. Anderson et al., p. 34.

2. "Homework, Sweet Homework," p. 15.

3. Karweit, p. 33.

4. On this point, also see Hinchey, p. 14.

5. Levin 1984, p. 3.

6. Ames, p. 268.

7. Smith, p. 46. This view directly contradicts the widespread notion that education is always hard work, an idea that proceeds from a specific and usually unstated set of assumptions about what's being taught, and how. Some kinds of curriculum, and some instructional techniques, can *make* learning unpleasant, but the unpleasantness isn't inevitable.

8. Anderson et al., p. 34.

9. Putnam et al., p. 129. Note that this doesn't mean ToT loses its relevance for mathematics in the later grades; it means it's less important at *all* grades when the subject is taught in a way that emphasizes understanding.

10. "Teachers reported that the main reason they assigned homework in the elementary grades is to give students time to practice skills from class lessons" (Epstein and Van Voorhis, p. 182).

11. Watson, p. v.

12. Brownell 1935, pp. 10, 12. Emphasis added. Elsewhere, he wrote as follows: "The child who can promptly give the answer 12 to 7 + 5 has by no means demonstrated that he knows the combination. He does not 'know' the combination until he understands something of the reason why 7 and 5 is 12, until he can demonstrate to himself and to others that 7 and 5 is 12. . . and until he can use the combination in an intelligent manner—in a word, until the combination possesses meaning for him" (Brownell 1928, p. 198).

13. Putnam et al., p. 89. Lauren Resnick and other experts have made the same point.

14. In so doing, it also invites them to think critically about those ideas. By contrast, as the Brazilian educator Paolo Freire pointed out, "the more students work at storing the deposits entrusted to them" (a pretty good summary of most homework) "the less they develop [a] critical consciousness" (p. 54). This raises the interesting possibility that while a reluctance to ask provocative questions may help to perpetuate the institution of homework, as I argued in Chapter 5, the institution of homework may also discourage students from asking provocative questions.

15. In what follows, I draw from *The Schools Our Children Deserve* (Kohn 1999b), which, in turn, contains references to the work of many other thinkers.

16. Brownell 1928, p. 200.

17. Windschitl, p. 352.

18. Kamii, p. 67.

19. Constance Kamii, personal communication, February 2006.

20. Langer, p. 13.

21. DeVries and Kohlberg, p. 374.

22. This is exactly what the eminent educator John Goodlad discovered in his "Study of Schooling" across the United States: "A very large percentage of children [in elementary schools] reported to us that they frequently did not understand the directions for the work they were to do. The consequence of this is that they did not get much done at school and so had a good deal to do at home—but did not understand the work in the first place. In other words, if there was any

reinforcement in the behavioristic sense, homework probably provided reinforcement of the wrong way of figuring out a mathematics problem" (personal communication, November 2005).

23. "Teachers complain, quite correctly, that they don't have time to tailor homework to the diverse interests of 30 fifth graders, night after night. In practice, they say, children in the same classroom usually take home identical assignments" ("Homework," p. 2).

24. Karen Schupack is now an administrator at the Bethlehem Children's School in Bethlehem, New York. Personal communication, December 2005.

25. Jim DeLuca. Personal communication, January 2006.

26. Leonard, p. 2.

27. Phil Lyons is a high school social studies teacher in California. Personal communication, February 2006.

28. Maja Wilson (p. 90) teaches high school English in Michigan. Similarly, William Morris, a teacher with more than three decades' experience, found that when he stopped assigning homework and had students do their writing in class, "the class actually became better." First, he explains, the assignments he came up with for them were better, perhaps because he knew "they had to be done at once and all in a room." Second, "the students came to class ready to write and share their writing with each other." They were more willing to read aloud what they'd written, and the feeling of learning from each other was more "intense." Finally, "the neatest thing was the students assumed I would write and share as well. And because everything was being done in real time there was no reason why I shouldn't. It helped me to add my work to the class and it formed a closer bond between all of us. Since I risked, they were willing to try anything" (personal communication, February 2006).

29. Schupack. See note 24 above.

30. All of this also applies to more sophisticated homework, by the way. Even if the rationale is to promote "integration of skills" (a current buzz phrase) rather than the mere rehearsal of those skills, the reality is often that "the only skills being integrated are those of procrastination and panic" (Waldman).

31. For more on this, including some supporting research, see Kohn 1999b, especially chapter 2.

32. For example, see Coutts; Corno 2000.

Chapter 7

1. Kolata. This excerpt incorporates an account by statistician and historian David Freedman.

2. U.S. Department of Education 2003.

3. The idea of blaming educational problems on the children who suffer their effects might seem so illogical, not to mention heartless, that even the most reactionary commentator would have to hint at this rather than coming out and saying it directly. But in the *Atlantic Monthly*, a leading mainstream magazine, writer Jonathan Rauch is given space not only to repeat the usual bromides about the need to "raise the achievement levels of American students" and to assert that our children "don't do much homework," but to explain that the reason is "many American students are lazy." He then sets about selling us on the miraculous, low-cost, achievement-boosting effects of forcing children to do more homework. Incredibly, Rauch contends that "the word 'homework' goes all but unspoken" in discussions about school reform, implying that he alone has been brave enough to break "the silence"—and, in particular, to stop talking about how schools are failing our children and start pointing the finger at "our children [for] failing their schools."

4. "Homework, Sweet Homework."

5. For example, see Berliner and Biddle; Bracey; Rothstein.

6. Labaree, p. 51.

7. I explored this connection in an article titled "Test Today, Privatize Tomorrow" (Kohn 2004).

8. For more on this, see Kohn 1999c.

9. Never mind; I'll save you the trouble. The first definition from the *Random House Unabridged Dictionary,* second edition: "characterized by rigor; rigidly severe or harsh, as people, rules, or discipline." The definition in the *American Heritage* is similar and is followed by an invitation to "See Synonyms at *burdensome.*"

10. Dewey 1913, p. 58. Even earlier, Voltaire observed, "That which is merely difficult gives no pleasure in the end."

11. National Research Council: Hoff. 2006 study: Viadero. (Research by Philip Sadler and Robert Tai was presented at the February 2006 meeting of the American Association for the Advancement of Science. When other variables were held constant, A.P. courses were found to provide almost no advantage to students in their college courses.) "Schools have eliminated": see Hammond; and Stettler and Algrant.

12. Large.

13. One of many examples: The Heritage Foundation, a conservative think tank that has had an enormous influence on the Bush administration's education policies, has worked tirelessly to advance an agenda of "tougher standards" and high-stakes testing while simultaneously trying to privatize public schools.

They've also published a report entitled *Why More Money Will Not Solve America's Education Crisis*.

14. Strickland is quoted in Routman, p. 43. For more about the inequitable effects of standardized testing, see Kohn 2000, especially the chapter "Poor Teaching for Poor Kids." For a devastating look at how those inequities play out in real classrooms, see Kozol.

15. See, for example, Reardon and Galindo; Marchant and Paulson; and Jacob. The extent of the problem has been camouflaged to some extent by misleading measures of graduation rates. Walt Haney at Boston College and other researchers have shown that students are dropping out of school earlier these days, which means it's necessary to look at a cohort of students in, say, eighth grade and then see how many of them have graduated four or five years later. Only then does the egregious impact of high-stakes testing become clear, particularly with respect to the most vulnerable students.

16. Barber, p. 55.

17. Ziegler 1992, p. 603. This conclusion is based on studies reviewed earlier by the same author: Ziegler 1986, p. 23. Ronald Ferguson and his colleagues, meanwhile, found that "minority students tend to be in the lower level classes that require less homework, so across the school as a whole, they spend less time on homework than white students do" (personal communication, March 2006).

18. Dawn Billings, who was then the curriculum director for the Oregon Department of Education, is quoted in Jaquiss.

19. Stipek; quotation appears on p. 558. The nature of the in-class instruction, not surprisingly, was parallel to the nature of the homework. "The more low-income students, children of color, and poorly achieving children in the school, the more didactic teaching and the less constructivist teaching were observed. Didactic, scripted teaching was particularly prevalent in schools and classrooms with a high proportion of African-American children" (p. 561) despite the fact that such instruction "can undermine young children's motivation, lower their self-confidence and expectations for success and create dependency and stress" (p. 563)—to say nothing of its limitations with respect to promoting understanding.

20. Stevenson et al. Minority parents, too, were more supportive of homework than were white parents in this study. Writer John Buell acknowledges that some low-income parents of color regard "homework [as] their children's ticket out of the ghetto." At the same time, he reports having spoken with "many other families in poor communities for whom homework was the single largest factor driving them from the public schools" (p. 4).

21. Larson et al. It wasn't clear from this investigation how much, if any, of the differences in total time students spent on homework was a function of the

amount assigned by their (inner-city versus suburban) teachers. Another study looked only at racial differences in time spent on homework, holding constant the course level and the type of district (because all 40,000 of the middle and high school students surveyed attended high-performing suburban schools). It turned out that African American and Latino kids spent the same amount of time on their homework that white kids did but were less likely to complete the assignment. "Group differences in homework completion appear most related to gaps in skills and resources at home, not effort or time on task." (Ronald Ferguson was interviewed in Sparks; quotation appears on p. 44.)

22. Deborah Meier; personal communication, April 2006.

23. Darling-Hammond and Ifill-Lynch, p. 10.

24. Rothstein 2004, p. 19. By the same token, he adds, even if all parents read aloud to their children, the effects would likely differ along class lines. That's true, first, because *how* parents read to their children is as important as *whether* they do so, and "an extensive literature confirms that more educated parents read aloud differently. . . ask[ing] questions that are creative, interpretive, or connective [rather than factual, and]. . . are more likely to read aloud to have fun, to start conversations, or as an entrée to the world outside." Second, it matters not only whether parents sit down to read with their children but whether children see their parents doing their own reading on a regular basis. This, too, varies by class (p. 18).

25. Baker and Letendre, p. 132. Likewise, Kralovec and Buell conclude that "homework may just be one of those schooling practices, like tracking, that in fact serve to sort students according to class and to magnify the class differences inherent in our society" (p. 66).

26. Andy Dominguez; personal communication, January 2006.

27. Douglas Both is quoted in Rosenberg 2004. He adds, "We're also dropping subject matter down a grade. We're teaching algebra in sixth grade."

28. Winerip, p. 40.

29. Vail. Piscataway's attempt to set a (rather high) ceiling on homework assignments was exaggerated in media reports—and deemed newsworthy in the first place—because, in the current climate, even a tentative admission by school administrators that homework may be excessive is seen as extraordinary.

30. Ziegler 1986, p. 4. And again: "Public attitudes toward homework have been more closely tied to the prevailing broader social philosophy and to national and international economic trends than they have to the research on homework's effectiveness" (Cooper and Valentine, p. 146).

31. Quoted in Winerip, p. 28.

32. Quoted in Gill and Schlossman 2003, p. 319.

33. This particular editorial, which appeared under the headline "Despite the Hassle, Homework Pays Off for Serious Students," was published on February 9, 2006 in the *News Journal* of Wilmington, Delaware. Chances are good that one just like it has recently appeared (or will soon appear) in your hometown paper.

34. For more on this, see Kohn 1999b, chapter 7, and the sources cited there.

35. Levin 2001, p. 40.

36. Bracey 2002. At first pass, the test results account for only 5 percent of the variance in economic competitiveness scores. But when seven countries that were near the bottom on both measures are removed, "the correlation between test scores and competitiveness actually becomes *negative*" (p. 738).

37. Rothstein 1998, p. 112.

38. Ray and Mickelson 1993. For more evidence to challenge the claim that school quality is responsible for economic productivity, see Cuban; Paris.

39. For more on this general topic, see Kohn 1992.

40. For provocative arguments from two economists, see Gordon; and Krugman.

41. Daro.

42. Bronner.

43. I'm reminded of a series of studies in which children were asked to play a specially constructed board game. Not only did they compete when their own success didn't require it, but they failed to see a cooperative solution that would have benefited both players. In fact, many of the children preferred a strategy that had the effect of taking a toy away from the other child even when doing so didn't help their own position in the game; they did so "for apparently no other reason than to prevent the other child from having it." This gratuitous rivalry was less a function of age than of nationality: American children acted that way far more often than did their counterparts from another culture (Kagan and Madsen 1971, 1972; quotation appears on p. 53 of the latter article).

44. Swenson.

45. I review some of the extensive literature on authentic assessment in Kohn 1999b, chap. 10.

46. See Kohn 2005a, esp. chap. 5.

47. Winerip, p. 40.

Chapter 8

1. "Students develop": Corno 2000, p. 545. Fifth grader: quoted in Coutts, p. 185. Parent: Julie King, a California mother of three; personal communication, October 2005.

2. Tom Little is head of the Park Day School. Personal communication, November 2005.

3. My analysis in this chapter is adapted from Kohn 2005b.

4. Katz, p. 16.

5. For one of many sources, see National Association for the Education of Young Children. Among the reasons this is true: First, young children are rarely able to communicate the depth of their understanding in the formats typically used by standardized assessments. These tests therefore do not produce an accurate picture of what children can do. Second, the stress that tests create in young children is particularly intense. Anecdotal reports abound of five-, six-, and seven-year-olds bursting into tears or vomiting in terror, their incipient self-confidence dissolving along with their composure. Finally, standardized testing is based on the premise that all children at a particular grade level must become academically proficient at the same things at the same time. Indeed, the tests are often yoked to grade-by-grade standards that explicitly say "All nth graders will be able to . . ." This is a dubious proposition where n equals 10. It is indefensible where n equals 1 or 2. Skills develop rapidly and differentially in young children, which means that expecting all students of the same age to have acquired a given set of capabilities creates unrealistic expectations, leads to one-size-fits-all (which is to say, bad) teaching, and guarantees that some children will be defined as failures at the very beginning of their time in school.

6. Iowa principal quoted in Ripley. California principal quoted in Ragland.

7. For more details and substantiation, see Kohn 1999a and 1999b on grades, and Kohn 1992 on competition.

8. Bempechat, p. 193.

9. England and Flatley, pp. 11–12.

10. Another analogy I've heard to make the same point is that BGUTI is comparable to denying people food in order to prepare them for a forthcoming famine.

11. Hyson is quoted in Jacobson, p. 14.

12. Personal communication with Phil Lyons, February 2006.

13. Waldman.

Chapter 9

1. See Mike Males's data-filled books (1996, 1998) that debunk widespread assumptions about teenagers' alleged recklessness, violence, and immorality.

2. See the 1997 and 1999 surveys entitled "Kids These Days" conducted by Public Agenda, a public opinion firm. (For details about the former report, see

Applebome; for details about the latter, see www.publicagenda.org/specials/ kids/kids.htm.) Mike Males (1998, p. 339) points out that the results of such a poll reveal nothing about children; they merely provide "an ugly self-portrait of adults' prejudices."

3. I've been unable to confirm the authenticity of this quotation, or of similar comments attributed to Socrates ("Children today love luxury too much. They have detestable manners, flout authority, and have no respect for their elders. What kind of awful creatures will they be when they grow up?") and the thirteenth-century priest Peter the Hermit ("The young people of today think of nothing but themselves. They have no reverence for parents or old age. They are impatient of all restraint. They talk as if they knew everything, and what passes for wisdom with us is foolishness with them.") But you get the point: Youth bashing is nothing new.

4. Personal communication, 1995.

5. If that depressing assumption is unfounded (which, happily, it is), then it might be enough to offer descriptive feedback or to engage children in conversation about the impact of their actions on others rather than offering them verbal rewards. For more on the assumptions underlying, counterproductive effects of, and alternatives to praise, see Kohn 1999a, 2005a. For evidence against cynical claims about children's (and all humans') motives, see the considerable research literature summarized in Kohn 1990.

6. McGregor. Notice how Theory X is entirely consistent with the behaviorist view of motivation: All organisms are essentially inert unless their actions lead to their receiving some sort of extrinsic reinforcer.

7. Interested readers can look up the work of Gordon Allport as well as findings concerned with the fundamental human impetus to attain a sense of competence (Robert White), to be self-determining (Richard deCharms, Edward Deci, and others), to satisfy our curiosity (D. E. Berlyne), or to "actualize" our potential in various ways (Abraham Maslow).

8. Dan Scharfman is a father in the Boston area; personal communication, January 2006.

9. Gartner.

10. Walberg, p. 14. He sees the worst in teachers, too, asserting that the reason they don't assign even more homework is that they "might be reluctant to correct" it. It's not a lack of time, or a legitimate concern about the lack of value in increasing the quantity of assignments; in Walberg's mind, only the fact that educators can't be bothered to correct homework could account for the fact that they don't give students more of it.

11. Sheila Cushman of Manassas, Virginia, is quoted in Odum.

12. Bryan and Burstein, p. 217.

13. Waldman.

14. While many writers who regard children as basically lazy are strong supporters of homework, it doesn't necessarily follow that those who challenge this view of children will also challenge the necessity of homework. See, for example, pp. 97–98.

15. See Cooper et al. 1999; Gerber; Lamborn et al.; Mahoney and Cairns; Mahoney et al. Of course, it's possible to overschedule children; the fact that it can be rewarding to participate in one or two extracurricular activities doesn't mean that it would be even better to participate in four or five, especially if they've been chosen by the parent.

16. Personal communication with Mary Jane Cera of the Kino School, July 2005.

Chapter 10

1. June Shoemaker's comment appears in "Should We Do Away with Homework?"

2. A poll of 1,085 parents conducted in early 2006 for the Associated Press and America Online by Knowledge Networks found that 57 percent of parents felt the amount of homework assigned to their children was about right ("A Look at AP-AOL's Homework Poll").

3. Ratnesar.

4. Bryan and Burstein, pp. 213–14.

5. For example, see Odum.

6. Krista Gypton teaches in Cienega High School in Vail, Arizona. Personal communication, January 2006.

7. For example, when Loveless says that "if parents believe their child has too much homework, they should talk to the teacher," it's in the context of his larger point that "if a homework problem exists, solutions should come from parents and teachers, not policy interventions" (p. 26). The effect is to ensure that the underlying source of the problem is never addressed.

8. Personal communication, November 2005.

9. According to interviews with high school students in New York, "time and again teachers, it seems, underestimate the amount of time it will take students to complete their assignments" (Black, p. 50). This seems to be true elsewhere as well, based on parents' testimony (Hui 2003).

10. Bethany Nelson; personal communication, November 2005.

11. Rosenberg 2004. Emphasis added.

12. Heller.

13. Voigt and Williams are both quoted in Egawa.

14. Robert Richmond, an English teacher in Salinas, California; personal communication, January 2006.

15. Sizer, p. 11. And from another source: "What we can expect from mandates for regularly assigned homework is a plethora of assignments that are neither imaginative nor individualized. . . precisely the kind of 'busywork' that both proponents and opponents of compulsory homework have cautioned against for decades" (Marek). In some cases, the result is assignments that are both longer and harder. But one study found that teachers who typically give "more extensive assignments tend to prefer cognitively less demanding exercises" (Trautwein et al., p. 41). Of course, we can't conclude anything about the intellectual value of an assignment just from knowing whether it's easy or difficult (see Kohn 1999c).

16. For example, see Cooper 2001, p. 28.

17. For more, see Kohn 1999b; Zemelman et al.; and some of the many sources discussed in both of these books.

18. Meier.

19. Dennis and Swick.

20. By analogy, some teachers recognize that traditional discipline policies— a list of specific rules and adult-imposed expectations, along with rewards for compliance and punitive consequences for noncompliance—are not merely ineffective but positively counterproductive. However, they may face a bureaucratic requirement to use, or even to post, some sort of classroom discipline policy. The solution may lie in taking the precepts of a democratic classroom community, including principles of problem solving, conflict resolution, and student participation, and redefining it as a "discipline" or "classroom management" program to satisfy administrators.

21. For example, see Krashen.

22. Hyde teaches at the Central Park East 1 Elementary School in New York City. Personal communication, November 2005.

23. Christopher Ward Ellsasser teaches high school in southern California. He's also an assistant professor of education at Pepperdine University. Personal communication, November 2005.

24. Julie King; personal communication, October 2005.

25. Personal communication, January 2006.

26. Christine Olinger of Silver Spring, Maryland, is quoted in Chenoweth.

27. I mentioned Tschudin's research on page 44. Haberman, meanwhile, conducted more than a thousand interviews in schools that serve low-income students and identified a relatively small number of "star teachers." Among the

many features that distinguished them was the fact that they "do not assign homework in the traditional sense, i.e., 'Do page 58 in the arithmetic book.' They try to create assignments that youngsters are able to do independently and successfully. These assignments are frequently planned with the children and grow out of some class activity" (p. 10).

28. Personal communication, July 2005.

29. Stevenson, p. 529.

30. Personal communication with Mark Springer, November 2005. For more about the Soundings program, see Brown.

31. Rogoff, p. 152.

Chapter 11

1. William Morris; personal communication, February 2006.

2. Haberman, p. 10. Thus, Sonia Medrano, a third grade teacher in New York City: "When I do assign homework, I make it relevant to what we are learning in school and not some handout. I also have the children check their homework with each other—as opposed to me going around checking—not to see if it was done, but to get different ideas from each other or to have the students assist each other with it" (personal communication, June 2005).

3. See the research reviewed in Kohn 1999a and 1999b.

4. Noddings, p. 257. Even the more traditionally minded Harris Cooper says, "The practice of grading homework [should] be kept to a minimum, especially if the assignment's purpose is to foster positive attitudes toward the subject matter." (Which might lead us to ask, When would that *not* be a key consideration?) "Grading might provide external reasons for doing homework that detract from students' appreciation of the intrinsic value of the exercise" (1989a, p. 183).

5. See Kralovec and Buell, pp. 92–94. More conventional proposals to increase the length of the school day as a way of "raising standards" should be supported "only to the extent they offer relief from homework," these authors add (p. 94).

6. Rothstein 2001.

7. The quotations in this section are all derived from personal communications with the individuals who are named, as follows: Frothingham, November 2005; Judith Barnes at Christa McAuliffe, July 2005; Bethany Nelson at Sparhawk, November 2005 and April 2006; Marta Beede at Bellwether, November 2005; Diane Meier at Wingra, July 2005; Erika Sueker at Golden, November 2005; Tanya Sullivan DeLeón at New City, November 2005.

8. An international survey found that textbook problems were "by far the most common type of [math] homework teachers use, closely followed by

worksheets. Indeed, textbooks and worksheets combined were the dominant form in virtually all countries" (Baker and Letendre, p. 123).

9. Schofield 2004.

10. Schofield 2005.

11. Hazlewood.

12. Maeroff, p. 164.

13. Gardner.

14. For more on this idea, see Kohn 2002.

15. Personal communication, February 2006.

16. Personal communication, February 2006.

17. Personal communication, February 2006. As for the reactions of her colleagues to a policy of little or no homework, Oliver says, "The younger teachers have been inquisitive and wonder how I get away with it, and they are not confident enough to look different. They also still believe that they need to get kids 'ready' for the hammer next year. I just say, what if you didn't do it, what would happen? They are afraid they wouldn't be respected by parents/teachers mostly. I tell them the research info, and I just don't think they believe it. Also, several of the younger teachers don't have kids of their own, and don't understand yet how it can be such a battle."

18. Samway, pp. 352–53, 355.

REFERENCES

Abrams, Pam. "Homework Hassles." *Parents*, February 2004.

Allington, Richard L. "How to Improve High-Stakes Test Scores Without Really Improving." *Issues in Education* 6 (2000): 115–24.

_____. "Ideology Is Still Trumping Evidence." *Phi Delta Kappan*, February 2005: 462–68.

Ames, Carole. "Classrooms: Goals, Structures, and Student Motivation." *Journal of Educational Psychology* 84 (1992): 261–71.

Anderson, Richard C., Jana Mason, and Larry Shirey. "The Reading Group: An Experimental Investigation of a Labyrinth." *Reading Research Quarterly* 20 (1984): 6–38.

Applebome, Peter. "Children Place Low in Adults' Esteem, a Study Finds." *New York Times*, June 26, 1997: A25.

Austin, Joe Dan. "Home Work Research in Mathematics." *School Science and Mathematics* 79 (1979): 115–21.

Baker, David P., and Gerald K. Letendre. *National Differences, Global Similarities: World Culture and the Future of Schooling*. Stanford, CA: Stanford University Press, 2005.

Barber, Bill. "Homework Does Not Belong on the Agenda for Educational Reform." *Educational Leadership*, May 1986: 55–57.

Begley, Sharon. "Homework Doesn't Help." *Newsweek*, March 30, 1998: 50–51.

Bempechat, Janine. "The Motivational Benefits of Homework: A Social-Cognitive Perspective." *Theory into Practice* 43 (2004): 189–96.

Berliner, David C., and Bruce J. Biddle. *The Manufactured Crisis: Myths, Fraud, and the Attack on America's Public Schools*. Reading, MA: Addison-Wesley, 1995.

Betts, Julian R. *The Role of Homework in Improving School Quality*. University of California–San Diego, February 1997. ftp://weber.ucsd.edu/pub/jbetts/Papers/hw0297.pdf.

Black, Susan. "The Truth About Homework." *American School Board Journal*, October 1996: 48–51.

Boe, Erling E., and Sujie Shin. "Is the United States Really Losing the International Horse Race in Academic Achievement?" *Phi Delta Kappan*, May 2005: 688–95.

Boser, Ulrich. "Overworked and Underplayed?" *U.S. News & World Report*, October 13, 2000.

Bowles, Samuel, and Herbert Gintis. *Schooling in Capitalist America: Educational Reform and the Contradictions of Economic Life*. New York: Basic, 1976.

Bracey, Gerald W. "Test Scores, Creativity, and Global Competitiveness." *Phi Delta Kappan*, June 2002: 738–39.

_____. *Setting the Record Straight: Responses to Misconceptions About Public Education in the U.S.* 2nd ed. Portsmouth, NH: Heinemann, 2004.

Bronner, Ethan. "Long a Leader, U.S. Now Lags in High School Graduate Rate." *New York Times*, November 24, 1998: A1, A18.

Brown, Dave F. "Self-Directed Learning in an 8th Grade Classroom." *Educational Leadership*, September 2002: 54–58.

Brownell, William A. *The Development of Children's Number Ideas in the Primary Grades*. Chicago: University of Chicago, 1928.

_____. "Psychological Considerations in the Learning and the Teaching of Arithmetic." In *The Teaching of Arithmetic*. Tenth Yearbook of the National Council of Teachers of Mathematics. New York: Teachers College, 1935.

Bryan, Tanis, and Karen Burstein. "Improving Homework Completion and Academic Performance: Lessons from Special Education." *Theory into Practice* 43 (2004): 213–19.

Buell, John. *Closing the Book on Homework: Enhancing Public Education and Freeing Family Time*. Philadelphia: Temple University Press, 2004.

Campbell, Jay R., Catherine M. Hombo, and John Mazzeo. "NAEP 1999 Trends in Academic Progress: Three Decades of Student Performance." *Education Statistics Quarterly* 2, no. 4 (2001). http://nces.ed.gov/programs/quarterly/vol_2/2_4/e_section2.asp.

Chen, Chuansheng, and Harold W. Stevenson. "Homework: A Cross-cultural Examination." *Child Development* 60 (1989): 551–61.

Chenoweth, Karin. "From Home, a Sampling of Views on Homework." *Washington Post*, January 30, 2003: T5.

Chomsky, Noam. *The Common Good*. Interview by David Barsamian. Tucson, AZ: Odonian, 1998.

Cool, Valerie A., and Timothy Z. Keith. "Testing a Model of School Learning: Direct and Indirect Effects on Academic Achievement." *Contemporary Educational Psychology* 16 (1991): 28–44.

Cooper, Harris. *Homework*. White Plains, NY: Longman, 1989a.

———. "Synthesis of Research on Homework." *Educational Leadership*, November 1989b: 85–91.

———. *The Battle over Homework*. 2nd ed. Thousand Oaks, CA: Corwin, 2001.

———. "This Issue: Homework." *Theory into Practice* 43 (2004): 171–73.

Cooper, Harris, Kristina Jackson, Barbara Nye, and James J. Lindsay. "A Model of Homework's Influence on the Performance Evaluations of Elementary School Students." *Journal of Experimental Education* 69 (2001): 181–99.

Cooper, Harris, James J. Lindsay, Barbara Nye, and Scott Greathouse. "Relationships Among Attitudes About Homework, Amount of Homework Assigned and Completed, and Student Achievement." *Journal of Educational Psychology* 90 (1998): 70–83.

Cooper, Harris, Jorgianne Civey Robinson, and Erika A. Patall. "Does Homework Improve Academic Achievement? A Synthesis of Research, 1987–2003." *Review of Educational Research* 76 (2006): 1–62.

Cooper, Harris, and Jeffrey C. Valentine. "Using Research to Answer Practical Questions About Homework." *Educational Psychologist* 36 (2001): 143–53.

Cooper, Harris, Jeffrey C. Valentine, Barbara Nye, and James J. Lindsay. "Relationships Between Five After-School Activities and Academic Achievement." *Journal of Educational Psychology* 91 (1999): 369–78.

Corno, Lyn. "Student Volition and Education: Outcomes, Influences, and Practices." In *Self-Regulation of Learning and Performance: Issues and Educational Applications*. Edited by Dale H. Schunk and Barry J. Zimmerman. Hillsdale, NJ: Lawrence Erlbaum, 1994.

———. "Homework Is a Complicated Thing." *Educational Researcher*, November 1996: 27–30.

———. "Looking at Homework Differently." *Elementary School Journal* 100 (2000): 529–48.

Coutts, Pamela M. "Meanings of Homework and Implications for Practice. *Theory into Practice* 43 (2004): 182–88.

Cuban, Larry. "The Corporate Myth of Reforming Public Schools." *Phi Delta Kappan*, October 1992: 157–59.

Darling-Hammond, Linda, and Olivia Ifill-Lynch. "If They'd Only Do Their Work!" *Educational Leadership*, February 2006: 8–13.

Daro, Philip. "Math Warriors, Lay Down Your Weapons." *Education Week*, February 15, 2006: 34–35.

Davenport, David. "Life Support: A Beastly Burden." *Pittsburgh Post-Gazette*, June 13, 2002.

Dennis, Lawrence, and Kevin Swick. "How to Turn Homework into Home Learning." *Teacher*, November 1973: 42–43.

DeVries, Rheta, and Lawrence Kohlberg. *Constructivist Early Education: Overview and Comparison with Other Programs*. Washington, D.C.: National Association for the Education of Young Children, 1990.

Dewey, John. *Interest and Effort in Education*. Boston: Houghton Mifflin, 1913.

———. *Experience and Education*. 1938. New York: Collier, 1963.

Dillard, Annie. "To Fashion a Text." In *Inventing the Truth*. Edited by William Zinsser. Rev. ed. Boston: Houghton Mifflin, 1998.

Dorn, Betsy. "Mom and Dad the Homework Helpers," 1998. www.familyeducation.com/article/0,1120,66-400,00.html.

Dressel, Paul. "Facts and Fancy in Assigning Grades." *Basic College Quarterly* 2 (1957): 6–12.

Dudley-Marling, Curt. "How School *Troubles* Come Home: The Impact of Homework on Families of Struggling Learners." *Current Issues in Education* 6, no. 4 (2003). http://cie.ed.asu.edu/volume6/number4.

Egawa, Kathy, Joanne Hindley Salch, Artie Voigt, and Annie Darley. "Developing a Homework Plan." *NCTE* [National Council of Teachers of English] *Elementary Cyberbrief,* December 1999. www.ncte.org/library/files/Files/Cyberbriefs/Homework_Plan.pdf.

England, David A., and Joannis K. Flatley. *Homework—And Why*. Bloomington, IN: Phi Delta Kappa, 1985.

Epstein, Joyce L. *Homework Practices, Achievements, and Behaviors of Elementary School Students*. Center for Research on Elementary and Middle Schools. Report no. 26. ERIC Document 301 322, July 1988.

Epstein, Joyce L., and Frances L. Van Voorhis. "More Than Minutes: Teachers' Roles in Designing Homework." *Educational Psychologist* 36 (2001): 181–93.

Finstad, Elaine. "Effects of Mathematics Homework on Second Grade Achievement." Course paper at Sam Houston State University. ERIC document 291 609, December 1987.

Foyle, Harvey, et al. *Homework and Cooperative Learning: A Classroom Field Experiment*. ERIC document 350 285, May 1990.

Freire, Paulo. *Pedagogy of the Oppressed*. New York: Continuum, 1970.

Garan, Elaine M. "Beyond the Smoke and Mirrors: A Critique of the National Reading Panel Report on Phonics." *Phi Delta Kappan*, March 2001: 500–506.

Gardner, Howard. "A Prescription for Peace." *Time*, January 25, 1999: 62.

Gartner, John D. "Training for Life." *National Review*, January 22, 2001.

Georgiou, Stelios N. "Parental Involvement: Definition and Outcomes." *Social Psychology of Education* 1 (1997): 189–209.

Gerber, Susan B. "Extracurricular Activities and Academic Achievement." *Journal of Research and Development in Education* 30 (1996): 42–50.

Gibbs, W. Wayt, and Douglas Fox. "The False Crisis in Science Education." *Scientific American*, October 1999, pp. 87–92.

Gill, Brian P., and Steven L. Schlossman. "A Nation at Rest: The American Way of Homework." *Educational Evaluation and Policy Analysis* 25 (2003): 319–37.

_____. "Villain or Savior? The American Discourse on Homework, 1850–2003. *Theory into Practice* 43 (2004): 174–81.

Glasser, William. *Schools Without Failure*. New York: Harper & Row, 1969.

Goldstein, Avram. "Does Homework Help? A Review of Research." *Elementary School Journal* 60 (1960): 212–24.

Good, Thomas L., Douglas A. Grouws, and Howard Ebmeier. *Active Mathematics Teaching*. New York: Longman, 1983.

Gordon, David M. "Do We Need to Be No. 1?" *Atlantic Monthly*, April 1986: 100–108.

Gorges, Todd C., and Stephen N. Elliott. "Homework: Parent and Student Involvement and Their Effects on Academic Performance." *Canadian Journal of School Psychology* 11 (1995): 18–31.

Grolnick, Wendy S., Suzanne T. Gurland, Wendy DeCourcey, and Karen Jacob. "Antecedents and Consequences of Mothers' Autonomy Support." *Developmental Psychology* 38 (2002): 143–55.

Haberman, Martin. *Star Teachers of Children in Poverty*. West Lafayette, IN: Kappa Delta Pi, 1995.

Hammond, Bruce G. "On Dropping AP Courses: A Voice from the Developing Movement." *Education Week*, January 19, 2005: 32.

Harlow, Harry F. "Fundamental Principles for Preparing Psychology Journal Articles." *Journal of Comparative and Physiological Psychology* 55 (1962): 893–96.

Hazlewood, Patrick. "Homework—A Burden of the Past?" *Teaching Expertise,* Summer 2006: 45–47.

Heller, Kalman M. "Solutions to the Homework Dilemma." No date. www.drheller.com/homework.html.

Hinchey, Patricia. "Rethinking Homework." *MASCD* [Missouri Association for Supervision and Curriculum Development] *Fall Journal*, December 1995: 13–17.

Hoff, David J. "Scholars Critique Advanced Classes in Math, Science." *Education Week*, February 20, 2002: 1, 12.

Hofferth, Sandra L., and John F. Sandberg. "How American Children Spend Their Time." *Journal of Marriage and Family* 63 (2001): 295–308.

Holt, John. *How Children Fail*. Rev. ed. New York: Delta, 1982.

"Homework." *Harvard Education Letter* 1 (1985): 1–3.

"Homework Hell." *Teacher*, May 1999: 59.

"Homework, Sweet Homework." *Economist,* May 6, 1995: 15–16.

Hoover-Dempsey, Kathleen V., Angela C. Battiato, Joan M. T. Walker, Richard P. Reed, Jennifer M. DeJong, and Kathleen P. Jones. "Parental Involvement in Homework." *Educational Psychologist* 36 (2001): 195–209.

Hui, T. Keung. "Too Much of a Good Thing?" *Raleigh News & Observer*, December 4, 2000.

_____. "Homework Headaches." *Raleigh News & Observer*, January 5, 2003.

Jacob, Brian A. "Getting Tough? The Impact of High School Graduation Exams." *Educational Evaluation and Policy Analysis* 23 (2001): 99–121.

Jacobson, Linda. "Playtime Is Over." *Teacher*, May 2004: 13–14.

Jaquiss, Nigel. "Homework Rebellion." *Willamette Week*, December 13, 2000.

Jongsma, Eugene. "Homework: Is It Worthwhile?" *Reading Teacher* 38 (1985): 702–4.

Kagan, Spencer, and Millard C. Madsen. "Cooperation and Competition of Mexican, Mexican-American, and Anglo-American Children of Two Ages Under Four Instructional Sets." *Developmental Psychology* 5 (1971): 32–39.

_____. "Experimental Analyses of Cooperation and Competition of Anglo-American and Mexican Children." *Developmental Psychology* 6 (1972): 49–59.

Kamii, Constance. *Young Children Continue to Reinvent Arithmetic—3rd Grade: Implications of Piaget's Theory.* New York: Teachers College Press, 1994.

Karweit, Nancy. "Time-on-Task Reconsidered: Synthesis of Research on Time and Learning." *Educational Leadership*, May 1984: 33–35.

Katz, Lilian. "The Disposition to Learn." *Principal*, May 1988: 14–17.

Kohn, Alfie. *The Brighter Side of Human Nature: Altruism and Empathy in Everyday Life.* New York: Basic, 1990.

_____. *No Contest: The Case Against Competition.* Rev. ed. Boston: Houghton Mifflin, 1992.

_____. "Choices for Children: Why and How to Let Students Decide." *Phi Delta Kappan*, September 1993: 8–20. www.alfiekohn.org/teaching/cfc.htm.

_____. *What to Look For in a Classroom. . . And Other Essays.* San Francisco: Jossey-Bass, 1998.

_____. *Punished by Rewards: The Trouble with Gold Stars, Incentive Plans, A's, Praise, and Other Bribes.* Rev. ed. Boston: Houghton Mifflin, 1999a.

_____. *The Schools Our Children Deserve: Moving Beyond Traditional Classrooms and "Tougher Standards."* Boston: Houghton Mifflin, 1999b.

_____. "Confusing Harder with Better." *Education Week*, September 15, 1999c: 68, 52. www.alfiekohn.org/teaching/edweek/chwb.htm.

_____. *The Case Against Standardized Testing: Raising the Scores, Ruining the Schools*. Portsmouth, NH: Heinemann, 2000.

_____. "Education's Rotten Apples." *Education Week*, September 18, 2002: 48, 36–37. www.alfiekohn.org/teaching/edweek/rotten.htm.

_____. "Test Today, Privatize Tomorrow." *Phi Delta Kappan*, April 2004: 569–77. www.alfiekohn.org/teaching/testtoday.htm.

_____. *Unconditional Parenting: Moving from Rewards and Punishments to Love and Reason*. New York: Atria, 2005a.

_____. "Getting-Hit-on-the-Head Lessons." *Education Week*, September 7, 2005b: 52, 46–47. www.alfiekohn.org/teaching/edweek/bguti.htm.

Kolata, Gina. "Thinning the Milk Does Not Mean Thinning the Child." *New York Times Week in Review*, February 12, 2006: 3.

Kouzma, Nadya M., and Gerard A. Kennedy. "Homework, Stress, and Mood Disturbance in Senior High School Students." *Psychological Reports* 91 (2002): 193–98.

Kozol, Jonathan. *The Shame of the Nation: The Restoration of Apartheid Schooling in America*. New York: Crown, 2005.

Kralovec, Etta, and John Buell. *The End of Homework: How Homework Disrupts Families, Overburdens Children, and Limits Learning*. Boston: Beacon, 2000.

Krashen, Stephen D. *The Power of Reading*. 2nd ed. Portsmouth, NH: Heinemann, 2004.

Krugman, Paul. "Competitiveness: A Dangerous Obsession." *Foreign Affairs*, March–April 1994: 28–44.

Labaree, David F. *How to Succeed in School Without Really Learning: The Credentials Race in American Education*. New Haven: Yale University Press.

Lambert, Pam. "Overbooked." *People*, January 20, 2003.

Lamborn, Susie D., B. Bradford Brown, Nina S. Mounts, and Laurence Steinberg. "Putting School in Perspective: The Influence of Family, Peers, Extracurricular Participation, and Part-Time Work on Academic Engagement." In *Student Engagement and Achievement in American Secondary Schools*. Edited by Fred M. Newmann. New York: Teachers College Press.

Langer, Ellen J. *The Power of Mindful Learning*. Reading, MA: Addison-Wesley, 1997.

Large, Jerry. "Find a Place for Family in Society Driven by Homework." *Seattle Times*, December 4, 2005.

Larson, Reed W., Maryse H. Richard, Belinda Sims, and Jodi Dworkin. "How Urban African American Young Adolescents Spend Their Time." *American Journal of Community Psychology* 29 (2001): 565–97.

Leonard, George. *Education and Ecstasy*. New York: Delta, 1968.

Lepper, Mark R. "Theory by the Numbers? Some Concerns about Meta-Analysis as a Theoretical Tool." *Applied Cognitive Psychology* 9 (1995): 411–22.

Levin, Henry M. "Clocking Instruction: A Reform Whose Time Has Come?" *IFG Policy Perspectives*, Spring 1984: 1–4.

_____. "High-Stakes Testing and Economic Productivity." In *Raising Standards or Raising Barriers? Inequality and High-Stakes Testing in Public Education*. Edited by Gary Orfield and Mindy L. Kornhaber. New York: Century Foundation Press, 2001.

Levin, Iris, Rachel Levy-Shiff, Talya Appelbaum-Peled, Idit Katz, Maya Komar, and Nachshon Meiran. "Antecedents and Consequences of Maternal Involvement in Children's Homework: A Longitudinal Analysis." *Journal of Applied Developmental Psychology* 18 (1997): 207–27.

Levine, Mel. *The Myth of Laziness*. New York: Simon & Schuster, 2003.

Lewis, Catherine C. *Educating Hearts and Minds: Reflections on Japanese Preschool and Elementary Education*. Cambridge: Cambridge University Press, 1995.

"A Look at AP-AOL's Homework Poll." *USA Today*, February 7, 2006.

Lord, Mary. "Burdened by Their Book Bags." *U.S. News & World Report*, October 23, 2000.

Loveless, Tom. *Do Students Have Too Much Homework?* Brown Center on Education Policy. Washington, D.C.: Brookings Institution, October 2003. www.brookings.edu/gs/brown/20031001homework.htm.

Maeroff, Gene I. "Reform Comes Home: Policies to Encourage Parental Involvement in Children's Education." In *Education Reform in the '90s*. Edited by Chester E. Finn Jr. and Theodor Rebarber. New York: Macmillan, 1992.

Mahoney, Joseph L., Beverly D. Cairns, and Thomas W. Farmer. "Promoting Interpersonal Competence and Educational Success Through Extracurricular Activity Participation." *Journal of Educational Psychology* 95 (2003): 409–18.

Mahoney, Joseph L., and Robert B. Cairns. "Do Extracurricular Activities Protect Against Early School Dropout?" *Developmental Psychology* 33 (1997): 241–53.

Males, Mike. *The Scapegoat Generation: America's War on Adolescents*. Monroe, ME: Common Courage, 1996.

_____. *Framing Youth: Ten Myths About the Next Generation*. Monroe, ME: Common Courage, 1998.

Marchant, Gregory J., and Sharon E. Paulson. "The Relationship of High School Graduation Exams to Graduation Rates and SAT Scores." *Education Policy Analysis Archives* 13, no. 6 (2005). http://epaa.asu.edu/epaa/v13n6.

Marek, Ann M. "The Research on the Benefits of Homework." In *The Whole Language Catalog*. Edited by Kenneth S. Goodman, Lois Bridges Bird, and Yetta M. Goodman. New York: McGraw-Hill, 1991.

Marzano, Robert I., Debra J. Pickering, and Jane E. Pollock. *Classroom Instruction That Works: Research-Based Strategies for Increasing Student Achievement.* Alexandria, VA: Association for Supervision and Curriculum Development, 2001.

McClelland, David C. "Testing for Competence Rather Than for Intelligence." *American Psychologist,* January 1973: 1–14.

McDermott, R. P., Shelley V. Goldman, and Hervé Varenne. "When School Goes Home: Some Problems in the Organization of Homework." *Teachers College Record* 85 (1984): 391–409.

McGregor, Douglas. *The Human Side of Enterprise.* New York: McGraw-Hill, 1960.

McReynolds, Kate. "Homework." *Encounter,* Summer 2005: 9–13.

Meier, Deborah. "Homework: Theory and Reality." *Mission Hill School News,* September 10, 2001: 1.

Melroy, Linda L. "Effects of Homework on Language Arts Achievement in Third and Fourth Grades." Ph.D. diss., University of Iowa. 1988. *Dissertation Abstracts International* A49/04: 725.

Muhlenbruck, Laura, Harris Cooper, Barbara Nye, and James J. Lindsay. "Homework and Achievement: Explaining the Different Strengths of Relation at the Elementary and Secondary School Levels." *Social Psychology of Education* 3 (2000): 295–317.

Mullis, Ina V.S., Michael O. Martin, Albert E. Beaton, Eugenio J. Gonzalez, Dana L. Kelly, and Teresa A. Smith. *Mathematics and Science Achievement in the Final Years of Secondary School: IEA's Third International Mathematics and Science Report.* Boston: International Association for the Evaluation of Educational Achievement, Lynch School of Education, Boston College, 1998. http://isc.bc.edu/timss1995i/MathScienceC.html.

Mullis, Ina V.S., Michael O. Martin, Eugenio Gonzalez, Kathleen M. O'Connor, Steven J. Chrostowski, Kelvin D. Gregory, Robert A. Garden, and Teresa A. Smith. *Mathematics Benchmarking Report—TIMSS 1999: Achievement for U.S. States and Districts in an International Context.* Boston: International Association for the Evaluation of Educational Achievement, Lynch School of Education, Boston College, 2001. http://timss.bc.edu/timss1999b/math-bench_report/t99b_math_report.html.

Napolitano, Jo. "School's Lesson Plan: No More Homework." *Chicago Tribune,* May 7, 2005.

National Association for the Education of Young Children. *Testing of Young Children: Concerns and Cautions.* Washington, D.C.: NAEYC, 1988.

National PTA and National Education Association. *Helping Your Student Get the Most Out of Homework.* Pamphlet. 1993. Adaptation available at: www.nea.org/parents/homework.html.

Natriello, Gary. "Hoist on the Petard of Homework." *Teachers College Record* 98 (1997): 572–75.

———. "Failing Grades for Retention." *School Administrator*, August 1998: 14–17.

Natriello, Gary, and Edward L. McDill. "Performance Standards, Student Effort on Homework, and Academic Achievement." *Sociology of Education* 59 (1986): 18–31.

Noddings, Nel. *Happiness and Education*. Cambridge: Cambridge University Press, 2003.

Odum, Maria E. "A Tough Assignment for Teachers." *Washington Post*, May 2, 1994.

Paris, David C. "Schools, Scapegoats, and Skills: Educational Reform and the Economy." *Policy Studies Journal* 22 (1994): 10–24.

Paschal, Rosanne A., Thomas Weinstein, and Herbert J. Walberg. "The Effects of Homework on Learning: A Quantitative Synthesis." *Journal of Educational Research* 78 (1984): 97–104.

Putnam, Ralph T., Magdalene Lampert, and Penelope L. Peterson. "Alternative Perspectives on Knowing Mathematics in Elementary Schools." In *Review of Research in Education*, vol. 16. Edited by Courtney B. Cazden. Washington, D.C.: American Educational Research Association, 1990.

Ragland, Jenifer. "In Santa Paula, Kindergartners Put to the Test." *Los Angeles Times*, October 6, 2001.

Ratnesar, Romesh. "The Homework Ate My Family." *Time*, June 30, 2003.

Rauch, Jonathan. "Now, for Tonight's Assignment." *Atlantic Monthly*, November 2004.

Ray, Carol Axtell, and Roslyn Arlin Mickelson. "Restructuring Students for Restructured Work: The Economy, School Reform, and Non-college-bound Youths." *Sociology of Education* 66 (1993): 1–20.

Reardon, Sean F., and Claudia Galindo. "Do High-Stakes Tests Affect Students' Decisions to Drop Out of School? Evidence from NELS." Working Paper 03–01. Population Research Institute, Pennsylvania State University, April 2002. www.pop.psu.edu/general/pubs/working_papers/psu-pri/wp0301.pdf.

Ripley, Amanda. "Beating the Bubble Test." *Time*, March 1, 2004.

Rogoff, Barbara. "Becoming a Cooperative Parent in a Parent Co-operative." In *Learning Together: Children and Adults in a School Community*. Edited by Barbara Rogoff, Carolyn Goodman Turkanis, and Leslee Bartlett. Oxford: Oxford University Press, 2001.

Rosenberg, Merri. "When Homework Takes Over." *New York Times*, April 18, 2004.

Rosenberg, Michael S. "The Effects of Daily Homework Assignments on the Acquisition of Basic Skills by Students with Learning Disabilities." *Journal of Learning Disabilities* 22 (1989): 314–23.

Rotberg, Iris C. "Interpretation of International Test Score Comparisons." *Science* 280 (1998): 1030–31.

Rothstein, Richard. *The Way We Were? The Myths and Realities of America's Student Achievement*. New York: Century Foundation Press, 1998.

_____. "How to Ease the Burden of Homework for Families." *New York Times*, May 23, 2001.

_____. "Class and the Classroom." *American School Board Journal*, October 2004: 16–21.

Routman, Regie. *Literacy at the Crossroads: Crucial Talk About Reading, Writing, and Other Teaching Dilemmas*. Portsmouth, NH: Heinemann, 1996.

Ryan, Richard M., Richard Koestner, and Edward L. Deci. "Ego-Involved Persistence." *Motivation and Emotion* 15 (1991): 185–205.

Sadler, Philip M., and Robert H. Tai. "Success in Introductory College Physics: The Role of High School Preparation." *Science Education* 85 (2001): 111–36.

Samway, Katharine. "'And You Run and You Run to Catch Up with the Sun, But It's Sinking.'" *Language Arts* 63 (1986): 352–57.

Savage, John F. "Homework: Put Your Policy Where Your Aims Are." *American School Board Journal*, June 1969: 24–26.

Scherer, Marge. "On Schools Where Students Want to Be: A Conversation with Deborah Meier." *Educational Leadership*, September 1994: 4–8.

Schmitz, Bernhard, and Ellen Skinner. "Perceived Control, Effort, and Academic Performance." *Journal of Personality and Social Psychology* 64 (1993): 1010–28.

Schofield, Kevin. "The Head Who Banned Homework." *Scotsman,* April 28, 2004.

_____. "Ditching Homework Adds Up to Better Grades." *Scotsman,* April 5, 2005.

"Should We Do Away with Homework?" *NEA Today*, October 2003: 45.

Sizer, Theodore R. *Horace's School: Redesigning the American High School*. Boston: Houghton Mifflin, 1992.

Smith, Frank. *Insult to Intelligence: The Bureaucratic Invasion of Our Classrooms*. Portsmouth, NH: Heinemann, 1986.

Solomon, Yvette, Jo Warin, and Charlie Lewis. "Helping with Homework? Homework as a Site of Tension for Parents and Teenagers." *British Educational Research Journal* 28 (2002): 603–22.

Sparks, Dennis. "We Care, Therefore They Learn." *Journal of Staff Development* 24 (2003): 42–47.

Spring, Karen. "Parents Ask." *M: The Magazine for Montessori Families*, January–February 2006: 7.

Stettler, Rachel Friis, and Joseph Algrant. "Changing Course for the Better." *Independent School*, Winter 2003: 40–47.

Stevenson, Harold W. "A Study of Three Cultures: Germany, Japan, and the United States: An Overview of the TIMSS Case Study Project." *Phi Delta Kappan*, March 1998: 524–29.

Stevenson, Harold W., Chuansheng Chen, and David H. Uttal. "Beliefs and Achievement: A Study of Black, White, and Hispanic Children." *Child Development* 61 (1990): 508–23.

Stipek, Deborah. "Teaching Practices in Kindergarten and First Grade: Different Strokes for Different Folks." *Early Childhood Research Quarterly* 19 (2004): 548–68.

Strauss, Valerie. "Homework Dreaded—by Parents." *Washington Post*, March 12, 2002: A10.

Strother, Deborah Burnett. "Homework: Too Much, Just Right, or Not Enough?" *Phi Delta Kappan*, February 1984: 423–26.

Swenson, Janet. "Can You Hear Me Now? Composing Connections Between Classrooms and Communities." Keynote address, Society for Information Technology and Teacher Education conference, Orlando, FL, March 2006.

Tanner, Daniel. "A Nation 'Truly' at Risk." *Phi Delta Kappan*, December 1993: 288–97.

Townsend, Stacy. *The Effects of Vocabulary Homework on Third Grade Achievement*. Kean College of New Jersey. ERIC document 379 643, April 1995.

Trautwein, Ulrich, Olaf Köller. "The Relationship Between Homework and Achievement: Still Much of a Mystery." *Educational Psychology Review* 15 (2003): 115–45.

Trautwein, Ulrich, Olaf Köller, Bernhard Schmitz, and Jürgen Baumert. "Do Homework Assignments Enhance Achievement? A Multilevel Analysis in 7th-Grade Mathematics." *Contemporary Educational Psychology* 27 (2002): 26–50.

Tschudin, Ruth. "The Secrets of A+ Teaching." *Instructor*, September 1978: 65–78.

Tsuneyoshi, Ryoko. "The New Japanese Educational Reforms and the Achievement 'Crisis' Debate." *Educational Policy* 18 (2004): 364–94.

Tymms, P. B., and C. T. Fitz-Gibbon. "The Relationship of Homework to A-Level Results." *Educational Research* 34 (1992): 3–10.

U.S. Department of Education. *Homework Tips for Parents*, May 2003. www.ed.gov/parents/academic/involve/homework/homeworktips.pdf.

_____. *How Important Is Homework?* No date. www.kidsource.com/kidsource/content/how_important_homework.html.

_____. *Strategic Plan—2002–2007, March 2002.* www.ed.gov/about/reports/strat/plan2002–07/plan.pdf.

U.S. Department of Education, America Counts. *TIMSS Overview and Key Findings Across Grade Levels.* 1998. www.ed.gov/inits/Math/tmpres2.html.

U.S. Department of Education, National Center for Education Statistics. *NAEP 2004 Trends in Academic Progress.* 2005. http://nces.ed.gov/nationsreportcard/pdf/main2005/2005464_3.pdf.

Vail, Kathleen. "Homework Problems." *American School Board Journal*, April 2001.

VanDeWeghe, Rick. "'How's It Coming?': Homework and Struggling Learners." *English Journal*, March 2004: 76–80.

Vazsonyi, Alexander T., and Lloyd E. Pickering. "The Importance of Family and School Domains in Adolescent Deviance: African American and Caucasian Youth." *Journal of Youth and Adolescence* 32 (2003): 115–28.

Viadero, Debra. "Scholars Warn of Overstating Gains from AP Classes Alone." *Education Week*, February 15, 2006: 14.

Walberg, Herbert J. "Does Homework Help?" *School Community Journal* 1 (1991): 13–15.

Walberg, Herbert J., Rosanne A. Paschal, and Thomas Weinstein. "Homework's Powerful Effects on Learning." *Educational Leadership*, April 1985: 76–79.

Walberg, Herbert J., and Timothy Shanahan. "High School Effects on Individual Students." *Educational Researcher,* August–September 1983: 4–9.

Waldman, Ayelet. "Homework Hell," October 22, 2005. www.salon.com/mwt/col/waldman/2005/10/22/homework/print.html.

Warton, Pamela M. "Learning About Responsibility: Lessons from Homework." *British Journal of Educational Psychology* 67 (1997): 213–21.

Washburne, Carleton. "How Much Homework?" *Parents*, November 1937: 16–17, 68–71.

Watson, John B. *Behaviorism.* Rev. ed. Chicago: University of Chicago Press, 1930.

Wildman, Peggy Riggs. "Homework Pressures." *Peabody Journal of Education* 45 (1968): 202–4.

Wilson, Maja. *Rethinking Rubrics in Writing Assessment.* Portsmouth, NH: Heinemann, 2006.

Windschitl, Mark. "Why We Can't Talk to One Another About Science Education Reform." *Phi Delta Kappan*, January 2006: 349–55.

Winerip, Michael. "Homework Bound." *New York Times Education Life*, January 3, 1999: 28–31, 40.

Wingard, Leah. "Parents' Inquiries About Homework: The First Mention." *Text & Talk* 26 (2006).

Zehr, Mary Ann. "Advocates Note Need to Polish 'Bilingual' Pitch." *Education Week*, February 1, 2006: 12.

Zemelman, Steven, Harvey Daniels, and Arthur Hyde. *Best Practice: Today's Standards for Teaching and Learning in America's Schools.* 3rd ed. Portsmouth, NH: Heinemann, 2005.

Ziegler, Suzanne. *Homework.* ERIC document 274 418, June 1986.

_____. "Homework." In *Encyclopedia of Educational Research*. Edited by Marvin C. Alkin. Vol. 2. 6th ed. New York: Macmillan, 1992.

ACKNOWLEDGMENTS

Thanks to my superb editor Marnie Cochran for her professionalism, her patience with me, and her dedication to this project; to my agent Gail Ross for her support; to Alisa, Abigail, and Asa for their forbearance during the time I was up in my office doing my, um, homework; to Lois Bridges and Smokey Daniels for helping to jump-start my research; to Cathy Vatterott for letting me go first; and especially to all the teachers and parents who generously shared their thoughts and experiences. The fact that many of them feel as though they're alone in questioning the conventional wisdom makes their stance even more courageous, but the good news is that they actually have plenty of company.

INDEX